Praise for

ENTREPRENEUR TO
MILLIONAIRE
and **KENT BILLINGSLEY**

"Just one of the principles in *Entrepreneur to Millionaire* helped my last company, Resulté Universal, generate $5.7 million in one meeting when it used to take a whole year to generate that much revenue. This book will transform your business."

—**REX KURZIUS,** CEO of Asset Panda, LLC

"This is a game-changing guide. Kent Billingsley's framework was responsible for taking one of my companies from 17 percent sales win rates to more than 80 percent for years—without lowering our prices or discounting. We have won major accounts in blind RFP bids with up to 12 competitors. Those accounts have generated millions of dollars when our average sale used to be about $100,000."

—**KISHORE KHANDAVALLI,** CEO of iTech US, Inc.,
and founder of Seven Tablets, Inc.

"When we first met Kent, our company was pre-revenue. His methodology helped us create a variable growth model and win several major contracts. It eventually sold for $12 million. If you are starting a business, you must learn and apply the ideas in this book!"

—**DEBBIE LEMON,** Cofounder of Rent A Toll, Inc.

"My firm has spent more than $1 million on coaching and training with different companies. The process Kent details in this book has provided the greatest ROI of all—we have achieved over 40 percent compounded growth for years. We help our clients manage their wealth, and Kent helps people create wealth with their companies. If you want faster and more profitable no-cost growth, this is the book for you."

—MITCH KRAMER, founder and CEO of Fluent Financial®

"I personally know at least a dozen entrepreneurs who have been using the Entrepreneur to Millionaire principles and have become multimillionaires. Kent Billingsley has earned his title: the Revenue Growth® Architect! We are using his methodology to create even more explosive growth at GLO."

—MICHELLE LEMONS POSCENTE, founder and CEO
of Global Leaders Organization, Inc. (GLO)

"I had all the leaders in my company learn and implement the concepts Kent shares in *Entrepreneur to Millionaire*, and that helped us increase our sales more than 300 percent in our target markets. Everyone on your team must read this!"

—DAVID BOGATY, CEO of WorldNet, Inc.

"Kent's methodology generated a significant increase in sales. His approach helped us transition from salespeople operating independently to a powerful strategic sales system. These concepts allowed us to compete and win against major competitors in complex selling pursuits. Our company eventually sold for more than expected because of the strong sales and cash flow these ideas helped create."

—MITCH GERVIS, CEO of NeoSpire, Inc.

"I know many entrepreneurs and their employees who have created fast-growth companies and become quite wealthy following the principles in *Entrepreneur to Millionaire*. My teams started applying these concepts after hearing Kent speak at an event over 10 years ago. His methods for transforming messaging alone can change your company's trajectory almost immediately. If you want to be a successful entrepreneur and become embarrassingly rich, you must learn and master what is in this book."

—TAD MCINTOSH, founder and CEO of HumCap, LLC

"Following Kent Billingsley's four-part process has helped us lead our industry in organic sales growth for the past five years in a row."

—JOHN POWTER, CEO of GDP Advisors, LLC

"The chapter on sales system conversion is extremely powerful. I reread it three times. Mastering and implementing the concepts in this chapter will enable you to deliver profitable growth."

—BRUCE K. PACKARD, Esq., Partner at Riney Packard, PLLC

"My company follows the strategies in this book, especially the one on pipeline acceleration. That alone accelerates contracts through the funnel about 5–10 times faster and produces sales worth millions more without hiring a sales army."

—SHANE LONG, Partner and President of Seven Tablets, Inc.

"If you are an entrepreneur, CEO, or business owner, this book is an indispensable read. It provides the right approach, strategic design, and implementation road map to offer more value to your clients and achieve greater financial results for your organization. If you liked *Traction*, how to run a better company, you will love *Entrepreneur to Millionaire*, how to become wealthier running a company."

—CARLOS ALBARRAN, CEO of Aurum Capital

ENTREPRENEUR TO
MILLIONAIRE

How to Build a Highly Profitable, Fast-Growth Company
and Become Embarrassingly Rich Doing It

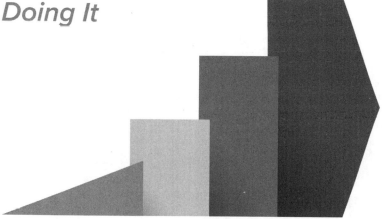

KENT BILLINGSLEY

New York   Chicago   San Francisco   Athens   London   Madrid
Mexico City   Milan   New Delhi   Singapore   Sydney   Toronto

1 2 3 4 5 6 7 8 9   LCR   25 24 23 22 21

ISBN   978-1-264-25712-6
MHID   1-264-25712-0

e-ISBN   978-1-264-25713-3
e-MHID   1-264-25713-9

This publication is designed to provide accurate and authoritative information in regard to the subject matter covered. It is sold with the understanding that neither the author nor the publisher is engaged in rendering legal, accounting, securities trading, or other professional services. If legal advice or other expert assistance is required, the services of a competent professional person should be sought.
—*From a Declaration of Principles Jointly Adopted by a Committee of the American Bar Association and a Committee of Publishers and Associations*

Library of Congress Cataloging-in-Publication Data

Names: Billingsley, Kent, author.
Title: Entrepreneur to millionaire : how to build a highly profitable, fast-growth
   company and become embarrassingly rich doing it / Kent Billingsley.
Description: New York : McGraw Hill, [2020] | Includes bibliographical
   references and index.
Identifiers: LCCN 2020040265 (print) | LCCN 2020040266 (ebook) |
   ISBN 9781264257126 (hardback) | ISBN 9781264257133 (ebook)
Subjects: LCSH: Revenue management. | Small business—Growth. |
   Strategic planning. | Success in business. | Entrepreneurship.
Classification: LCC HD60.7 .B55 2020 (print) | LCC HD60.7 (ebook) |
   DDC 658.02/2—dc23
LC record available at https://lccn.loc.gov/2020040265
LC ebook record available at https://lccn.loc.gov/2020040266

"The mass of [entrepreneurs] live lives of quiet desperation."

—Adapted from Henry David Thoreau

CONTENTS

Foreword by Mark Cuban   vii

Acknowledgments   ix

INTRODUCTION   A Smarter and Faster Path to
Entrepreneurial Success   1

CHAPTER 1   New Will and Different Way   15

PHASE I
Revenue Ready

CHAPTER 2   Your Company Genesis: The FMP   29

CHAPTER 3   Business Modeling   43

CHAPTER 4   Multiple Revenue Streams   59

PHASE II
Market Ready

CHAPTER 5   Targeting Your Sweet Spot   75

CHAPTER 6   Packaging for Value   89

CHAPTER 7   Power Messaging Tools   103

CHAPTER 8   Tiered Pricing Strategies   115

PHASE III

Go to Market

CHAPTER 9   Marketing Demand Creation   131

CHAPTER 10   Sales Conversion System   149

CHAPTER 11   Partnering for Demand   167

CHAPTER 12   Pipeline Acceleration   179

PHASE IV

Own the Market

CHAPTER 13   Blueprinting Optimization   195

CHAPTER 14   Competitive Dominance   209

CHAPTER 15   Talent Optimization   223

CHAPTER 16   From Learning to Implementation   239

             Appendix: Additional Resources   245

             Index   249

FOREWORD BY MARK CUBAN

One of the great business lies of all time is that sales is all that matters. What matters is profitable sales and, more importantly, profits. If you as an entrepreneur are working untold hours, stressing out and worried about your health and that of your family, and thinking there must be a better way to run a business, you have come to the right place.

I've known Kent Billingsley for 40 years. I still remember the first time I met him in our apartment parking lot. From that day forward, we became lifelong friends. Over all those years, I have come to know Kent and have admired his business skills and his ability to find profitable solutions to problems. Frankly, I've always wondered why it has taken him so long to write this book!

Kent has finally taken his decades of experience turning businesses into profit-generating machines and put that knowledge into one easy-to-read book. This is not yet another book about how businesses are run in Silicon Valley, Los Angeles, or New York. This is a book for entrepreneurs who have put everything they have on the line, who have been grinding for years, and are not sure why they haven't reached the level of success they think they should have. This is for entrepreneurs who have a growing business that looks incredibly successful from the outside— lots of sales, lots of employees, and lots of visibility—but who can't quite get to the point of generating the cash flow and personal bank account they have worked so hard to achieve.

Kent does an incredible job of showing entrepreneurs that a successful business is not built on closing any deal but on focusing on and closing the most profitable deals—that you can make more money focusing on the right prospects rather than every prospect. With *Entrepreneur to Millionaire*, Kent provides a road map any entrepreneur can use.

I wish I had this book when I was first getting started. It's a must-read!

ACKNOWLEDGMENTS

I'd like to thank the leaders who inspired, challenged, and made it possible for me to gain the experience and expertise to write this book: Mark Cuban, the greatest technology entrepreneur I have ever known; Ross Perot Sr., the most inspirational leader I have ever worked for; Edward Yang, the most benevolent and smartest "East meets West" international leader; Valerie Lyons, the best entrepreneurial corporate leader; Greg Q. Brown, the best entrepreneurial CEO, now running Motorola Solutions, Inc.; Mickey Austin, a great sales leader; Mike Donohue, the best entrepreneurial strategist leader; and Michelle Lemons Poscente, the most connected entrepreneurial leader I know.

I'd also like to thank the clients, entrepreneurs, partners, publishing team, and friends who listened to me, read my manuscript, polished my content, and applied and implemented my programs in their companies: Dianna Booher, David Bogaty, Bob Claycomb, Casey Ebro, Jim Eckelberger, Mitch Gervis, Chris Graham, Ron Hall, Kishore Khandavalli, Mitch Kramer, Rex Kurzius, Bruce K Packard, Debbie Lemon, Shane Long, Carol Mann, Tad McIntosh, Vince Poscente, John Powter, Pat Reinheimer, Phil Resch, Rick Sapio, and Kevin Winters.

To my beautiful and lovely wife, Terri, and son, Turner, thank you for helping me stay focused and keeping the house quiet, in spite of our dog, Coco, cats, Leo and Cleo, and eyelash crested gecko, Galileo.

Introduction

A Smarter and Faster Path to Entrepreneurial Success

Kicking off a speech to several hundred entrepreneurs at a global summit in Montreal, Canada, I asked the exuberant attendees these questions: "How many of you run companies that offer great products and services and deliver *exceptional value* to your customers and clients?" All hands shot up. "Perfect." Money—more sales, revenue, and profits—and especially creating company wealth or your personal fortune, must never be your sole focus, but the by-product of the *value* you and your company bring to your clients and the marketplace.

To achieve business growth, who has done or is doing the following:

- ▸ Spend more money on marketing: advertising, SEO, social media, or digital marketing
- ▸ Hire more employees like salespeople
- ▸ Spend more on training
- ▸ Lower prices to win new clients
- ▸ Add more products and services

"How many of you are spending every waking hour and every dollar to achieve greater business growth? Is everyone working harder and smarter too?" Each question raised more hands. Soon every attendee had an arm raised. No one wanted to be left out. Several entrepreneurs looked around to proudly confirm their unanimity.

I paused to let the hands slowly lower.

"If you want to become embarrassingly rich from your business, my highly successful clients have proven you can stop doing *all* of those things—*immediately*," I stated slowly and clearly.

Confusion and doubt overcame the audience, each trying to remember the actions they had just agreed they were doing. Didn't we all agree, they wondered? How can we all be wrong?

"Remember a few minutes ago when everyone raised their hand? Meaning what they are doing—*you are doing*.

"You'll never have radical results if you follow the same path as your competitors. As an entrepreneur your vision might be to make the world a better place, but you won't get paid for it if you don't think and execute differently than everyone else.

"We—you and I—have all been lied to and taught to religiously execute those business growth strategies I just asked you about. It's been pounded into our head. To be successful you had to go out and aggressively market, sell, and promote your products and services and achieve business growth.

"You've been sold to do what it takes and spend what it takes. I've been starting and building companies for over four decades, and I read those messages when I first started, and I still hear them today. There are thousands of speakers, books, and websites all designed to help you grow your business. I receive about a dozen unsolicited emails a week from companies wanting to help me with leads, marketing, social media, and digital efforts.

"Do you think I'm going to tell you that to be successful, you have to stop focusing on growing your business?

"Yes. Transformational success requires radical change in how you think and act," I advised.

We've all been living myths about entrepreneurial success. I've worked inside—physically in the offices and boardrooms—of several thousand organizations, many in foreign countries, who are growing fast and slow. Want to know the real behind-the-scenes performance in most firms? Growing or not?

> *The majority of companies barely make any real money.*
> *They struggle with cash, cash flow, and working capital.*

And 99.9 percent of entrepreneurs and small business owners eke out a living, sacrifice their lives, grind out their employees, work through nights and weekends, and neglect their health. They fight anxiety for years to decades, clinging to hope that someday they will become wealthy from their business. A few will. Most won't. Entrepreneurs end up settling, quitting, going back to work for a big company, retiring, or even selling their venture at a loss.

Why do most entrepreneurs live lives of quiet desperation?

Because of this amazingly simple premise: Entrepreneurs are burning too much money focusing on how to start, run, and grow a business. But they're not learning how to *create wealth*. They don't know how to *make* serious money—huge sales, massive revenues, and ridiculous profits—from their company.

Billions are spent by training, coaching, consulting, and speakers convincing you to increase your spending and activities to grow faster. They sell the continuous myth that spending more money, especially with them, will increase your success. Let me share a secret: that's how they make their income, by taking some of yours. The lie perpetuates because entrepreneurs mistakenly conflate that a growing business makes more profit. They believe that growth and profitability go together. They don't.

Fable: Business Growth Will Create Wealth

Where does the "business growth makes the entrepreneur a lot of money" fairy tale come from? It starts with a flawed measurement of business success. You've been taught that to have a successful company you must accomplish these objectives: add more clients and customers, add more contracts, add more employees, add more products and services, add more locations, add more SKUs, add more salespeople and sales transactions. Add more of everything.

And that is the giant flaw. When you add a good thing, you'll most likely also add a bad thing. When you add all of those items listed above, you will add more expense, add more overhead, add more costs, add more infrastructure, add more management, add more time, add more resources. And you'll also add more headaches, more people issues, and more stress. What's the common denominator? *Adding.*

> *When you add a good thing to your business,*
> *you'll most likely also add a bad thing.*

I know what you might be saying: "Well that's just understanding what it takes to run a growing firm," or "That's how you grow," or, "Yes, it's the nature of business—you have to take the bad with the good." Or maybe you've bought into the lie that to add top line you might have to accept less bottom line.

Or do you?

The first list above was all about adding—increasing sales and revenues. The second list was also about adding—costs, expenses, and headaches. If you most likely add both upside and downside to grow, then you'll experience "running on the never-enough-money treadmill." If your growth goes up and so do all your costs and headaches, is your business really better? Are you more successful?

This paradox is what scares entrepreneurs and small business owners concerning fast or explosive growth. No matter how fast they run, they're still in the same financial squeeze they were in before. Except now they have increased headaches, stress, frustration, and fewer hours for life. That is the failure of trying to survive with the "hope for profit" business growth philosophy—eventually dying from exhaustion or burning out your entrepreneurial spirit.

More from More

The classic business model for success I just discussed can be summarized in this phrase: *more from more.* This philosophy is good for *incremental* results. It's a universal practice from the last century, but not a superior approach to making huge profits against the current destructive market forces. Sadly, 99.9 percent of companies and their leaders execute to this paradigm and count on greater business growth for making more money. However, this approach can never achieve *optimized profit production.*

Here is the counter. A bigger business might produce more overall profit, but at what cost? It's usually *incremental growth with incremental profits*—nowhere near the maximum profit potential of a well-designed company.

If you're happy with slow to average growth and just earning some income, then you can stop reading right now and stay on your current slow money-making path. However, if your competitors learn and follow my approach to revenue growth, as I'm going to explain, they will make every day you're running your business harder, more frustrating, and less profitable. Ironically, many entrepreneurs believe their businesses are stable or growing when in reality their businesses are dying. Google the fable about the boiling frog to understand this point.

Why Focusing on Business Growth Is Flawed

If you and your team have the insatiable drive and burning desire for fast or even explosive growth, with huge profits, then you must think and act in a different way. We need to shatter some common and classic paradigms and clichés that will keep you locked in last century's thinking and mediocre results. Have you ever heard this business saying?

You have to spend money to make money.

That's why most entrepreneurs have money problems or their companies fold. They either justify wasting money to try to achieve growth or they unconsciously burn money—profits—hoping for success. Listen to the argument—you can't grow without spending money. I don't know about you, but I love hearing someone tell me I can't do something.

For a split second, did you just start to question your current business growth belief system? Or maybe you experienced an "aha" epiphany that maybe you can achieve higher levels of success without spending any more budget or increasing headcount? Congratulations. Your business profit making transformation has begun.

More from Less: Superior Concept Misapplied

Now you know the business paradigm "more from more" only produces incremental success. It can never achieve the highest growth levels using the fewest resources. What's a smarter and superior path to maximize profits? To create wealth and become embarrassingly rich from your business, you must follow a more modern philosophy.

More from less.

Have you heard that maxim, "more from less," before? The theory and thinking isn't new. However, most leaders misunderstand the "more from less" philosophy and get it backward. Entrepreneurs who misapply this concept can make short-term gains but create long-term pains.

For example, I'll never forget during one of the frustrating years in my corporate life. The company I worked for was led by a CEO whose first name was Lester. The enterprise was in cost-cutting mode as expenses were rising too fast. I had been complaining to my manager because, after shattering my quotas for several years, my salary wasn't increasing. His response was, "Don't forget we all work for Les"—meaning that the corporation needed to keep more so I had to accept less. Frustrating.

Being cheap, or a fiscal freak, is just one way of misapplying "more from less." However, it's sadly played out in companies every day. As an attempt to be more successful, entrepreneurs and leaders become overly tightfisted, cut costs, or abuse relationships with employees and vendors.

For example, employees who used to have one job now have three roles to lower costs. In other situations, team members are burdened with old or outdated equipment to save money. Another way of misapplying this principle is consistently cutting back on compensation benefits or other employee perks to reduce costs. Abusing your people hurts all stakeholders. It lowers morale, increases talent turnover, and repels the high performers you need.

Another misapplication is when business owners beat down their vendors' prices or terms to increase their own margins. Or leaders drag out accounts payables to where suppliers are forced to use factoring to receive a fraction of their money. The belief that "more from less" means someone else suffers couldn't be further from the positive intent and potential power of this idea.

More from Less: Scaling Revenue Growth

You've just learned two important points. First, "more from more" will take forever to become wealthy. Second, "more from less" is a superior approach, but usually misapplied. Then how are aggressive entrepreneurs exploiting "more from less" to create millions faster? And keeping their employees, suppliers, and clients smiling?

If you had to choose growing faster or making more money, which would you choose? Many entrepreneurs would say growth, believing that ridiculous profits will come from larger size. They don't. An extraordinarily successful company is not measured by the revenue it makes (unless valued by market share) but the money *it can keep*. Are you rich if you can pay your bills? Or are you wealthy when you have 10 times more after covering expenses?

I know what you're saying. "We use our profits to 'spend more to make more.'" Great. You've completely missed the point of the principle. That's why entrepreneurs waste money and burn their profits. If they make it, they spend it. What if you could achieve explosive growth and still generate embarrassing amounts of profit?

This is the best-kept secret to achieving amazing top-line growth and ridiculous bottom-line results consistently: instead of focusing on business growth, you must learn to focus on "revenue growth." By that I don't mean just "growing top line." Mistakenly too many businesspeople interchange the term "business growth" and "revenue growth." But it's right here that the subtlety and unique application of "more from less" will make your company, your employees, and yourself a fortune.

Did you notice that the name of my firm isn't The Business Growth Company? Instead it is branded and trademarked The Revenue Growth® Company, LLC. It's the subtlety and counterintuitive application of the term "revenue growth" that is the method to making so many entrepreneurs and employees wealthy. Let me explain.

Revenue growth—*more from less*—is when your business produces more of all the good things without adding the bad things. Revenue growth, as you must learn, master, and apply, happens when your business can produce more revenue from every company asset. For example, you can produce more revenue from every:

- Contract
- Client
- Employee
- Sales pursuit
- Product or service
- Store location
- Asset
- New offering
- Geographic expansion
- Acquisition

You can produce more revenue from everything.

Periodically you must look at the results of areas of your business to see how much revenues increased. Did you spend more money, yes or no, driving up the top line?

You should be ready to jump out of your chair, unless you're on an airplane, to go measure your organization and revenue growth in different categories. This will show if your enterprise is getting bigger *and* more profitable. However, a warning first. The right way to apply this principle—*more from less*—has enormous challenges.

First, it's not culturally accepted because most businesspeople mentally live in the last century. Second, it's not supported by third parties who support you because they need you to increase your spending with them. Third, it's rarely ever measured. The few times I see this principle applied is with retail locations, "same-store sales" (SSS) year over year. But SSS is only a measurement. The secret to "more from less" success is the strategies that increase top line while maximizing bottom line.

Here is a quick example of "more from less" being applied. In one start-up situation, a team applying these principles helped a salesperson carrying a $750,000 quarterly quota sign a new contract valued at more than $13 million. That's 18 times her sales target. Using the old business growth "more from more" paradigm, to generate $13.5 million the company would have needed 17 more salespeople, each of them working several additional sales cycles, to win 17 more sales contracts. But that doesn't include the enormous costs of all these extra salespeople, sales expenses, support expenses, and so on.

Across all industries, around the world, our research shows the average sales win rate is about 25 percent, meaning that if salespeople work four opportunities, they win one. Which means this group, to generate $13 million, would have to multiply 17 times 4, which equals 68 unique sales cycles.

Do you know the costs of a typical but complex and lengthy sales pursuit? Do you know that every time you add a salesperson you have added eight categories of profit-eating costs to your business? Chapter 10, "Sales Conversion System," will detail those eight sales costs. Do you know how long it would take this organization to work through another 68 sales cycles? An entrepreneur following the classic business growth approach would spend millions to make millions, leaving little profit—in addition, wasting years for this small return. This company generated more than

$13 million in revenue with the costs of one salesperson, with a quick four-month sales cycle. That is "more from less."

A Counterintuitive and Startling Performance Fact

Years of researching past client engagements and successes identified dozens of places where the "more from less" principle is game-changing. Nine out of 10 entrepreneurs don't need more of most things they believe they need to grow and make money. They need less. Far less. To achieve faster, more profitable revenue growth, here is what entrepreneurs and teams want but usually don't need:

- ▸ They don't need more leads—they need fewer leads of much higher quality.
- ▸ They don't need more salespeople—most already have enough headcount to double and triple sales.
- ▸ They don't need more proposals flying out the door—they need to learn how to win more and lose less.
- ▸ They don't need more prospect or sales pursuits—they need to stop working the average of 50 to 75 percent of those prospects who will never buy.
- ▸ They don't need more marketing materials or brochures—most information doesn't accelerate the sale.
- ▸ They don't need more customers—they need higher-quality customers who pay more.
- ▸ They don't need more contracts—they need bigger, better, and longer-term agreements.
- ▸ They don't need more clients—they need clients who leave less often.

The Difference Between Business Growth and Revenue Growth

To become embarrassingly rich from your business, here is another way to cement this radical but business success-changing thinking. As I have explained, the core principle behind inferior business growth is "adding." Add more to make more. However, revenue growth is not adding. Revenue growth, as I want you to learn and apply the concept, is the most powerful form of "scaling."

Yet, the term "scaling" is another overused business expression that is quite often misunderstood. When I ask entrepreneurs and CEOs their ability to scale, they usually answer like this:

▸ We can scale up operations as we are not running third shift.
▸ We can scale the sales organization and easily hire more salespeople.
▸ We can scale up marketing through using more advertising mediums.
▸ We can scale the organization by investing in more technology.

Are these examples of scaling? Not by my application. If you look closely, they are really "more from more." That's adding. Authentic and profit-based scaling is achieving more *without adding any costs or resources—* in some cases, even lowering costs and achieving greater production. One client had five salespeople generating less than a million dollars of sales a year. Three years later after a few retired or left, they have two salespeople generating several million annually. That is real revenue growth, and it is helping create a ridiculously profitable company.

Revenue growth scaling is when assets (of any kind)
produce more revenue while barely increasing costs.

For example, say you have product or service X that sells 1,000 units. For faster growth, many entrepreneurs add more products like product Z to sell another 1,000 units, when in most cases product X could have sold 2,000 without adding all of the costs, infrastructure, and headaches associated with product Z. I know that is a simple formula. Yet you would be shocked at how few entrepreneurs tap the huge potential of what they already have on hand. In every company sits a treasure chest of profits from existing assets waiting to be unlocked.

Here is a question to drive revenue growth scaling: How much more revenue or percentage of revenue did you produce this year versus last year? For example, in my last corporate role as an executive helping run a public company, I judiciously tracked the average size of contracts we signed. The first year our average contract size was just less than $200,000. In the third year the average size exceeded $400,000.

Why is this important for you? Because adding massive amounts of revenue per client, minimizing marketing and sales, using fewer resources, and requiring minimal support retains cash. Every time you add a client, your organization requires more administration, more support, and more infrastructure to manage each one. Those resources shred profits, taking longer for you and your team to become embarrassingly wealthy.

Barriers and Resistance to Success

I hope reading to this point you see how much easier it will be to make a pile of cash from your venture. Would you like more proof to give you greater confidence in this concept? Every principle in this book has been corporately field-tested, some more than a thousand times, to prove they work. When these concepts are matched with the right *will*, in the right sequence, astonishing results happen. This unique revenue growth application has created thousands of embarrassingly successful entrepreneurs and employees who have become millionaires around the globe.

But wait, even if your team is ready to walk through fire, there are huge roadblocks and change-resistance challenges ahead. With more than two decades of experience in thousands of different situations, I've identified about two dozen major resistance issues to transforming performance. One issue by itself can kill a company, but no entrepreneur faces just one.

All resistance issues fall into one of two categories: external or internal. Most businesspeople aren't naive about barriers to success. But they mistakenly believe the worst threats are external to their company. Wrong.

The strongest forces killing success are found inside a firm.

Internally, every idea or decision is politically positioned or emotionally charged. Ironically, the most ruthless saboteurs to success work either in or for a company. These may be leaders or employees putting themselves first, or investors, third parties, or board members following last century's approaches. In other cases, internal people will hear the words you say but not apply the right meaning. The term *revenue growth* versus *business growth* is just one of hundreds of examples of mistaken interchange.

Most often, these people mean well, but they're operating from stale, flawed, or inaccurate paradigms. I will warn you now: new thought leadership is lonely. You will have difficult to challenging conversations with people who haven't read this book or don't understand these counterintuitive principles. I know, because I've been fighting against change resistance issues with employees, teams, executives, and board members for decades. Why do I keep working to drag people kicking and screaming out of the last century? For the joy of watching them experience mind-blowing results when they learn to do things a new way.

Everyone in your company must be on the same path—*optimized revenue growth*. You'll quickly identify the "more from more" flawed thinking people—especially outside experts and vendors. Don't worry. I or this book will help you show them how to partner with you to compete and dominate in this new era.

Here are some examples of how people will try to sabotage your transformation efforts from business growth thinking to a more powerful revenue growth measurement. This is the language or thoughts that most saboteurs use. Try not to laugh when someone says this in a meeting.

- ► *Historical success.* "We've always done it that way, and we've had business success." Or "Our business is doing fine." Or "If it's not broke, don't fix it."
- ► *Historical failure.* "We've tried things like this, but they never worked out." Or "We've spent a lot of time trying to do things that way, but we didn't get the results."
- ► *Delusions of competency.* "We're already doing this (or these things); it's nothing new."
- ► *Living in the past.* "That's not how I was taught to run a business." Or "Here is how we did it, and we were successful before."
- ► *Passive aggressive—cooperate to graduate.* "Sounds great, I'll start doing it now." Or "Sure, let's try it for a while." Or "Anything will be better than what we've been doing."
- ► *Flawed expertise.* "That new approach sounds awesome, but . . . I read on the Internet/my buddy said they did it a certain way/my CEO or entrepreneurial business group (none of whom are experts in business transformation) suggested doing it a different way." Or "I heard a speaker last week suggest this idea that is different."

At this point, you understand why so many entrepreneurs and small business owners fail. They never learn how to make serious money—earnings, cash, and profits—with their business. Which means hitting any size iceberg can sink their ship. Even the best entrepreneurs can follow the wrong path of business growth. But not you or your team. Hopefully, you have the burning desire to follow the right way: the revenue growth way of scaling all assets to achieve maximum profitability.

You and your team also have new language and standards. For example, you should ask before every major action, Is what we are doing "more from more"? Or is there a way to produce more sales, revenue, and profits using the resources we have—"more from less"?

Why Take This Radical Counterintuitive Advice from Me?

As a speaker at a CEO entrepreneur event at MIT in Boston, I joined the group in the morning to meet some of the attendees during breakfast. One of the CEOs came up and asked to join my wife and me at our table. After we'd introduced ourselves, she asked, "What makes you qualified to speak to our group?"

The question didn't bother me, but I could tell my wife was put off by the aggressive inquiry. There were two ways I could have answered her question. First, let me share with you how I wanted to respond to this "in your face" inquiry and then what I actually said.

Initially, I thought about giving her the following bullet points from my biography:

- Delivering more then 10,000 hours of business transformation content in speeches, workshops, and programs in 36 countries.
- Helping small businesses *and* large corporations generate billions to tens of billions in new sales, impacting the lives of more than one million employees.
- Redesigning, transforming, and turbocharging more than a thousand organizations around the world—from strategy and structure to culture and compensation, from people and process to technology and measurement.

- Fast-tracking to become chief strategy officer (CSO) and chief marketing officer (CMO) of a billion-dollar technology services firm with thousands of employees.
- Managing teams in 16 different Asia-Pacific countries, while living in Hong Kong, with a marketing budget in the tens of millions of dollars.
- Building out part of a public software start-up from $2 million to $36 million in about two and a half years—with my sales teams achieving an astonishing win rate of 48 out of 50 contracts (96 percent) for three years against IBM, HP, CA, Tivoli, BMC, and Harris software companies. The company, Micromuse (MUSE), was eventually bought by IBM in 2005, making several hundred employees millionaires.

Although those are highlights from four decades of global business success, I knew she wanted to hear what distinguished my background from that of any other speaker. She needed to hear jaw-dropping results for entrepreneurs, so I shared this:

"I have developed a phased road map of proven principles and methods that have helped thousands of entrepreneurs and employees become millionaires and multimillionaires with their businesses—some in less than 12 months. In addition, I have spent decades proving that every business can double or triple their sales, revenue, or profits and not have to spend another dollar on marketing or hire another salesperson, creating massive profits."

Then I asked her, "Have you helped your employees become millionaires with your business?"

She responded with a much more polite tone: "No."

"Then I think you will enjoy learning my road map and methods so you can do that," I said, smiling.

CHAPTER 1

New Will and Different Way

Over the last two decades I've been analyzing the characteristics, traits, and results of the thousands of entrepreneurs in our customized high intensity programs. When running our Revenue Growth® program, called RAMP®, I (or a team member) am physically at the client site every week turbocharging the organization. Some weekly session engagements of two to eight hours have lasted more than five years. This on-site, deep-in-the-engine embedment, building all parts of the organizations for years, gave me insights, opportunities for testing, and proof that were not possible through just observation, research, or training. The participant results neatly split into two groups, ranging from solid results to ridiculously profitable growth and success.

Group One included those who experienced really good or great results. Group Two were those entrepreneurs and employees who quickly (within months or a few years) became millionaires and multimillionaires. Meaning the second group of participants made massive returns from what they learned and applied. Having excited and fanatical wealthy clients is awesome for them and for us. However, my vision is creating companies that help the employees and stakeholders become successful and make the world a better place. Never forget: business should be fun and a win for everyone!

After analyzing thousands of session notes of program delivery and client results, this was the big "aha": Those who created wealth and became embarrassingly rich, Group Two, exhibited the most "high spectrum entrepreneurial" traits. The most consistent characteristic of Group Two was the entrepreneur *and* team members' unwavering willingness to do things differently. No matter how uncomfortable.

Group One, those entrepreneurs and teams who had varying degrees of success but didn't achieve *retire tomorrow* level results, had this characteristic: They had little willingness to be radically different. They thought and executed more like small business thinkers and owners. The takeaway? The businesspeople who didn't achieve astonishing results had this commonality:

> *They might call themselves entrepreneurs—*
> *but they're not "entrepreneurial."*

What does that mean? Most of those entrepreneurs were basically "small business managers." They never thought, executed, or operated with an entrepreneurial mindset or drive. Other entrepreneurs in Group One might have started with "high spectrum entrepreneurial" characteristics and drive but lost their way. They fell into the "small business owner ditch" and were unwilling to climb out. For example:

- ▸ They were innovative creating their idea of a hot new product or superior service, but now they market and sell their unique offerings like their competitors.
- ▸ These participants might have taken risks when starting a business, but they haven't taken any major or calculated risks since.
- ▸ They may have invested to start their venture, but now only spend money to make their business bigger, instead of investing to make it extremely profitable and cash rich.
- ▸ They started with a vision for greatness and to sell in a few years, but now they're jogging on the small business treadmill barely making money or struggling with cash issues.
- ▸ They began with an attitude to dominate, but now they're happy to get along and win their fair share.
- ▸ They experienced winning all the time in the beginning, but as the business grew, their new goal was just winning more often than losing.
- ▸ They were all about change and doing things differently when they started, but now they're scared of change and resist any effort of transformation.

How important is thinking and acting entrepreneurial? It's foundational to becoming embarrassingly wealthy from your business. This book is not designed to teach you how to become a millionaire in 25 years, but one-tenth that time. However, you and your team must understand that it is impossible to go from A to B if you're not starting at point A. In other words.

You can't quickly go from entrepreneur to millionaire if you
don't start as a true entrepreneur and be entrepreneurial.

This was research based on our clients, but I believe it's true in the marketplace. The mass of entrepreneurs are not actually entrepreneurial—*they're small business owners.* They think small. Act small. Make small changes. And over time accept small results.

You can call yourself an entrepreneur, CEO, or anything else you want. And you can act the popular entrepreneurial aphorism of "fake it till you make it" for validation. But titles, name tags, and facades won't make you rich.

Being or labeling someone a small business owner is not an indictment or judgment. I'm both a small business owner and an entrepreneur. Being an entrepreneur does not make someone superior. It's not the title, it's *your expectations.* What leaves me frustrated is the thousands of small business owners who come to me complaining about how hard it is to make money, moaning about the challenges of being successful as a small business owner. They want my help but aren't willing to radically change how they think and act to achieve optimum results. Or worse, they don't show leadership and they tolerate change-resistant team members.

When the Student Is Ready, the Teacher Will Appear

"Why did you become an entrepreneur?" I asked a new prospect to see if she just needed surgical fixes or was a fit for our high intensity transformational RAMP® program. She shared with me the pain and sleepless nights she had been experiencing over the past five years struggling with her business.

She explained in a controlled tirade, "I hated my corporate career as I felt like a cultural misfit. I was penalized for creative ideas and marginalized for questioning the doctrines. My silent mantra became 'go along and get along.'

"I wanted to try new ideas, do things differently, but any innovative thinking was squashed. My breaking point was when our CEO spoke to our leadership team after we missed our year-end numbers. He challenged us, demanding we think and act more entrepreneurial. It was a total crock of crap. Nothing in our culture, rewards, or recognition supported being entrepreneurial. So, I quit."

She continued, "I had a unique idea for a service that I didn't see anyone providing, which my company didn't want to try. With several years of savings, I decided to take the proverbial plunge and do it by starting my own business."

I responded, "I totally understand how you feel. CEOs ask me to make their teams more entrepreneurial. I tell them I can't make anyone do anything. But I can help create the culture, systems, and environment to foster that kind of behavior. Did you achieve the freedom and control you wanted?" I politely probed.

"No," she half smiled. "I've discovered I traded corporate stress for small business anxiety. As a corporate VP I didn't worry about money once the budgets were finalized. However, running a start-up business, all I worry about—*and I agonize day and night*—is money. No one warned me that running a business is all about money. I didn't envision being consumed with earnings, income, paying bills, making payroll, paying vendors, managing credit cards, and juggling cash flow 24-7. I have too little time with prospects, clients, and employees."

Then she added, "The stress has increased. After burning through my savings and then some bridge loans, we took on an investor a couple of years back. The investor's help felt like a godsend in the beginning. They offered valuable support and guidance. I thought this was my savior as the cash injection made all the money challenges go away. *For a short time.* Then the cash struggles came back. The investor is more demanding, questioning my decisions. I've added fear to my worries. It's suffocating."

"What do you want to change most?" I probed.

"I want my business to make real money. Cash in the bank that I don't need, a reserve fund. I feel like I can't breathe. A sizeable bank account would give me a mental cushion to think clearly. I want enough excess capital to get through ups and downs. I'm so tired of playing the money games of moving cash around, floating bills, apologizing to vendors, only paying the minimums on credit cards," she said, exasperated.

NEW WILL AND DIFFERENT WAY 19

"Would a million in your bank account solve that problem?" I asked.

"Absolutely," she exclaimed.

"Is that your goal—to make a million from your business to become liquid?" I probed.

"Money was never my goal. It is now." She hesitated, then spoke slowly. "I always thought that if I provided a really great service and made my clients happy, issues like money wouldn't be a problem. I was so naive it's embarrassing. A million dollars in the bank would give me what I wanted from being an entrepreneur—freedom and control over my career and life."

"First of all, I'm confident your company offers excellent services and you have a rock star team. Second, you already know how to run a business. But you've never learned the most important lesson about business success. You have to learn how to turn on the parts of your company, not only your employees, to generate revenue and profits for you," I explained.

"I'm so ready I can't stand it. However, I've pounded into my team to put the client first and money second," she stated.

"Perfect. However, putting the client first will not guarantee profit or growth. You have to do both. To attain a seven-figure bank account, you will need to make two radical transformations. The first change is developing a different *will* to succeed. Second is following an uncommon *way*. Many clients have said changing their will and way were harder than starting and running their companies. One last point. In 25 years, we don't have a case study where anyone earned millions without the whole company, especially key employees, being in total unison following the new thinking and path," I shared.

The New Will

"You've heard the adage don't work harder, work—"

She interrupted, "Smarter. Yes, that's what we're all about."

"Great. Now stop thinking like that. If you want to create wealth as quickly as possible, then don't follow that flawed advice. That phrase, which sounds clever, will sabotage success. It means you and your employees are doing all the work. Remember, you or your employees can't scale rapidly, be leveraged, or act as an enterprise acceleration point. Many entrepreneurs or individual heroes are the choke point, barrier, or roadblock. Even if they work smarter," I explained.

"The 'will' you must follow is different than work ethic or intelligence. It's not the will to work hard, be persistent, or learn from your failures and persevere. Can you name a serious businessperson you know who doesn't have a strong will to succeed? The myth of 'working hard and grinding it out' is why entrepreneurs will never quickly earn millions. Even worse, without the right will to change, they'll stay running on a treadmill," I said.

"We have strong wills. My leaders have team huddles every day pushing that subject," she declared.

"How are your morning rah-rahs working out?" I pushed. Taking a breath, she reflected while accepting the irony of strong will and mediocre results. "See, that's the problem," I noted. "Most every entrepreneur, small business owner, and employee has the same strong will as you. And more daily motivation sessions won't help. The wrong will is the reason you're not outdistancing your competition.

"The will you must develop is the drive and desire—*not to work harder or smarter*—but to ignite and leverage key parts of your company to do more work. I want you to fire up all parts of your company, not only your people. When you intelligently wake the sleepy parts of your enterprise, business becomes fun and making money becomes easy," I said.

"I don't understand," she questioned. "What you said about strong will and desire goes against everything I've ever been taught."

"Perfect," I replied as I smiled. She slanted her head showing confusion. "Your transformation has begun," I quickly added. "The genius entrepreneur Einstein said it best. Doing things the same way and expecting different results is insanity."

I then shared an analogy that had helped my clients mentally own this powerful dichotomy of "you doing the work versus your company." Picture both an unmotorized treadmill and an escalator in an office building. The unmotorized treadmill means the people, you and your employees, are the motor.

To make the large treadmill belt move, you have to walk or run and never stop. If you don't work at pushing the belt, it won't turn. Like most businesses, the company only runs as hard as you work. But as you've experienced on the unmotorized treadmill, it stays flat and you don't seem to get anywhere.

Think of an escalator. It has many parts, similar to an enterprise. There are the motors, trusses, belts, balustrade, panels, steps, and handrails. How much effort is required to reach a higher level? None. When the escalator parts move in the right sequence, you gracefully rise with no sweat, tears, or stress. With the unmotorized treadmill, like a small business, you can run all day and you're still in the same spot.

The will you must develop is to make critical parts of your enterprise work for you. Design and operate areas of your company to create leverage, accelerate, and scale to take your business to higher levels. Every organization has one to two more levels of potential easily available requiring no extra effort or energy. Small business owners who are not entrepreneurial become work martyrs sweating on the treadmill running as fast as they can. They think, "Look at me, look how hard I work," while on the inside painfully realizing they're still in the same place financially.

Every company has parts to leverage, accelerate, and scale to produce faster, no-cost growth and profit performance. Even more amazing is that machinery, like escalator components, can run all day for years. But you must develop the will to learn, master, apply, and leverage those parts of your company. Each part will help you create stronger client demand and convert that demand into new contracts and cash sooner. Your new will is the first major change to making a fortune 10 to 100 times faster.

"I'm sold. I want our company to operate like an escalator and get me off the darn treadmill. What are the parts and how do we begin? I'll get my leadership team," she stated.

Different Way

"Team, I want to introduce you to our new in-house expert. He is a Revenue Growth® Architect. His role is being our business transformation guide. We are changing our path," she said.

The leader of operations quipped, "Where are we going?"

She looked at the team. "We are going to change how we've been doing things. We will continue to put clients first, while also achieving profitable and explosive growth." Turning to me, she said, "Tell them."

"You're going to learn a smarter, easier, more effective way to double and triple sales, revenue, and profits. Without working any harder. But first we have to begin on the right path. This road map consists of four major phases," I said.

One of the leaders jumped in, "Like Start, Growth, Maturity, and Decline?"

"Not exactly. That is called a business life cycle or maturity graph, moving from start-up to decline or death. That chart shows the natural progression of a business in relation to time and revenues or profits earned. But it doesn't offer strategies in how to stay in growth mode forever and make a continuous fortune.

"The road map we will carry out is about creating optimized company performance, meaning producing maximum profits and revenue using minimum resources. A company that doesn't focus on optimized performance can quickly travel the path you mentioned, headed toward maturity and demise. Death or dominance is a choice.

"Like many, you have been following a common but flawed path called 'more from more.' Last century that was the road less traveled. This century that overcrowded trail wastes time, burns resources, and eats profits," I said.

"The road map, the Way, to making the most money with your business while utilizing the fewest resources, has four distinct phases." I provided an overview of each phase.

Phase I: Revenue Ready—*Validation*

This foundational phase puts in place the building blocks to optimize growth. However, it doesn't begin by fixing what's underperforming on the inside of your company. The phase starts outside, with the marketplace problem to solve, accurately framing the genesis of how and why your company began. What is your venture's reason for being? This is where most entrepreneurs and businesses get off track. Yes, even before an entrepreneur creates a formal business structure, too many ventures are set up for mediocrity or worse, failure.

Phase II: Market Ready—*Preparation*

This is the phase that every company, big and small, skips, cheats, or checks the boxes and jumps over. This is all about the preparation required to create the best strategies for most wins and fewest losses. The principles in this phase prepare your company for maximum performance and results, using the least amount of people, time, and investment. If you were a general in the military, would you send your soldiers into battle without the right strategy, gear, protocols, methods, and structure? Many entrepreneurs fight unprepared and treat the casualties (business losses) as a badge of courage.

Phase III: Go to Market—*Winning*

This phase is where the battle becomes the war. You are now fighting to win quality contacts, new clients, and cash in the shortest time possible. It's about winning, conversions, and speed. This phase is easy when you begin your venture. But start earning a little money, start winning some contracts, and you will have competitors everywhere. Typically, people think of this phase as marketing efforts and selling activities, but that narrow thinking is last century's application. When the Go to Market phase is set up properly and implemented correctly, minimal efforts can rain new clients and cash.

Phase IV: Own the Market—*Dominating*

This phase is about domination. You are winning all the time in your segment and space. Amazing and shockingly positive results happen in this phase. Superior talent wants to work for you. Investors and lenders beg for your business. High-quality clients pursue you. Although your teams are still executing with strong will and incredible discipline, the money making is easy. In many cases, cash flow can be raging like a river after a storm. This phase gives you and your team total control over your destiny, success, and future. Running a business while in this phase is fun and exhilarating.

When I finished my explanation, the CEO entrepreneur commented, "Those four phases don't sound that hard."

"I understand what you're thinking," I replied. "However, achieving proficiency of this four-phased road map is challenging for numerous reasons. First, it's hard to mentally own the concepts because entrepreneurs are taught to work, not to spend time thinking and learning. Second, the markets, buyers, and competitors are constantly changing, which means you must be evolving and adapting. Third, there is no quick payback. Some revenue growth principles won't show impact for months. Our digital *now* culture, delivered to your door the same day, instant gratification reward system has destroyed the virtue of patience," I said.

"You mentioned proficiency, what do you mean by that?" she asked. I explained as follows.

Levels of Proficiency

To quickly unlock the riches of your company and create a fortune, you must understand proficiency. This is skill or competency in doing something. In my road map it's the levels from awareness to mastery level. All parts of your company, not just your people, must achieve high proficiency levels for each phase and its principles.

Proficiency is commonly used for measuring fluency with language. How effectively can someone communicate in a foreign language? There are hundreds of models, pyramids, and stacks to illustrate different levels of proficiency, most starting with no knowledge or beginning skill.

Martial arts is the best international example of proficiency levels by using colored belts. No matter which discipline, they all start with white belt—white meaning blank, no color or no skill. Some traditions have a rainbow of progressive belt colors. Most have six. The pinnacle of achievement is black belt. Although there are "dans," or stripes, for higher achievement, black is the highest belt color. Black belt is the universal symbol for the mastery level of martial arts. Yet if you talk to most people who have earned a black belt, they will tell you that their learning has just begun. I am confident you will feel the same way after you start mastering, integrating, and leveraging the principles in this book.

Here's another example for my golfing friends. Most people believe golf proficiency is the ability to shoot a low score. Scoring in golf is the result of a player's proficiency level. Quick, how many different ball flights can come off a golf club face (sans putter)?

If you said one or a few, you are an amateur, beginner, and unaware. Sorry. Professionals know there are nine unique flight patterns for launching a golf ball. Golf mastery is being able to execute one of nine perfect ball trajectories at the right time, right distance, in any kind of weather. You will hear golf announcers describe proficiency this way: "That golfer has all the shots." I hope that helped your game.

Your team must read, learn, apply, and achieve mastery level with these phases and principles as core competencies. Please don't forget your path to business wealth is only as fast as your weakest proficiency. Pro golfers who dominate say they "let the club do the work." In the same way, you will learn to have parts of your company *do the work* for you.

Entrepreneurial success comes from creating, integrating, and leveraging "company proficiencies," not just people effort.

Now you understand the new will—*letting parts of your company do more of the work.* The different way—*what parts of your company to turn on and leverage in the right sequence.* Let's move from theory (why do it) to application (how to do it). The following chapters are the most powerful profit-producing principles from the 600-plus modules in our Revenue Growth® high intensity programs. I have applied these principles to create high growth and profit transformation in companies ranging from start-ups to billion-dollar enterprises all over the world.

One last important point to keep in mind. At some point, you have probably been in an internal business meeting and working to answer this question: "How do we attract more clients, quickly increase sales, and make more money—without spending more time or effort?"

The following chapters will provide field-tested and proven answers to your team for every type and size of company and every kind of situation.

Revenue Ready
(VALIDATION)

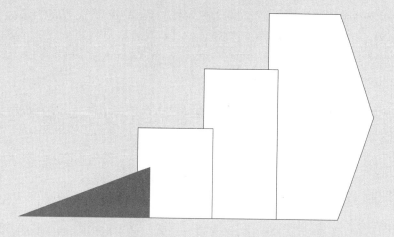

Only one in a thousand companies is ready to generate all the revenue, profit, and sales possible using the fewest resources. Why so few? In most cases, major mistakes and flawed assumptions were made or followed before the venture started. In other situations, what was true when the business began has changed.

Entrepreneurial journeys are like the voyage of the RMS *Titanic*. Were you taught that one of the worst maritime disasters of all time was caused by the massive cruise liner hitting an iceberg? Was that block of ice the real cause?

The truth is the *Titanic* voyage failed well before the ship set sail. Similar to most companies, the ship and venture were not set up for success but for disaster. Here are a few failure points: falsely believing the ship was unsinkable, not having enough lifeboats, using inferior steel to save money, leaving port with a raging fire in the boiler room, sailing too fast, and not sending SOS codes but their own proprietary codes. In trying to avoid the iceberg, the captain of the *Titanic* turned the ship, exposing its weakest part. Experts argue he should have rammed the large mass of ice head-on, using the reinforced stem (front edge of the bow).

Starting your venture and revenue growth journey on the wrong foot can be disastrous, but you may not know it for a while. However, there is one thing that can solve almost every business problem you will face: more profits that produce a strong cash flow. Without money, every problem is an iceberg waiting to sink your ship. Let's set sail the right way, by being Revenue Ready.

CHAPTER 2

Your Company Genesis: The FMP

W here does a great business begin?

Most people would say a business starts with an idea.

Some would say a business starts with a product or service.

Others would say that legally forming a company, corporation, or LLC starts a business.

These, or a combination, might be how a business starts, but it's not how a remarkably successful, ridiculously profitable, money-making company actually begins.

Years back, on an American Airlines flight from Los Angeles, California, down to San Diego, I sat next to an elderly gentleman who was shuffling through business reports. We exchanged greetings and then started talking about what we did. I shared with him my career in the technology sector: outsourcing computer operations of large corporations. My specific company was EDS, a multinational information services firm started by Ross Perot. He smiled politely.

"And what about you?" I probed.

He responded gleefully, "I'm having more fun than ever. I own six companies, including a winery in Temecula that I'm flying down to visit." He continued, "However, there is one new venture that has me quite excited." His passion for this start-up endeavor was contagious. "I've acquired this new golf company, and we have an innovative driver coming out that is going to change golf. . . . Golf is such a hard sport for so many people. Our new metal oversized driver will make hitting the ball off the tee easier and drive it a long, long way."

I nodded in agreement, "Yes, the first tee shot is stressful and difficult, and anything that gives any golfer more distance with control solves a lot of golfers' frustrations."

We talked more about golf and his winery. When the plane landed, he turned to me and politely said, "It was nice meeting you. Here is my card. My name's Ely Callaway." The name didn't mean much at the time. However, meeting him and knowing the outcome of his story sure does resonate today, a few decades later.

If you play golf, you know all about Callaway clubs and how their "Big Bertha" changed driving forever. If you don't play golf, Callaway Golf created the first oversized technology-based metal driver that solved several golf challenges. Because of how the "Bertha" improved golf, Callaway Golf went on to become a billion-dollar company.

Why should you care about this story? It's understanding where an extremely successful business—*a serious money-making company*—begins. *It starts with a problem.* In this case, the problem was a gap between how golfers play and how they want to play.

Callaway started and became successful because the current drivers weren't addressing the frustration golfers were experiencing in hitting the ball. Swinging a Bertha allowed new and old golfers the ability to bomb their shots off the tee. The Bertha driver was so effective at producing longer, straighter shots, many golf courses around the world had to be redesigned by adding yards to every hole. Ely didn't only help golfers, he changed golf.

This chapter will reveal the foundational principle of how and where sustainable, fast-growth, high-profit companies actually begin. Understanding this core concept is the first and most critical step to start and build a successful enterprise. If you get this first step wrong, it won't mean you can't have a decent business. It will simply mean the risks of failure are greater, the time to make money is longer, and the effort to become a millionaire might never happen. Applying the key elements of this concept is the difference between grinding your life away in a company forever or making millions fast.

Fundamental Marketplace Problem (FMP)

Back to the most basics of business questions: Where does a great company actually begin?

With a problem . . .

Every business—let me repeat that to be crystal clear—every brilliant and sustainable enterprise starts by identifying a marketplace problem that exists today or will exist in the future. That marketplace problem is not currently being solved, or the market is underserved, creating a gap or opportunity. A marketplace problem creates a commercial opportunity for someone—hopefully you—to close the gap and make millions. The gap is a current state of pain or lack of pleasure that keeps the buyers from being where they want to be.

I've coined this concept as a "Fundamental Marketplace Problem," or "FMP."

Without a problem, representing a gap, to be solved, why should any business exist? Who would pay you to fix or offer something that doesn't need to be changed? Every FMP falls somewhere on the spectrum of "wants and needs."

However, not every want or need is the genesis for a sustainable, extremely profitable, successful company.

The more complex and the more widespread the FMP, the faster your enterprise can grow and the more wealth you can create.. Through space exploration, we know that the planet Mars holds vast amounts of precious minerals and elements that could quickly advance humanity's ability to thrive in the solar system. Some scientists estimate that mining Mars would be worth trillions of dollars. But access to Mars is a classic FMP.

Humans can't get to other planets because of the costs and logistics of transporting groups of people through space. The weight and equipment required to feed a space crew for several years are two of the biggest challenges. However, imagine a solution to the travel FMP—say, for example, people hibernating so they could sleep their way to Mars. That would dramatically reduce the food and water needed. Where is the idea to solve that FMP of traveling to and mining Mars? Scientists and companies are studying how bears can hibernate for so long without eating or drinking.

If you want to be an entrepreneur and start a business, that's one thing. However, if you want to make millions from a company, then identify an FMP to be solved and then figure out the best way to solve it. I will cover the how-to—the solving part—in more detail in the Market Ready and Go to Market phases of this book.

Once an FMP is identified, you must start crafting, creating, and imagining the idea to fix the problem or close the gap. However, the synergy between an FMP and your idea to solve it is still only a solution—not a serious money-making company yet. But it's that synergy—problem meets solution—that creates the potential to turn a gap into gold.

FMP Is Foundational to Earning Millions

Think of the FMP as the fertile soil required for the seeds of a successful venture. To identify the potential of an FMP, you must analyze all three parts: the foundational cause, the marketplace scope and scale, and the degree of pain.

Foundational Cause

An example of the foundational cause for an FMP that almost everyone has experienced is buying a new or used car. Few consumers would agree that dealing with a car salesperson and the auto-buying process is fun, safe, low risk, or enjoyable. Owning a new car is a joy. Dealing with car salespeople can be torture. Yet what is the underlying cause or basis of this pain? Why does the "I want a new car but hate dealing with a salesperson" fundamental problem exist?

People dread car salespeople because of the underlying premise in the car-buying and selling relationship. In almost all cases, no matter when or where you're buying an automobile, there is a serious conflict of interest. For the salesperson to make a lot of money (commissions and bonuses), the buyer needs to lose money. In other words, the more the buyer pays for the car, the more commission the salesperson makes. That's the foundational cause of this marketplace problem.

You know that trust is a critical element to a successful business relationship. How can there be trust when the car-buying game is set up as a "win-lose" proposition? This same conflict of interest is found in many industries with direct commissioned salespeople such as insurance, broker-age, and real estate. Most sales compensation plans reward the salesperson for larger and higher margin or more profitable transactions, which means the buyer will usually overpay.

How have companies tried to deal with this fundamental conflict of "wanting to avoid car salespeople"? In the past, auto dealers tried train-ing programs. They tried "no-haggle" car buying. Some dealers have openly admitted they try to hire only women as salespeople because buyers tend to consider females more honest and trustworthy. That's sexist and discriminatory.

None of those ideas truly solves the fundamental problem of bro-ken trust. Many auto dealers today have taken a completely different approach—shifting the problem. They don't let their salespeople sell at all or be paid on commissions. They have them act as ambassadors or humble shepherds to get the buyer back to the "finance department," where the real professional salespeople are now hiding.

Most new car dealers don't make money selling new cars; they make money selling financing, warranties, and add-ons. And that's where the sales conflict is today. Car dealerships have never solved the root cause of the trust problem. Sadly, they've quietly shifted the broken relationship issue to another department. That means there is a car buying FMP worth tens of millions to whoever can solve it.

Marketplace Scope and Scale

The "marketplace" part of the definition determines the scope and scale of the FMP. I gave you an example of an extremely broad problem of dealing with car salespeople. However, there is huge money to be made in narrow FMPs too.

For example, consider drug manufacturers. They might have to invest a billion dollars on some drugs to march them through the FDA-approval gauntlet only to help a small fraction of afflicted people. Buying a car is not a life-or-death situation. So, the dollar exchange—the potential—is based on a massive number of transactions. Conversely, regarding life or death, the potential for a lucrative business is not dependent on a numbers game, but the cost of each transaction.

One way for you to determine the scope and scale of an FMP is to cat-egorize the situation on the spectrum of "want" or "need." A new or used car is usually a want, and only on occasion a need. Medicine to cure a life-threatening problem is a need. It's a "must-have."

Degree of Pain

Once you identify a foundational cause and there is good scope and scale, it's time to discuss the third part—the discomfort of the problem. Frame the problem by levels of pain or pleasure. Why hasn't the car-buying process been solved when there is a clear conflict of interest and massive scope and scale? It's because of the low level of pain. People buying cars have come to accept that purchasing a car (or other transaction with commissioned salespeople) has an inherent agony. Most buyers begrudgingly swallow that anguish because "that's just the way it is—part of the process."

Either the "level of pain" or degree of positive emotion experienced is what motivates buyers to buy. The higher the pain or amount of pleasure, the more people will pay. and the faster they'll give you their money. Why is the newest high-end restaurant always sold out for weeks or months? Is it because people are hungry? No. It's the gap. It's because people want to pay for a culinary pleasure not available anywhere else.

A quick way to test the level of pain is to ask buyers how serious the problem or issue is to them. Ask if they'll write you a check to solve it. Their action, or lack thereof, is all you need to know about the problem and pain level of your FMP.

Back to golf. If you play the game, how much would you pay to hit the ball 30 yards farther than your golfing buddies? A fortune, right?

FMPs Evolve

In your pursuit to become a millionaire as an entrepreneur, you must know FMPs come and go. They evolve at different times and speeds. Marketplaces are constantly changing. Wants and needs are continuously evolving, and the speed of change is ever increasing. Meaning those who are first to market aren't always the best at solving the FMP or making the most money. However, last to market can be bad, too. Timing is critical.

Probably there is no better example of FMPs evolving and old solutions being destroyed than the advent of the smartphone. The handheld device has become the technological wrecking ball of so many FMPs and solutions offered by other items.

The smartphone, at last count, has replaced more than 50 different tools and items including cameras, flashlights, video cameras, compasses, radios, boom boxes, books, specialty e-book readers, calculators, voice recorders, carpenter's levels, TVs, bar-code scanners, landlines, alarm clocks, wristwatches, calendars, notepads, airline tickets and boarding passes, remote controls for TVs, and so on. How many companies have had their single products replaced or wiped out by the smartphone? The number keeps increasing.

All of those products at one time solved different FMPs. However, those items created FMPs by having to carry, haul, buy, or maintain them. Traveling and taking high-quality pictures 10 years ago would have required an SLR camera or a dedicated bulky video recorder if you wanted to capture high-definition pictures and movies. Now, many smartphones are better than thousand-dollar cameras used to be.

FMPs being destroyed is the bad news. What's the good news? Needs didn't go away. Those solutions simply created new FMPs. For example, some smartphones need dedicated apps to take certain types of pictures and videos. There is a huge new market for specialty lenses that snap onto your smartphone for professional-level photography. Thousands of people on YouTube are enjoying lucrative careers by teaching people how to use the innovative functions of their smartphones. Money-making content creation jobs like those didn't exist decades ago.

FMPs Lead to Millionaires and Billionaires

Mark Cuban is a great American entrepreneurial success story. A self-made multi-billionaire, he has bought and sold numerous companies as the richest investor on ABC's prime-time TV show *Shark Tank*. Besides his stint on *Dancing with the Stars*, another popular TV show, he is also owner of the Dallas Mavericks NBA basketball team, a franchise valued at more than $2 billion. Here is a story about how Mark earned his first million and then billion using the concept of FMP.

Mark and I attended the same college, Indiana University (IU) in Bloomington, Indiana. He graduated in 1981 and moved to Dallas, Texas, as did I a year later. We became close friends while living next to each other in the Village Apartment complex in the heart of Big D (Dallas). Mark was selling software in a retail store, and I was working for a division of PepsiCo, Frito-Lay.

Mark was ahead of his time in understanding and writing columns about technology and so decided to leave the retail space and start a new business. The company Mark created was to help business owners solve a new and huge Fundamental Marketplace Problem. The FMP that Mark exploited in the 1980s evolved because companies were buying numerous computers and workstations. However, those devices couldn't talk to each other, and they couldn't share expensive devices like freestanding laser printers. Mark started a firm that offered software and installed LANs (local area networks) to leverage a company's hardware investment.

One of the joys Mark and I had attending our college in the late seventies and eighties was the excitement of our school winning National Championships in basketball. In 1976, the IU basketball team went 32 wins with zero losses all the way through the NCAA championship, a record that has never been broken. Mark and I were both attending IU when the basketball team won the NCAA championship in 1981. The coach, Bobby Knight, was one of the most colorful and fiery coaches of all time in any sport. As IU alumni, we breathed basketball and winning championships.

Once we graduated from IU and left Bloomington, being able to follow the basketball team and see or hear the games was difficult. In Dallas, we would call around to sports bars to see who might show the next game. Mark and I would meet at different restaurants, and after several beers often find out they wouldn't be able to receive the satellite feed for the game. How frustrating! There's an FMP.

While Mark and I were living in Manhattan Beach in Los Angeles in the early nineties, Mark connected with Todd Wagner back in Dallas about an Internet radio company. Mark and Todd actively started soliciting the rights to broadcast radio and professional sports live on the Internet. Hearing any sports broadcast, any time, free over the Internet was unimaginable at the time. The company was initially called Audio.net but was later renamed Broadcast.com.

Remember I said the amount of money you can make from solving an FMP is determined by the scope and scale of the problem? Because tens of millions of people wanted to listen to all kinds of content on the Internet, Yahoo bought Broadcast.com for $5.7 billion. Mark sold most of his stock in 1999, earning his first billion.

FMPs Are Everywhere

If you're not excited about being an entrepreneur on your way to becoming a millionaire or billionaire, you should be. There are more FMPs today than ever before. There are more ways to start and grow businesses because change, good or bad, creates opportunities in every market, industry, country, and continent. To help you grasp the concept of FMPs, let's talk through a few globally recognized examples.

Apple

Quick quiz: What FMP did Apple solve? Most people don't know this because they don't see the world through an entrepreneurial mindset. Going back in time to the beginnings of Apple, the real computer giant at the time was IBM. Along with IBM, there were other major hardware (or legacy systems) manufacturers. However, computers and processing at that time were geared toward commercial enterprises. The market was a business-to-business (B2B) play. Computers hadn't made it into the home for many reasons. The original hardware was room size, expensive, and designed to process massive chunks of data (punch cards). But the biggest problem of all was that computers were too sophisticated for the consumer market.

To tap the consumer technology FMP, IBM and many other companies started making personal computers (PCs). However, to run these PCs users had to know some basic programming and start everything with the ubiquitous Command Prompt to run DOS (Disk Operating System). For most consumers that had a "yuk factor." Apple came along and said in my language, let's solve the FMP: People who own personal computers don't want to know programming.

Apple identified the FMP: Computers are nerdy. Their solution: We will make computers fun!

What the people at Apple make is fun, how they retail it is fun, even their commercials are fun. They were and are the anti-boring, non-nerdy, don't be geeky, answer to computers since—ready for this—1976! And they continue to make hundreds of billions keeping computers, smartphones, and technology fun.

Google

What FMP did Google solve? With the creation of the Internet came the information ocean. The problem: People found themselves drowning in information. Finding things on the Internet was frustrating, time-consuming, and in many cases, quite limited. There were, and still are, many companies trying to solve that problem.

However, Google had the best solution set for the FMP: how to acquire the most popular or highest quality information in the fastest time. It's interesting how fantastic Google is at search, but not all types of Internet exploration. For example, Google's Shopping search is extremely limited. Shopping on the net is a huge FMP waiting to be solved, and it will be interesting to see who solves it and monetizes the opportunity best.

Amazon

As the smartphone has been the destroyer of devices, Amazon has become the e-commerce death star for many retailers. But how many people know how Amazon actually started, and what FMP the company initially solved? Take a minute and answer that question. Do you know the original name of Amazon? The answer: Cadabra. Back to its reason for being . . .

Access to a wide range of books was limited to what could be found in brick-and-mortar stores. If you went into a Barnes & Noble, you might find three books available for purchase on a certain subject, while there might be hundreds of books written for that topic. Bookstores were more than happy to *order* any book for you after a search to see if the book was still in print. However, ordering a book could take two to four weeks. When do most people want a book? Immediately. Waiting up to a month was like an eternity. Jeff Bezos decided to sell books via e-commerce since the number of web users was growing at 2,300 percent a year. Today, Amazon continues to identify more FMPs, and like that tractor beam on the death star, assimilates their solutions into its bowels. Its next FMP is gobbling the FMPs in the shipping industry.

Biggest Entrepreneurial FMP Mistakes

It would take a massive book to discuss the many mistakes made with FMPs. One mistake already mentioned is that not every want or need is a FMP to be solved. Or, if you solve it, the solution may not meet the criteria for a sustainable, profitable business. And failure to frame the FMP correctly is still another huge mistake.

Let's go back to the Apple example because it has stood the test of time and is still followed today. Back in the mid-seventies when Steve Jobs and Steve Wozniak dropped out of college, they could have started Apple for many reasons.

Think back to when personal computers first started. Here are some examples of probable FMPs for consumer computers:

- ▸ Computers are all the same shade—putty.
- ▸ Computers are large.
- ▸ Computers require knowing a language like DOS.
- ▸ Computers have only 256K of storage, have limited applications, are like boat anchors, and can't be carried around.
- ▸ Computers are too expensive, can't print, aren't connected to anything, and are nerdy.

Any or all of those are FMPs. As an entreprenuer, what you must figure out is which of these, or what combination of all of these, should be solved. In addition, what makes this challenging is to determine which FMPs not to worry about. Many companies have failed because they tried to be all things to all people—meaning they became essential to no one.

Priority determines strategy. How would you rank the list of problems above? Which one is first? Yes, that was easy—fun as already mentioned. But which one is second, third, or fourth?

Why Focus on FMPs Now

Identifying, framing, and then prioritizing the FMP will deliver powerful benefits to your entrepreneurial aspirations. Of the dozens of benefits, these three have proven to be most consequential to entrepreneurial success: speed, costs, and risk mitigation.

Increase Speed

How fast can you put in place a solution, model, or offering that solves an FMP and turn it into money? Business is about speed or time to market. Bad timing kills deals, ruins growth, destroys careers, and eats cash. The clearer and better framed your FMP, the faster you can make your millions.

Lower Costs

Companies without clear and compelling FMPs burn money, waste resources, and eat profits. The less you must spend to achieve growth, the greater the profits. If your FMP isn't clear, then you will spend hundreds of thousands to millions in marketing and sales—for no reason other than not doing your homework.

Reduce Risks

Every venture is filled with risks. Every decision, typically hundreds a day for most entrepreneurs, carries exposure to mistakes or business-shutting errors. A compelling FMP can be the rudder to keep your decision making clear and effective. For example, ask your team this question: Is what we are about to do to solve the FMP better than any other decision or path?

Sense of Urgency

After reading this chapter, I hope you see starting a business in general, and your company specifically, from a fresh perspective. Recently I led a new client, with about $10 million in sales, through my FMP analysis process. What they discovered is they had not framed the marketplace problem properly and were working off an unclear business rationale. After we recrafted their FMP positioning statement from several sentences down to about six words, the executive team sat back astonished. They realized their company would probably be twice their current revenues if they had been leveraging a stronger "reason for being."

What about your business? In my experience, only about one in 500 clients have framed the FMP correctly, and some of our work is with billion-dollar firms. Many companies have been around for years and can't yet figure out why growth stalled or why they aren't making more profit. In most cases, they were never connected to a compelling FMP, or it changed.

But that doesn't mean they're stuck forever. They simply need to reevaluate why they do what they do and then capture the correct or evolved FMP. Messaging, which I cover in a later chapter, is totally dependent on how well you and your team understand what's broken in the marketplace and why it's not yet fixed or satisfied.

Important note: You don't have to have a perfectly framed fundamental marketplace problem to start a business. A compelling and even quantifiable FMP is only critical if you want to make a lot of money and make it fast.

An FMP is *why* your business should exist and people will pay you. The next chapter is about modeling, *how* and *where* you make money and create wealth.

FMP Action Plan

Have your team choose two or three brand-name companies that have nothing to do with your business or industry, but everyone on your team knows. I recommend product or service companies that have been around for a long time. Have your team identify the problems each company focused on solving. What was missing or underserved in the marketplace? What is their top FMP? Has it changed? Are they still solving the original market flaw, or have they transformed?

Once you're comfortable with applying the FMP concept, move inside. What are all the marketplace problems your company was created to solve or is solving today?

Create a list of 5 to 10 problems. Next, prioritize or rank those in order of importance.

Work out the top choice in this way. How is it fundamental? What is the scope and scale? How big is the pain? Does it have all three?

Solving an FMP and creating an idea for a product or service is not the hardest part of entrepreneurial success. The inability to turn concepts into cash—lots of it—is where thousands of entrepreneurial dreams die every day. Now that you have framed an FMP, the next chapter, "Business Modeling," will show you how to convert problems into profits.

CHAPTER 3

Business Modeling

*Success by design is repeatable and
scalable. Success by luck isn't.*

Years back a friend finally decided to leave his corporate path and venture out as an entrepreneur. He hungered for the potential freedom, lifestyle, riches, and flexibility of calling his own shots. However, finding investors and funding is a great hurdle to starting a new business, especially one that is "capital intensive"—like the retail sandwich shop franchise he chose.

Fortunately, his background in finance and several corporate disciplines earned the respect of numerous high net worth friends. Plus, he had "done his homework" vetting dozens of franchisee models. He spent months crafting and polishing his pro forma financial statements and specific business prototype. He diligently identified and developed strategies to manage through the numerous risks and challenges of starting and running a new enterprise.

With investor financing in hand and good geographic mapping for potential and competitive threats, he quickly built his first brick-and-mortar sandwich shop. Up and running, his shop became a bustling stop for the lunch crowd and the late-evening teen traffic who loved the fresh cut fries made to order.

After several months of smoothing the kinks in the operations, he invited me to stop by and have a sandwich and talk about his business and being an entrepreneur. As I enjoyed one of the custom-made toasted turkey and swiss cheese sandwiches, it was clear the excitement of entrepreneurship was still in his heart. He bragged about his new store manager and the great feedback the establishment was receiving.

However, behind the happy face veneer of small business ownership, challenging structural issues were creeping into his venture. His partner, with tenured experience in the industry, had made many promises he was not keeping. This partnership, foundational to success, started failing on several levels. In addition, predicting peaks and valleys of traffic flow was more voodoo than science. If it rained, the store would be fully staffed with no customers.

Yet, no one had warned him of one problem in particular. A loaded school bus showing up on a normally quiet but rainy Thursday night could create a brand meltdown. Impatient teens, while standing in line, would broadcast fervently on social media, "We've been waiting for days. This place yuks."

His dreams, vision, and model of successfully opening eight locations by a hard calendar date went from quite possible to impossible. He confessed, "This path has to work as I can't go back to the corporate treadmill." He added, "I've leveraged friends and business relationships that have taken years to build to secure the funding. Hiring and training staff and leaders has been exhausting and stressful."

I asked, "What is the most important goal you have right now?" He stated to get all eight stores open. I restated my question, "Where do you feel the most stress?" He shared, "With my investors. They are constantly asking me how we're doing, and their folks are analyzing my statements now more like detectives."

"Do your investors care how they're paid back, or do they care more about the date—the when?" He looked at me wondering where the questions were headed. I followed with, "I love the food, like your plan, and respect your model. You have carried out so many steps perfectly. For example, not reinventing the wheel but leveraging a proven franchise model. With proper analysis, that approach can be smart." I continued, "However, if you want to make a lot of money much faster, I recommend you change or at least supplement your existing enterprise design."

"Right now, your model is to satisfy a Fundamental Marketplace Problem (FMP) in the business to consumer (B2C) market. I would recommend solving an FMP in the business to business (B2B) market. How much work have you done in the corporate event space, catering to companies?"

He said, "Just dabbled.

"What was your B2B experience?" I probed. His mental wheels began spinning.

He smiled. "Well, it was predictable. The events we catered were highly profitable."

He added, "The corporate clients loved our product as they're never served fresh french fries." He said he already had all the infrastructure. He went on to talk about several other aspects of corporate clients that he loved. He summed up our conversation saying that catering could be the path to gain greater control of growth and pay back the investors much faster.

I smiled. "Yes, however, to prepare you," I paused to drive the key point. "You will have to change or add different parts to your current retail model. A B2B market is radically different."

"What do you mean?" he said.

"First of all, you are moving from a walk-in traffic, reactive, simple transaction sale. B2B markets are a proactive, complex, multiphase, multibuyer, committee sales process. The money can be great, but how you market, sell, deliver, and support must be quite different."

Effective Modeling Design

Identifying a market problem and then creating a product or service idea to satisfy that FMP are two critical steps to starting a ridiculously profitable company. However, those two steps alone will never bring you major prospects or rapidly turn potential clients into massive earnings. You need the right enterprise structure and parts in a well-designed and differentiating model to make serious sustainable income.

This chapter will help you understand the idea and principles of basic business design. If you're new to entrepreneurship or the concepts of modeling, it might sound a little daunting. I understand. Sadly, many entrepreneurs don't want to take the time to comprehend these concepts; they want to quickly see money. However, I guarantee you will never optimize your company or personal riches if you don't make the effort to master this structural step.

To help you understand and then apply the modeling concept, I'm going to take you through the process of effective design—from starting your structure by looking at the market externally to finishing your model with the right flow internally. You will also read examples, specifically about one industry I know you've experienced, to help you master the principles of crafting unique business designs.

Fortunately, you have more modeling choices than ever. There are no limits to how you design your venture for growth and profitability. Ironically, all the options make business design easy and difficult simultaneously. The wide range of choices leads to many entrepreneurs using flawed and ineffective structures. And a weak model can become the number one reason your great ideas, unique services, and innovative products never transform into a mountain of cash.

What are poor modeling design results? Millions of dollars wasted. Millions in revenue lost. About 9 out of 10 times, I solve major marketing and sales issues by fixing flaws in model engineering. Before you spend more, hire more, do more, or become more frustrated, do the smart thing. Check if your enterprise design has flaws or the structure has become stale after you and your team read this chapter. Poor modeling or inferior design should no longer sabotage your growth once you master these principles.

Evolution of Business Modeling

To understand the present *and maximize your future*, you must study the past. To introduce modeling to new entrepreneurs and those who need to fix their model, let's take a quick review of the evolution of commerce. History provides pivot points where smart entrepreneurs adapt and make money. Other businesspeople miss the moment and live with disappointment and frustration.

For thousands of years the craftspeople who made wheels would trade those wheels for a like-valued offering. Somewhere around 5000 BC some cultures started using metal objects as money for the exchange. However, whether someone traded spices, textiles, or exchanged metal coins, commerce followed a simple two-part process: make and trade. Business was simple.

As populations grew into cities, a single wheel maker couldn't keep up with demand. Competitors rolled into the wheel production space.

However, that still wasn't a serious problem as supply and demand balanced themselves. Someone would rotate to blacksmithing if a village had too many wheel creators.

However, the last century was a commercial pivot point for most product makers. Large cities would experience an overabundance of wheel manufacturers. Consumers who wanted a new wheel had buying choices for the first time. That's good for buyers and bad for wheel makers, right? No, it's a problem for both. For the producer, how do they get buyers to choose them? For the consumer, which wheel company is the best?

Now wheel makers had to move to a more complex enterprise model. Instead of "make and trade," the model expanded to market, sell, deliver, and support. What had been ways to differentiate, such as price, location, or product type, were losing effectiveness. As time marched, corporate modeling became even more complex. Now wheel manufacturers had to manage returns, payment collections, and designs to meet ever-changing safety regulations. But strap on your seatbelt as the ride is getting bouncier.

Now because of technology and Internet of Things (IoT), commerce and modeling variations are expanding. Even worse, some business models, leveraging digital platforms and virtual relationships, are disrupting whole industries. For example, the largest retailer doesn't own brick-and-mortar stores (okay, a few). The largest hotelier doesn't own any real estate. The largest on-demand taxi service doesn't own any vehicles. Today organizational models can be pay by the drink, hire people fractionally, and rent don't own. Many workers making sizable incomes don't have a single or full-time job.

Are the massive and disruptive market changes bad? Quite the opposite. It means business, commerce, and models are constantly evolving, creating new FMPs. There are endless opportunities to create wealth if you follow the right road map to owning a market. But you must love change and welcome innovation. Your company commerce model and enterprise architecture must follow excellent design and superior execution.

What Is a Business Model?

A business model is how parts of a company work together to turn products and services into money. Effective revenue growth business modeling is the strategic design of how your venture will uniquely satisfy the FMP and create optimized and sustainable income. Intelligent business architecture requires answering basic high-level questions such as who, what, where and how for your offerings. You must answer each of those questions and hundreds more for every part of your model. Your answers will determine whether you survive or thrive.

There are four criteria to consider when crafting a basic business design model. It is best to consider all data inputs simultaneously to create a *close to perfect* model. However, no design can ever be flawless, as every type of business architecture has advantages and disadvantages.

Criterion I: Your FMP Market

What marketplace problem needs solving (FMP)? Where is this particular market segment? What best describes the market to compete: consumer, commercial, or government? Or a combination? What is the size of the market segments? Is this market growing or shrinking? Is your market vertical (single industry) or horizontal (common need in all companies)?

Criterion II: Your Offerings

What are the best ideas, solutions, or methods to solve the FMP? Will you be offering a product, service, or combination? If it's a product, can you buy it, or must you build it? If it's a service, can you buy it, or must you create it? If you're offering both products and services, are there synergies?

Criterion III: Your Vendors, Suppliers, and Partners

No company can be successful as an island. Every business must leverage vendors, suppliers, and partners. External providers are a blessing and a curse. A great model design means more of the former. Your enterprise model architecture will determine who and how providers help your company be successful.

Criterion IV: Competitors and Substitutions

What competitors are working to solve the FMP? Is the market saturated with choices, or are buyers frustrated with limited options? Besides traditional competitors, are there substitutions or "work-arounds" giving buyers reason not to buy your products or services?

Visualizing Modeling

Modeling can be difficult to picture, so here is a story to help you and your employees cement the concept. I walked into my four-year-old son's room while he was playing on the floor. He had opened his Christmas gift of wooden blocks and had them strewn everywhere. The blocks had standard shapes of circles, squares, triangles, and rectangles. However, those basic shapes varied in sizes.

"Tell me what you're building," I quizzed.

With passion and exuberance, he explained his vision as if leading the blind. "This is the city I'm building. These four pieces are the town hall." Pointing, "Right next to it are these different blocks which are the police station. The three blocks lying flat are where the hospital helicopter lands when bringing hurt people. Those blocks, over there, will make office buildings and a hotel."

"Wow, you have quite a functioning metropolis," I said proudly.

"Dad, it's not real. It's only a model," he clarified.

Did that story bring back memories of being a kid or watching children build things with blocks? If you have ever arranged parts to a picture puzzle, you know there is only one exact way to create the image. The placement is static. The puzzle piece fits, or it doesn't.

However, with building blocks, like a business, your design is dynamic. There are unlimited combinations in who, how, or if you perform each function. Similar to company model design, you can assemble, connect, stack, or align the blocks in any number of ways to create whatever structure or form you imagine. The blocks in an enterprise model represent the parts, functions, and departments.

Modeling Differentiation Examples

Pizza, according to Google searches and my family, is the number one food worldwide. But no matter your Italian "pie" toppings, the pizza market is tops for understanding modeling and making dough (yes, bad money pun). Since pizza is so popular and saturated (the market and the cheese), let's see how different business models are able to earn a slice of the US $38 billion market.

Pizza Hut was started in 1958 when a friend suggested to the Carney brothers of Wichita, Kansas, that they should open a restaurant that sold nothing but pizza. Restaurants offered pizza, but as a choice among other dishes. My favorite reward, in my youth, was earning pizza at Helen's Fine Dining in Evansville, Indiana. Helen's offered a 14-inch sausage pizza, buried halfway down on the right side of their menu. Pizza Hut became the first business model of "stand-alone" restaurants, dedicated to only serving pizza. Heaven.

Domino's Pizza, starting only a year later than Pizza Hut in Ypsilanti, Michigan, focused on speedy delivery. Again, two brothers started the company, and like Pizza Hut part of their growth model used the relatively new concept of franchising. Domino's became known as the "pizza delivery" company.

Instead of you having to get dressed and drive to the closest Hut, Domino's would bring your pizza to your door. This focused delivery model was astonishingly effective. To further differentiate their model, Domino's guaranteed their delivery time of "30 minutes or less." Great idea except some drivers caused wrecks meeting the delivery times.

Papa John's decided to take a bite out of the market using a different approach. Starting almost a generation later than Pizza Hut and Domino's, they saw an opportunity to differentiate. They knew you don't grow fast by following someone else's approach; you grow fast by solving an evolving FMP.

John Schnatter (the Papa) decided to fight the "pizza wars" not by "walk-in stores" or speed to your doors, but higher quality. Papa John's claim to fame was using fresher and superior items and toppings as compared to other pizza companies. So, he baked that strategy into the tag line: "Better Ingredients, Better Pizza." Pizza Hut sued Papa John's for their better pizza claims but lost the suit.

If you wanted to make serious dough in the retail pizza space, how would you compete and win against the giants? In our town a new franchised pizza player has emerged taking market share by believing consumers needed a lower-priced takeout.

Papa Murphy's, starting in Oregon in 1981, used a radical approach to gobble market share. Instead of table seating, delivery, or trying to compete on quality ingredients, they borrowed from the playbook of Subway and grocery stores. Learning from other industry models is a smart move you and your teams should do.

Papa Murphy's created several smart variations on the classic pizza store model. First, they allow customers to customize their pizza through an assembly line process in their stores. Second, they don't use ovens, so they don't bake. Their model is "take and bake."

Sometimes adding or removing steps from how your competitors operate creates a new superior model. For example, since Papa Murphy's doesn't need ovens, their stores require less space. Without baking and managing ovens, employees need fewer skills. No ovens mean fewer ways to get hurt or cause damage to the store.

Yet the greatest benefit to customers and owners involves taxes. Unbaked products are "nontaxable grocery items" in our state. That means Papa Murphy's pizzas are exactly 8.25 percent cheaper than other pizza joints. Imagine being able to offer your product almost 10 percent cheaper than your competitors without sacrificing quality or margins.

These pizza chains use the classic business building blocks of marketing, sales, operations, and support. They each perform them with slight variations. I hope the "aha" is that even in the most competitive, commoditized, low-margin market space, you can compete and make a fortune using a slightly different twist on existing models. Did this section make you hungry for success by thinking differently?

External Market Models

Your internal business model is *how* you compete. An external market model is *where* you compete. There are basically three external markets where you can participate: consumer, business, and government marketplaces. Think of a casino and playing craps, blackjack, or poker. Like markets, these are all games where you can make and lose money. However, the rules, strategies, and even cards versus dice are different. Choosing the right game or market to compete decides your fate.

Business to consumer (B2C) is where a company sells its products and services directly to the end user or customer. In almost all cases, a retail shop or location is a B2C model, where customers walk or call in and can purchase or use the service directly on-site—from groceries to nail salons, from banks to automotive service centers. This is typically viewed as a "consumer transaction model."

The B2C model existed when businesses were first formed and is still popular today, especially for services. Many people believe the retail model is dead with Amazon being the wrecking ball. However, most personal services will always require a fixed or physical location.

Business to business (B2B) is where one company sells to another business. The companies buying the product or service can be the end users. Other times they are the distribution channel moving the offering to a B2C model. B2B has more complex marketing and selling, with more decision makers and steps in the buying process.

Business to government (B2G) is where a company sells to the local, state, or federal government. Many entrepreneurs make the mistake that B2B is the same as B2G. Please don't be naive. Working in B2G in Washington, DC, showed me just how complex government selling and delivery can be. Years of painstaking marketing, sales, and relationship development can be wiped out with a change in administration. Government sales can be big, but so can the headaches.

Why You Must Understand External Markets

First of all, you can become embarrassingly rich in every market model. But how well you understand the external marketplace, where you decide to compete, will affect every part of your model design.

A reason many entrepreneurs don't strike it rich is they fail to grasp the nuances of their external market. Or they can't transition to a more profitable space. Consumers learn, choose, and buy differently than companies. And governments learn, choose, and buy differently than consumers or commercial businesses.

For example, most government procurements now have two separate and complex sales cycles. One sales process is for the provider to make the "Approved Vendor List (AVL)." The next is to excite an agency to buy from your company once it is on the list. Thousands of small businesses die every year by not executing the right model and strategies to survive and thrive in the B2G gauntlet.

Product or Service or Both

What will solve the FMP you identified best? A product, service, or both? Every business offers a product or service or combination of the two. Can you think of an enterprise that doesn't? To simplify things, I will in most cases refer to those three choices as an offering.

In this part of the process you don't need to get too complicated with your offering, but just develop a basic idea, design, or concept. The most important thing you must do is to make sure your offering solves the FMP faster, better, or more affordably than any other choice. You have to give your prospect or client a compelling reason to buy from you. Too many companies offer "look the same" offerings, and when buyers can't differentiate between choices, they usually buy based on known brand or low price—the two worst reasons to make a purchase decision.

Your Internal Enterprise Model

Now that you have decided on your offering, you need to make strategic and foundational decisions about your enterprise model. You can make these decisions in any order, but I don't know of a business that doesn't have to execute all four "client facing" core functions. Marketing, selling, delivery, and support are the ABCDs of an effective model.

Delivery and support can be considered "business operations." However, I split them because the term "operations" is too broad and is different in every company. This is the universal enterprise model flow:

Marketing + Sales + Delivery + Support = Revenue

Marketing. How will your business activities create attention and demand for your offerings? What is your basic marketing model and core strategy?

Sales. How will your business compete and win new customers and clients? And how will your sales function efficiently and effectively convert contacts into transactions and contracts? What must you have in place to sell if you're in a simple transaction, complex, or sequentially complex sales in the external market model?

Operations/delivery. How will your business physically or virtually create and deliver your products to its customers? How will you provide clients the services that are part of your offerings?

Support. Support is how your enterprise helps clients and customers with their purchase. Support includes assistance in using your products and services, implementing the offerings, or fixing and returning them.

Internal Support Functions

Your core functions listed above will need support to operate from what are called internal or "non-client-facing" departments. Unlike core functions, support organizations work behind the scenes or as needed. There are hundreds of books written on this subject, but here are a few essential internal support groups I recommend.

You will need some level of human resources (HR) to assist the core functions with issues such as employee hiring, management, benefits, culture, compensation, compliance, and development.

Every model must have some level of bookkeeping and accounting. Typically, this is called finance and will track, measure, and manage the money (sales, revenues, expenses, and profits) of your organization.

Your business will need legal help at different times, from setup and structuring to managing rights and risks. Usually small companies don't require full-time legal counsel, but they should have a relationship with attorneys before a crisis.

The technology area of your business can be outsourced or a full department. Off-site help is usually some sort of support or break fix. On-site would be more strategic, setting directions for efficiencies and competitive advantage.

Enterprise Modeling Mistakes

From my experience leading business transformation teams working with billion-dollar clients to optimize their growth starting in 1995, I can make this declarative statement. Every single venture from start-ups to multibillion-dollar firms have hundreds to thousands of mistakes, failures, and disconnects in their model and flow. However, those revenue and profit killing flaws persist because too many leaders don't grasp the amount of sales and resources wasted. There are reasons those holes in model and execution are rarely plugged.

Delusions of Competency

Our company is great. It just needs a few tweaks here and there. Or we just need a few great salespeople to help us. In every company, including yours, there are hundreds of weak points in every department. These holes are like oil and gas leaks in a car. You spend money and time filling up the tank and a fortune on maintenance and repairs.

Arrogance

Another big mistake is simply poor model design and flow execution. Too many entrepreneurs experiencing growth and profit have parts broken or missing from the beginning. In addition, they usually have things in their company they should stop doing. Instead, they're happy earning hundreds of thousands when they could be making millions with less effort.

Cheapness

I can't tell you how many entrepreneurs I know who own $100,000-plus cars. They won't hesitate to spend a thousand for a tune-up or maintenance. They wouldn't think of missing an oil change to protect their baby. But convincing some entrepreneurs to make an investment to optimize an appreciating asset—their company engine to make millions—and they freak out about spending a dollar.

Why Rethink Your Modeling Now

Your business model answers the "how" to become rich from your venture. An effective layout sets the foundation for "more from less." A poor design requires "more from more." Here are more benefits of an intelligent layout.

Speed

Success in business is how fast you make results happen. Speed to market, speed to client acquisition, speed to partners, speed to converting contacts into contracts. Your model is your accelerator.

Scaling

Another huge benefit of designing and executing the right model is the ability to scale revenue growth. Scaling is when your model can produce more sales, revenue, and profits from your assets without adding costs or headcount. One client started producing 10 times more sales with their existing sales force by simply dividing their sales model into two parts.

Attraction

The better your model, the easier it is to attract everything you want and everything you don't want. A unique corporate model will help you attract the best of the best clients—and besides attracting them, you will also retain them. Currently many of the clients in our high intensity programs today, with their second or third companies, were in our programs 10 or 15 years ago becoming millionaires with their first businesses.

One entrepreneur from our high intensity RAMP® program decided to sell while his company was experiencing explosive growth. Business brokers were so excited about the top-line trajectory that they started to bid against each other, creating an "auction effect." His company sold for tens of millions more than he had dreamed.

Sense of Urgency

You've now learned the principles of modeling, one of the most important concepts of creating scalable revenue growth. Modeling is the framework to help you rapidly go from entrepreneur to embarrassingly rich from your ideas and business. Please don't take this chapter lightly as it is essential to creating massive wealth.

Modeling is choosing and putting the critical building blocks of success—functions and departments—in place to tap the synergy of the FMP and your ideas. Don't fall in the trap of believing nonsense like "if our products or services are good enough, they will sell themselves." Billions have been lost following a flawed "if I offer it, they will come" philosophy.

Today there are unlimited ways to design and build successful company models. You don't need to own or run every department on-site, and I recommend that you don't. Once you decide the jobs to be executed, ask yourself this question: Could someone besides my team do this work? However, choose outsourcing carefully. Every type of model, including turning to third parties, has pluses and minuses.

One last critical thought: Your model should, and must, change periodically. But don't shift your design as an exercise. Make sure any re-architecture transforms your enterprise to achieve next-level revenue and profit growth.

Business Model Action Plan

You and your team should talk through the FMP to make strategic decisions regarding your model. The first place to start is to understand how, where, and why the external market is being underserved. What models are serving that market today?

How can you make your model different? Reread the pizza model stories. Each one was a variant. How could you design a better or different model than what is currently available?

Will you offer a product, service, or combination?

Go through each client-facing function. Who will do the work? How will it get done? Will you do your own marketing or outsource it? Do you need salespeople, or can you sell your offerings without human touch points?

You have mastery of modeling once you have created and can deliver on a design that provides superior value to your perfect client. Your offerings and model must solve the FMP by being faster, better, more cost effectively, or a combination of these, than the other choices in the marketplace.

Now that you have a business model that attracts and differentiates, it's time to find where you can make the most money with your offerings. The next chapter, "Multiple Revenue Streams," will show you potential sources of cash flow.

CHAPTER 4

Multiple Revenue Streams

You can't make a dime of profit until you
generate a dollar of revenue.

When my son turned five, I felt it was time for him to learn about the outdoors and become respectful of the environment. A wonderful way to do that was to have him join a Cub Scout pack. To learn environmental stewardship and leadership I believe Scouts of America (BSA) is one of the finest programs available. Plus, they offer business-related merit badges such as American Business, American Labor, Public Speaking, Salesmanship, and my favorite, Entrepreneurship. But for him to stay in Scouts for the years to earn those badges and achieve Eagle rank, like his uncles and dad, he would have to enjoy tent camping.

So, camping we must go. With another family we planned a six-day Thanksgiving outdoor getaway. Important strategies to enjoyable camping are a quality tent, functional gear, and the variety of food. In that order. Nothing ruins a camping experience worse than waking up during a rainy night and finding water on your tent floor and seeping through your sleeping bag. For that reason, I hiked the local sporting goods stores and trekked the Internet to purchase the highest quality tent, gear, and equipment available.

With our SUV overloaded inside, on top, and with a full rack on the back, we drove highways and byways to idyllic Inks Lake State Park, an hour west of Austin, Texas. It was fall, and the strong winds and a fine mist made it cold. Being late November, darkness arrived slightly after 5 p.m. Even with a raging fire, glowing lanterns, and warm drinks, both families became chilled and retreated to their tents slightly after 6 p.m. and cocooned in our shelters playing cards, reading, and telling stories.

So much fun the first night. However, by the third night my son muttered the death statement: "Camping is boring." By the fifth night, the wind had died and the stars were shining bright. However, with a chance of rain, we had to keep the tent shrouded in the no-see-through rain fly—a bulky tarp covering the tent from top to bottom.

At the end of six days, while driving home, I reflected on the good and bad experience of our first family camping trip. The food, drinks, and campsite next to the lake were awesome. However, because the evenings became boring, the tent camping experience was unfulfilling. Due to the darkness and cold, we didn't spend much time enjoying camaraderie with our friends. That was frustrating. I feared my wife and son would not like camping. The vision of my son staying in Scouts or earning Eagle were fading.

Like many of my male camping friends, I don't mind mother nature being a little mean. The colder, rainier, darker, windier, and snowier, the bigger the badge of outdoor survival honor. Primitive, technical, or roughing-it camping is fun for some. But for families with kids, with any type of inclement weather the fun factor dies. Add wind, rain, bugs, or cold, and most families cancel their trip.

I spent months mentally grinding this question. How can family tent camping be fun, enjoyable, comfortable, and a pleasant experience, no matter the weather? It became an all-consuming dilemma. No longer was I only thinking about my son, but also quality family time being outdoors, with friends, away from technology. Yes, a camping FMP.

Researching the Internet and videos about how to make camping more enjoyable for families and groups, I discovered a fascinating statistic. In Europe, families will tent camp for four to six weeks. How is that possible? In America, a camping trip lasts on average two days and one night. How can Europeans camp in tents for a month or more and have a great experience? Why can't Americans have that level of experience?

My "aha" discovery was that the family tents "across the pond" are about 10 to 15 years more innovative and technologically advanced than US equipment. For example, more than 50 percent of tents sold in the

United Kingdom don't have metal poles. Their family tents are larger and more luxurious, and they pitch faster and easier using inflatable air tubes. In addition, unlike the American tents that use canvas and mesh, the European tents have large clear plastic windows. The Euro air tent material is so innovative and high quality that you don't need a suffocating and cumbersome rain fly.

I promptly ordered my first air tube family tent from a distributor in the United Kingdom. It was a Vango 600XL that could sleep six people. Our next camping trip was with friends to Dinosaur Valley State Park. With a wine closet in the living zone, we entertained up to eight people during the afternoons and evenings. Camping was now fun and glamorous. Boring tent camping transformed to family glamping—glamorous camping.

One day a senior park ranger stopped by as he had seen our European inflatable tent from the road. After squeezing one of the air tubes, he said, "I've been a park ranger for 30 years. I've never seen a tent of this size, quality, separated zones, air tubes, and windows. Where can I buy one?"

The FMP to make family tent camping more fun, enjoyable, and comfortable was solved by the Europeans. However, inflatable, windowed, zoned tents aren't sold or distributed in the States. You must know what to buy and how to order them from European companies. A distribution FMP to be solved. Helping Americans learn and gain access to these superior tents needed fixing.

Traditional B2C Model

Finding a marketplace problem and creating an offering and model to solve it does not guarantee a profitable or fast-growth company. If you want to become rich from your business, you are going to need to combine another Revenue Ready element: how and where you will make money, your revenue streams. Remember this.

> *As location, location, location is critical to real estate success,*
> *revenue, revenue, revenue is to a successful company.*

The FMP, lack of knowledge and access to the superior European inflatable tents, is clear and compelling. Plus, there is proof of a market for this type of gear in the United States. Not only me, but several friends have purchased them too. Air tents are so superior, I currently own five different models, and we have camped more than 50 nights on dozens of outings.

The question, as we learned in the previous chapter, is what's the right model to solve the camping tent learning and access FMP? The classic B2C camping equipment sales model would be to open a retail location and rent warehouse space for stocking and parts. However, technology and Amazon have disrupted the typical brick-and-mortar presentation and fulfillment approach.

I decided to create a digital platform with a virtual presence. The intent is to avoid buying, stocking, ownership, or fulfillment—or handle the dreaded returns and restocks. My digital model, to solve the FMP, would follow a three-pronged approach. First, create a web presence as an influencer and use YouTube as a content provider. Second, operate an access portal through a website for people to research, learn, and purchase the best tents and gear in the world. Third, leverage well-known affiliate marketing platforms and major distributors for fulfillment.

Typical retail or hard locations have basically one way to make most of their income, foot traffic. That retail structure is expensive, static, and limiting. My digital model could offer a dozen or more different income streams. That means generating sales, profits, and earnings and never hiring an employee or touching a tent.

The question you must answer is which methods of income work for you and your customers. What you won't know at first is which income methods might produce the most money. It takes time, learning, and adaptation. Over time, you will change or add earning strategies to find an optimized mix.

Below is a list of my finished income stream strategies and others in development. Some ideas are already making money. Other methods for income are in creation phase. There is no right or wrong number of earning strategies. Listed alphabetically are income streams for my brand InTents Glamping® and Glamping, LLC. Which of these would work in your model?

- ▸ Affiliate marketing (Amazon, Camping World UK, AWIN Affiliates)
- ▸ Clothing—trademarked and monogramed patches, hats, shirts, and other glamping items (all product prototypes completed)

- Downloads of content, handbooks, materials
- Free prerelease products from manufacturers to test, review, and then sell
- How-to products (books, handbooks, and materials)
- Paid consulting to influence manufacturers and distributors
- Manufacturing and retail endorsements
- Speeches and workshops on camping to glamping transformation, strategies, and hacks
- Sponsorships
- Subscriptions to site and online learning
- YouTube advertising (InTents Glamping channel)
- Video channel monetization
- Webinars and online coaching
- Website advertising

Understanding Revenue Streams

Did that hike through the camping FMP, model, and revenue streams have you excited and give you ideas for your business? I share personal and client stories to help you see multiple perspectives at different revenue optimization phases.

Before going further, I want to make sure everyone reading this book, from employee to entrepreneur, understands the meaning of income streams and why this concept is so important to your business success. If you said more streams would mean more money, you would be missing out on two other important reasons.

An income stream is the way a business earns money with its business model. Most companies produce revenue, also called income or top line, from the sale of goods or services. Think of a restaurant where walk-ins find a table and are then offered dining choices by the waitstaff. A single revenue stream is how the majority of small businesses and entrepreneurs start their venture. The single-source model has worked for thousands of years starting with trading. The sole earning strategy is still a popular model today because of its simplicity.

The word "revenue" means the aggregate of all sales and monies earned over a period. Multiple revenue streams exist when a company has numerous ways to generate income. Multiple streams have many advantages. However, a plural approach does add complexity.

Let's continue using the restaurant example, with three additional ways to earn income. A dining establishment could also offer takeout, delivery, and catering. Increasing revenue streams means you will need to augment or add operating parts to your model. Simply offering takeout, which many restaurants don't offer, adds many steps and items. The diner will need special bags and packages, new meal ordering information, even an area of the kitchen to prepare and package the takeaway meals.

Whether your growth model runs on one income stream or many, there are advantages and disadvantages. The beauty of a single source of income is speed of creation and simplicity to manage. The negative to a single-stream model is the risks. Any event, external or internal, can affect traffic and shutter your business. A natural catastrophe, pandemic, or internal issue with a key employee not showing up can be devastating.

The disadvantages of a single-source earning stream are the advantages to having multiple sources. The biggest upside is scalability and risk management. With more income options, your venture has more ways to scale sales. Restaurants dependent on in-house dining have a maximum amount in earning potential based on floor space, number of seats, and table turns.

Managing risks can be the greatest advantage to creating more income alternatives. During the COVID-19 pandemic of 2020, thousands of restaurants shuttered from being too dependent on foot traffic. Other restaurants that were already running multiple streams could continue operations and preserve business-saving cash flow.

Choosing the number of income sources is the difference between a small business mindset and becoming rich as an entrepreneur. It's a choice, not a judgment. Many people start or run a new venture to earn a simple, easy, noncomplicated lifestyle. Starting and running a small business is noble and needed by society. However, with the simplicity of single-source revenue comes exposure or closure from minor disruptions.

Streams Become Rivers

So that you and your employees never forget the powerful concept of multiple income streams, let me use a real river as a metaphor. While vacationing with my family in one of our favorite towns, Durango, Colorado, we enjoyed lunch seated at an outdoor table nestled on the banks of the magnificent Animas River.

The fresh mountain air is reason enough to visit this gentrified mining town, but the flow of the powerful Animas is captivating. Without peeking at this majestic 100-foot-wide tributary, you could hear the rushing thunder and feel the vibration of its strong current.

A typical tourist could become mesmerized by the grandeur of millions of gallons of mountain water rushing by. However, thinking like an entrepreneur building a company, it's more important to understand how great rivers begin. The mighty Animas River doesn't start out mighty but minuscule. It forms from rain and melting snow creating hundreds of tiny streams merging through cracks and folds down the Rocky Mountains.

Remember this when you become frustrated with your business growth as an entrepreneur. Billion-dollar companies don't start with billion-dollar incomes. Unless built through acquisitions, these streams of small earning sources flow into rivers of revenue.

Mountain streams come together to create the power and flow of this 126-mile tributary to the Colorado river system. Moving from metaphor to business, think of all the ways these streams form a river to create commerce—or revenue streams—for the city of Durango.

A single river can allow a city to create income in many ways. Selling the freshwater and fishing licenses, creating hydroelectric power, taxing businesses that offer tourists river activities (rafting, tubing, and kayaking), generating tax revenue from the restaurants and coffeeshops located on the riverbanks, selling or taxing pictures or calendars of the scenery, and even selling camp fees for tent and RV campers.

While listening to the river I heard the whistle of the famous Durango & Silverton Narrow Gauge Train. That coal-burning steam engine train takes thousands of tourists a year on the three-and-a-half-hour, 45-mile trip from Durango to Silverton along the deep gorges following the gorgeous Animas River.

All those activities listed above produce millions of dollars of income for the towns of Durango and Silverton. You may never visit Colorado, or these towns, but I hope you pictured how streams create a river and how a river of revenue creates business success. The more high-quality earning strategies you and your teams create, the easier and faster it is to making millions. It's the difference between paddling upstream versus letting the current swiftly and easily glide you downstream.

Forms of Revenue Streams

Direct sales revenue streams are the core income for most businesses. Those conventional income sources have multiple variations. There are four common earning strategies ranging from one-time to ongoing. Entrepreneurs should work to generate income from all forms. One of the methods I use to help clients become rich is showing them how to use one income form to drive their prospects and clients to another.

Instead of using a client or industry-specific example, let me use the ubiquitous product called a "widget." Today widgets have real meaning in the technology world. However, for decades business schools have used the "widget" nomenclature so students focus on learning concepts and are not distracted by a specific offering.

You are now the entrepreneurial CEO of Fast-Growth Widget Company. Your development teams created a new widget to market, sell, deliver, and support. Here are four different ways to produce income with your widget.

Transaction Revenue

A transaction sale takes place when someone, in any market model, makes a single purchase of your widget. It is a basic exchange of any type of offering for cash or credit. They can buy one or multiple widgets—the size of the sale doesn't matter, just that it's a "one-time purchase." In addition, your client can buy more widgets any time, but further purchases are not required. Transaction sale revenue is simple, quick, and complete, whether of a product or a service.

Project Revenue

This is an engagement to provide work for a client for some period of time. Projects have fixed periods or phases with specific deliverables. For example, the client who bought several of your widgets hires your firm to come implement those widgets into their workflow. Project revenue can be based on fixed price, time and materials, or some other variable. Like transactional revenue, your client might never come back, or they could call you for several projects of the same nature.

Services Revenue

This is creating income from work involving your employees. Your client who bought your widgets and is now happy with installation wants more help. They hire some of your experts to provide widget optimization training, knowing they will buy and use your product for years. They also commit to your team running development programs once a quarter. The difference between project and services is that a project is unique and performed one time. Services can be a one-time limited engagement or ongoing.

Recurring Revenue

Recurring revenue means the income flow never stops. Whether by need or by contract, your client buys your products consistently for long periods of time. Recurring purchases are also known as "subscription" services. Recurring revenue has become one of the most popular forms of top-line growth. If the buyer stays satisfied, then you keep seeing more income from the same source, requiring no additional marketing costs or sales efforts.

Important note: One method is not superior to another. Using several forms can allow prospects and clients to test, try, or evaluate your value without taking the painful risks of a long-term contract. Use a combination of methods to attract and rapidly grow your revenue river.

Unconventional Revenue Streams

After learning about conventional revenue streams, the next category is called "unconventional" income methods. To keep these two groups of income clearly separated, remember *where* the money is generated. Conventional income is what you make from direct sales of your products and services. Unconventional revenue is indirect earnings from non-product or service efforts.

Unconventional income is money from activities that are not generated by your standard offerings or manual service activities. For example, your CFO wisely invested all the extra millions of dollars your company has made from applying the principles in this book. The interest and dividends those investments earn would now be considered indirect income to your company, an unconventional income source.

An important note for entrepreneurs is that your business can change or evolve to where an unconventional income can become the foremost or daily revenue activity. For most entrepreneurs there are numerous ways to create earnings from your offerings without having to worry about unconventional forms of income. At the same time, don't make the mistake of having so many revenue streams that you don't execute any of them well.

Following are some examples of unconventional revenue streams:

McDonald's. The general public believes McDonald's is in the fast-food or burger business. McDonald's corporation is in the franchise and real estate business. Yes, McDonald's has sold billions of burgers all over the world. However, where they make their billions of dollars a year is through buying high-valued real estate, like hard corners, and then leasing it back to the franchisees for a premium. That brilliant land to lease operation generates tens of billions of dollars a year that doesn't represent a penny from selling a Big Mac.

Insurance companies. Most people know and believe that insurance companies make money from people paying their premiums. And yes, underwriting makes money for insurers when their payouts are less than the premiums they collect. However, the major money, the second pillar, to how insurance companies generate millions to billions is through investment income by investing those premiums into financial markets and equity instruments. Most insurance companies make far more money from leverage than they do from their traditional products and services.

Retail electronic stores. Think of a name brand audio video chain. As everyone knows, making a profit in retail is difficult if not impossible. Not too long ago, to stay in business, many electronics retailers had to start selling their products close to cost to stay open. With almost no margin in their offerings, they had to find other income streams, so they decided to sell insurance. Have you bought any type of electronic gear where you weren't offered an extended warranty? Well, that protection plan isn't to protect you. It's to protect the seller's bottom line.

One of the largest electronic stores stated in its 10K years ago that most of its profits came from extended warranties, not the razor-thin margins in their product sales.

Revenue Stream Mistakes

There are a number of mistakes to avoid when creating revenue streams.

Too Few Revenue Streams

Too many entrepreneurs are narrow in their thinking and keep their growth limited to conventional or offering-based income. Once you feel like you have all the conventional ways to generate traditional top line, start being creative. For example, if you're painting houses or commercial buildings as a transaction, create a periodic maintenance schedule where you come back every two years and provide touch-ups.

Too Many Revenue Sources

Many clients don't have enough income methods. Others try creating money from too many sources. It's not often that I walk into an office that is trying to make money a dozen different ways. Yet when I do, the strategies are frequently stand-alone with no synergy. That is why I gave you my example of how I use one income stream to "feed" another.

Not Managing and Optimizing the Income Strategies

Another mistake I see is not cultivating the flow of the monies. Like nature, streams become blocked, dry up, or seek the wrong path. You must manage the flows. For example, you should have a separate profit and loss (P&L) statement for each product or service to judge each one's level of production or optimization.

Why Create Multiple Revenue Streams Now

Multiple ways of generating revenue can create many wonderful benefits and speed to becoming wealthy. However, remember, all income streams are not equal. A reason for sharing my camping transformation story was to teach you to think about earning strategies as you're designing your enterprise model.

Speed to Profitable Growth

Time is your enemy, and the faster you can achieve audacious goals the better. More sources of income create that massive river of top-line growth. In my 40 years in business, I've never heard someone say, "We make too much money." But I know thousands of people who have been fired for missing income targets. In addition, without revenue there is no profit, and profits are what make you rich. Work hard to put in place the right number and mix of income streams.

Increases Valuation

One of the biggest reasons business buyers and brokers lower the value of a company is being too dependent on a single or too few income sources. The more and higher-quality methods to increasing the top line, the greater your enterprise valuation. Whether you're selling your business or not, you want your company to be worth as much as possible with the lowest risk. That way if you need working capital you will be offered the best terms and rates.

Fewer Resources Needed to Make Money

This is possibly the biggest benefit of all. This book is about optimizing explosive revenue growth. More income using fewer resources creates ridiculous profitability. Having more direct and indirect earning methods producing profit can scale top and bottom line without ceilings, hurdles, or barriers.

Lowers Risk

Tens of thousands of entrepreneurs and their companies fail every year for one reason: those businesses couldn't produce enough income. However, reasons for business failure are typically cited as poor management, bad marketing, or weak sales, when one more income idea might have saved the entrepreneur.

Surviving Entrepreneurship Naked and Afraid

Entrepreneurialism reminds me of the show from the Discovery Channel called *Naked and Afraid*. If you've seen a few episodes, you will catch the pattern to life and death survival. A man and woman must subsist with no help, in a remote location, with one basic tool each. Most participants choose a knife, machete, pot, fire starter, or even duct tape. They must outlast biting bugs, venomous snakes, flesh-eating tigers, and extreme temperatures without bringing outside food or water for 21 days. Buck naked. Isn't that quite like being an entrepreneur?

The pattern to surviving the three-week *Naked and Afraid* ordeal is the same: shelter, water, food. Most urban dwellers would think to find water or food first. Wrong. The contestants who don't follow the sequence or don't execute each part well fail. Always. Few make it.

There are proven patterns, formulas, and methods to success in nature, life, and business. Patterns have power. And those who don't learn, master, and follow those patterns don't survive. The starting pattern my clients have proven to becoming rich are the first three principles of FMP, model, and revenue streams. With poor execution or the wrong sequence the survival of your business is at risk.

Too many seasoned entrepreneurs, leaders, and teams believe they know and have mastered the concepts of creating income sources. That's unfortunate because developing, managing, and then optimizing your income streams is a fluid practice (OK, no more river puns). Many entrepreneurs become complacent with their income methods. Remember your competitors are constantly looking for more earning ideas to put you out of business.

Entrepreneur to Millionaire is not about making millions someday; the focus is on today. Speed to revenue must be a critical part of your business culture. The more streams, the greater the chances of making your company ridiculously profitable, which means you and your employees become embarrassingly rich faster. In addition, the number one reason entrepreneurs fail is that their top line dries up. Thriving, not surviving, is the biggest reason to have multiple sources of income.

Revenue Streams Action Plan

The first thing for you and your team to do is to inventory your current revenue streams. How many do you have? Now list them in descending order, beginning with the greatest income generator. Think about the restaurant example: walk-ins, to-go orders, delivery, and catering. Most restaurants might start with walk-in traffic, but, with good planning and design, scale their business through additional streams.

Brainstorm new revenue streams. Take your current revenue number and double or triple it. Then come up with new income ideas to hit those new numbers.

Now work on optimizing the mix. As you add new streams, are there some you should remove? Too many streams can become distracting.

Some new revenue streams will be easy to develop. Others will take years. That is another reason you must develop a long-range plan. For example, you can't monetize a YouTube channel until it exceeds a certain number of subscriptions. Build that into your plan.

You achieve mastery of revenue streams when you exceed your growing income and top line targets each year.

You and your team have just worked through three of the most important principles of Revenue Ready, which will accelerate entrepreneurial success the most. The next phase, Market Ready, and its four principles will put your venture in position to make the most money through sales, revenue, and profit in the easiest, fastest, and most cost-effective way.

Market Ready
(PREPARATION)

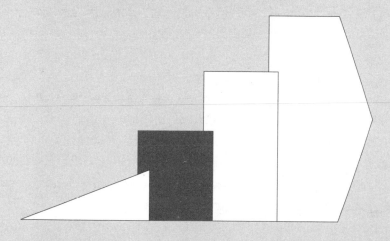

In the Revenue Ready phase, you learned about validating your business by connecting an FMP to a business model and to revenue streams. Once those principles are in place, most entrepreneurs mistakenly jump right to Go to Market, aggressively marketing and selling their offerings with all their energy and resources for business growth. That business growth path eats profits and limits fortunes. In the Market Ready phase you prepare for explosive revenue growth and maximizing the riches from your business.

Do you enjoy visiting other countries? World travel is one of my favorite hobbies. I've been fortunate to visit more than 60 countries and work in almost 40. Initially, personal travel was about meeting people, food, culture, and trying to visit all the great churches of Europe. It was exhausting. However, once I visited Warwick Castle in London and Neuschwanstein, King Ludwig's palace fortress in Germany (the inspiration for Cinderella's castle at Disney), I became hooked on castle hunting. From burgs and schlosses to citadels and palaces, I was hooked and awed.

My fascination with castles is rooted in understanding military strategy, defense, and offense during times of war. I am not a fan of war, but having been a chief strategy officer, I love learning all about the science of success and winning.

While I was touring a massive castle in Europe, the curator described the number of years and the efforts spent preparing for the Crusades between 1095 and 1492. I asked if the years of preparation were for motivation, focus, or discipline. The curator replied, "The real reason for the extreme preparation was to win the wars as quickly as possible while suffering the fewest casualties."

Quite applicable to business success, isn't it? Casualties in business come in many forms. For example, losing key customers, losing deals, employee turnover, and losing a critical supplier. One of those, if big enough, could close a company. Most entrepreneurs don't have years of time to prepare to make money and pay the bills. You may not even have weeks. But if you skip these steps, you will pay for it in lost years and millions, not to mention frustration and stress. Even if you have to "prepare to win" while engaged in battle, do it. Many clients have proven that following this Market Ready phase and its principles can hyper-accelerate maximizing fortunes in minimum time with minimal casualties.

CHAPTER 5

Targeting Your Sweet Spot

In trying to be all things to all people, you
end up being nothing to no one.

efore we zero in on this chapter on targeting, I need to be blunt. Of the thousands of clients I've worked with through the decades, this is the one area where there are always *massive* mistakes. When those errors are corrected it can quickly create millions in new sales, revenue, or profits. Every entrepreneur misses the mark with this Targeting proficiency, for many reasons. That means there is a high probability you have miscalculations in who, where, and how you target for success. Minor misalignment can set off major missteps and ruin your chance of becoming embarrassingly rich.

During an initial meeting with a new client's executive team, I led them through this road map checklist:

1. Compelling fundamental marketplace problem to solve. FMP. *Check.*
2. Great mix of products and services and business model to fix the marketplace issue. Modeling. *Check.*
3. Clients have paid to buy and use the offering. Revenue Stream validation. *Check.*
4. Fast, successful, profitable, and consistent sales growth. *No check.*

That result of three yeses and one giant no represents a million entrepreneurial businesses around the world. They believe in their heart of hearts they have successfully completed critical thinking in the Revenue Ready phase. However, now they're beyond frustrated with their weak marketing and sales results. The problem is the leaders skipped over some essential steps. Especially the most important Entrepreneur to Millionaire principle in the Market Ready phase—*effective and accurate Targeting*.

"Tell me about your clients," I asked.

"We love them. And they love our work," they gushed.

"Who is your perfect client?" I asked. They smiled and described specific customer names, companies, and their types of businesses. However, confusion and disagreement started growing among the leaders about the quality of each client.

"For argument's sake, let's say you are absolutely clear on who buys. Why does your buyer buy what your buyer buys?" I probed.

All were silent. The leaders stared at me wondering if that question was rhetorical. "How well do you feel that you know and understand your potential clients, how they think and what drives their decisions to choose you over someone else? Or worse, why they sometimes choose a different provider?" I continued.

More silence. One of the quieter attendees responded, "It appears we know our clients, but we really don't understand them."

If you want to make a fortune with your business and become embarrassingly rich, as fast as possible, you must thoroughly understand how your future clients think, feel, and make decisions.

To understand why your buyer buys what your buyer buys,
you must see the world through your buyer's eyes.

Who Is Your Perfect Customer or Client?

What is the difference between customer and client? Is there a distinction?

While I often use the word "customer" to refer to an individual who makes a one-time purchase and the term "client" to refer to a repeat customer—an individual or entity with whom one does consistent or reoccurring business—for the purpose of this book, I will use the words somewhat interchangeably.

Imagine playing any sport—golf, basketball, football, cricket, or soccer. Does it matter your level of skill if you don't know where you're aiming? Targeting accuracy is essential as it sets in motion every other strategic and tactical decision about your business. Yet effective targeting remains elusive in all size companies for two reasons. First, the entrepreneur and team never completed the aiming process correctly. Second, targets—specifically prospective clients—are dynamic and constantly changing in different ways. Sometimes their wants and needs shift abruptly and other times glacially. Failure to comprehend, apply, execute, and continuously calibrate targeting properly costs small businesses millions and corporations billions.

In later chapters I will unpack the statistic that two-thirds of all marketing and sales activities are a complete waste of time and money. Most often that profit robbing starts with inaccurate targeting. Ability to discern between buyer types remains a weakness because it's a difficult proficiency to master. It requires an entrepreneur and team members to apply a combination of principles, competencies, and ongoing validation.

First, effective targeting is a core concept, a fundamental truth, that serves as the foundation for a chain of reasoning in processes or systems. Second, there are numerous skills, a cluster of methods to be followed. And finally, the most common reason targeting is so flawed is because it's a collaborative process between quantifiable data and qualitative information. I'll provide more detail on that later.

The good news is that entrepreneurs and teams that master this principle can leapfrog competitors stuck in the proverbial mud of being all things to all people and nothing to no one. Effective targeting is connecting, engaging, and then building a perfect portfolio of the highest quality customers. This chapter will share the key concepts to spending the least amount of time and money identifying and pursuing your perfect client.

Targeting Your Perfect Client

To catch the most fish, you need a lot more than bait.

This is a sports example that audiences around the world tell me helps them "own" the concept of targeting.

Imagine you are going fishing. If you're an amateur, then spending time with kids or friends on a boat and lake might be your goals. The snacks and drinks you take along might be the next priority. Fishing is both a sport and a leisure activity, but running a business to become wealthy is not.

Let's say you become hooked on the sport and decide to become a professional angler to earn a living and lead a crew. A "fishing entrepreneur" so to speak. With your new endeavor, your team and family don't eat if you don't reel in a kettle of fish or win prize money for the largest catch.

The real difference between an amateur and a professional is that the former can afford mistakes, the latter can't. Success in entrepreneurship has the adage "eat what you kill" or in this case what you catch. And this is where the concept of targeting becomes so life or death (business speaking) important. For the amateur, fishing is basically grabbing bait, pole, boat, and snacks and drinks. Don't forget your kids. Next, head to the lake.

However, for professionals every decision represents a fork in the road to success or failure. Every single step—*every mental choice*—must start and end with the fish (metaphor for the target), including every detail such as type, size, habits, and number in your catch. Those standards, or goals, start a chain reaction of reasoning and mental judgment.

As you add or change goal parameters—to catch a certain type, size, or number of fish, by a specific time—hundreds of critical choices must be decided in the perfect sequence. Skipping or making mistakes in any of those steps creates huge risk and can drown success. So it is with the sequential principles in this book. One decision sets up the next choice. The first mistake makes every future step potentially flawed.

In addition, on the day you go fishing let's say you change the goal—*the type of fish*. Every decision that was made before could be wrong or lower your odds of success. And this is what I want you to understand about targeting for your business. Any slight variation in your target audience or target market sends a ripple effect or new validation through every subsequent step.

If you change the catch—*the target*—you will have to rethink everything about your angling goals and strategy. Here is a partial sample of the rethinking necessary when you change your target type fish:

- ▸ Fishing location—boat, dock, bank, fresh water, saltwater, etc.
- ▸ Fishing bait—types and size of lures, live, fake, or rubs or paste, etc.

- Fishing line—what pound test, what type of material, what length, etc.
- Fishing line accessories—weights, bobs, and where to put them
- Fishing depth—on bottom, near bottom, midway up, or near the surface
- Fishing time (unless dictated by a tournament)—morning, afternoon, evening
- Fishing tools—gloves, bags, knives, scissors, pliers, etc.
- Fishing team—by yourself, with a partner or several people
- Fishing food and drink—part of a day, all day, proper hydration
- Fishing clothes—hot, cold, waterproof, etc.
- Fishing shirt—what type and how many pockets, with sections for bait or tabs to hold poles, SPF, long or short sleeve, bright colors for safety or bland to not be distractive
- Fishing shoes/boots—what type, size, support, grip, etc.
- Fishing glasses—size, UV blocking, sunglasses, and bands or grips
- Fishing license—for type, size and number of fish for locations, and what time period
- Fishing safety gear—size of boat, number of people
- Fishing boat—this list could fill several books

Whether you're a fisherman or hate fishing, don't float over this powerful analogy. You are an entrepreneur, fishing for the perfect clients. What I want you to understand is that just 16 categories representing hundreds of decisions are key to putting you in position for fishing success. Yet there is *no guarantee of winning anything.* Look at all the choices you must decide to hope to catch a single fish.

If you change one small detail or goal, every other choice must be rethought or revalidated. Success as a fishing entrepreneur doesn't start with the boat, gear, equipment, clothes, and technology. Everything you and your team think and do starts with the proverbial fish. The fish is your target, and if you don't know and understand everything about your fish, then you cannot optimize making money. Ironically, most entrepreneurs don't understand themselves, let alone their buyers.

The mass of entrepreneurs and business leaders don't know their fish and make business-destroying gaffes in targeting. So how do they compensate for this focusing failure? You got it. "More from more."

Leaders spend more time, hire more fishermen, buy more equipment, and put more poles in the water hoping to catch more fish. That's a metaphor for spending more money on marketing, sales, and hiring and hoping to catch more customers. Even if they do hook more clients, they've wasted too much of their profits. If making a fortune with your business is your goal, then you must become proficient at knowing your buyer better than you know yourself.

What Is Targeting?

Targeting is the philosophy, process, and ability to select an object or a group for attention in investment or effort. Basic targeting for entrepreneurs means breaking large markets into smaller groups, and then identifying and ranking those specific slices of buyers and closely aligning their wants and needs to match your offerings of products and services. The underlying premise of targeting is that all prospects do not think and act alike. Treating all potential clients the same way will damage your business, dilute your efforts, or destroy your profits.

After understanding this basic concept, you're ready for the novice level, which is dividing segments into subsegments based on demographic facts like revenue size, location, industry, or number of employees. Using hard data is the most popular way entrepreneurs target. However, that approach has dangerous flaws and limitations as you will learn.

Once you've created your target groups, you're not finished. The highest level of targeting proficiency is identifying your "sweet spot" in the marketplace down to a *hard number*. A sweet spot is that group of buyers who love what you do and are willing to pay any price to buy what you offer. Finding the exact number of buyers in your sweet spot creates remarkable efficiency and effectiveness for marketing budgeting and sales planning. Generating optimized profit production is only possible through an accurate laser focus.

How should you identify your sweet spot? First you have to develop a clear and specific list of the attributes of an ideal buyer. This inventory becomes your "Perfect Client Profile," or PCP. How will you know you have the right set of characteristics of a PCP? You can confidently answer two categories of questions. You can explain *who* buys. Second, you can validate *why* they buy. Even if your company is new, there is a good chance you already have several profiles or baseline client characteristics.

Sweet Spot Targeting

If you play or watch sports that use clubs, rackets, or bats, there is one competitive truth: every piece of equipment has a spot that produces a different result when struck. That area is so important to winning it's nicknamed the "sweet spot." The part of the club or bat is where performance is optimized. When players can hit the ball or object in that zone, they can achieve maximum results with minimum efforts. Did you say to yourself, "more impact from less effort?" Yes.

Remember the story about my conversation with Ely Callaway and the Big Bertha driver? This is how he made billions. He engineered the Big Bertha driver head larger, allowing the sweet spot to be wider and higher, making the driver easier to hit and satisfying every duffer's ego.

Why is understanding your sweet spot so important? This area is special because it produces what is called the "trampoline effect." When the ball or object hits the sweet spot, it doesn't just ricochet back, it springs forth adding energy, control, and distance to the shot. That's what you need to demand from your business efforts. When you put effort into a market you don't want a simple return. You want the maximum springboard back. It's the difference between throwing a golf ball with your arm 50 yards, versus smashing the ball off your driver's sweet spot close to 300 yards.

In every market there is a sweet spot, a segment of prospects and clients where your focus and efforts will provide the greatest return. A market sweet spot is where there is clear alignment between what you offer and what the prospect wants or needs. More specifically, the potential clients believe, on an *emotional* and *logical* level, that your value proposition far outweighs their potential costs and risks of using your offering.

However, unlike the modern golf clubs and tennis rackets on which the best area is marked or shadowed, it's not that clear in business. Targeting your sweet spot means you and your team must diligently work to discover, calibrate, and validate it. Applying the sweet spot principle will give you more control over success and your business more consistency.

Classic Targeting Mistake

One of the first clients in our high intensity programs joined because they were so frustrated with their first-year sales efforts. There were two partners with one having expertise in product development and the other in major corporate sales.

Tension and stress started to tear at the two leaders because they were spending so much time and money traveling and presenting. Their sales pipeline was filled with prospects of massive well-known companies. Their CRM database had the names and titles of all the Fortune 100 CFOs.

We spent some time talking through the sales funnel and their contacts. As I quizzed them about their buyers the conversation became emotional in a positive way. Both partners were visibly proud of the potential clients they had spent a year cultivating. From a basic targeting approach, things seemed in order. However, there was a severe problem—*no sales*.

The flaw, like most entrepreneurs, was that their pursuit strategies were too heavily based on their personal emotions, not PCP and sweet spot logic. When I asked why they were pursuing multibillion-dollar companies, they shared the excitement of signing a major corporation. A well-known brand name contract would attract more investors and better employees, and be leverageable to more prospects.

I agreed with them. However, a small business needs new sales like a car needs gasoline to run. If your fuel gauge is on empty, don't keep driving around till you find the perfect new combo gas station with burrito bar and coffee barista. It's not what you want, it's what your business needs. Stop at the closest gas station and fill your tank.

From our sessions, their "aha" was several client profiling mistakes. They had not factored in how larger corporations, in their B2B market, require far longer and more complex sales cycles. They also misunderstood how bigger brand targets have more ruthless competitors. However, the biggest blunder of all, killing their sales, was an internal buyer issue. The potential client department heads didn't want to change and install an unproven product from a no-name start-up firm. There was too much risk.

We retargeted to mid-tier corporations with more approachable CFOs and crafted a compelling value proposition that balanced the investment versus the risks. They bumped into less resistance and fewer competitors and signed several high margin contracts after just a few months.

Their "aha" came when they realized that they were competing in a market they wanted, but the buyers didn't want them. Targeting is not only about who you go after, but also identifying those who are attracted to you and your value proposition. They were not in their sweet spot because the energy they put in was resisted, not returned, by the prospect. If your value doesn't far surpass the prospect's risks, then there is no fit. Retarget.

A Personal Example

This was one of my worst start-up targeting blunders. When I launched my performance transformation business about 20 years ago, I made a huge mistake that almost closed the company. Following everything you're learning in this book, I first identified and analyzed an immutable FMP. Sales organizations around the world are nowhere close to being optimized, meaning sales performance is inconsistent, unpredictable, not scalable, high stress, and low morale, with turnover issues.

Continuing the targeting process, I identified the prospect profile pain point of VPs of sales for Fortune 100 companies. These sales leaders are usually tortured from the top to hit more difficult targets every quarter, and they're frustrated from below because their salespeople are usually more lucky than competent. With years of experience optimizing sales departments nationally and internationally, I felt confident turning this value proposition into a successful business. It was my strong desire to help VPs of sales become heroes and rich.

Everything seemed in order—the FMP, model, client profile, field-tested value propositions, years of experience and certifications to prove my expertise. I felt confident in my efforts applying the Revenue Ready and Market Ready phases in my business. However, after six months and dozens of meetings with only a few small contracts, the results were frustrating. I questioned every principle and decision.

Then came my "duh" moment. If the bait doesn't attract the fish, either change the bait or change the fish. Had I made targeting mistakes? But who, what, or where should I target? I called back several VP of sales prospects to gain insight on why the compelling value proposition "more from less" wasn't motivating them to move forward.

My demographics were aligned and solid, but I had overlooked the emotional construct of my prospect profile. I blew it in the psychographic areas and alignment. My "aha" was how their feelings split into two categories, creating sweet spot targeting misalignment. The first category were those sales leaders who were having success. They were arrogant, cocky, and didn't want or need help. The second group were VPs of sales who were struggling with sales challenges. They were stressed, concerned, frustrated, and nervous. They were scared that I would accelerate their firing, even though in reality, I was their best hope of not being terminated and becoming successful.

I quickly changed everything about my client profile targeting. I stopped pursuing VPs of sales at billion-plus corporate, public, technology companies with thousands of salespeople. I also expanded the bait—offering holistic, systemic, and explosive revenue growth.

My new targeting and FMP strategy focused on ultra-aggressive and hypercompetitive CEOs and entrepreneurs of private companies under $100 million frustrated with slow growth or low profitability. I broadened to all types of prospect companies, not only technology firms. My new sweet spot included sales organizations ranging from first hire to several hundred, competing in complex enterprise pursuits. My focus were CEOs wanting fast growth who would invest to develop all their leaders, not only VPs of sales. With more effective targeting of a better aligned sweet spot, my business exploded with dozens of new clients in a matter of months.

More Targeting Mistakes

Effective ongoing targeting is so fundamental and critical to quickly making a fortune, why do so many entrepreneurs overlook it? Entrepreneurs give me hundreds of excuses for not effectively identifying their PCP and sweet spot, but they all fall into three categories.

They Don't PCP Target at All

The entrepreneur doesn't go through the steps of creating and validating a pursuit profile and segmentation to identify a sweet spot. The popular excuse for not targeting is, "We don't want to miss any business," or "Anyone can buy what we offer." *You might want to sell to anyone, but your buyers won't buy from anyone.*

They Target Halfway

Entrepreneurs might identify demographics but not work to prioritize their psychographics. Unfortunately, facts like company size or number of employees become the dominant segmentation tool, simply because they are tangible, identifiable, and measurable. However, how your prospects think and feel is intangible but more important. These emotional characteristics are harder to uncover and extremely hard to measure because they're subjective.

Been There Done That

Every prospect market is fluid. Your sweet spot and PCP characteristics need constant updates and evaluation. Marketplace, buyers, and competitive factors change at speeds never experienced before. In addition, any change in company performance should trigger a new targeting analysis. Too many entrepreneurs just keep pursuing the same profile ever year yet wonder why their growth slows down, their sales cycles stretch, or their sales losses increase.

Targeting Is Not Saying No—But Maybe

You might feel I'm telling you to say no to new prospects who don't fit your profile. Just the opposite. You should be willing to accept new business from anyone at any time if there is clear mutual fit, meaning there is a potential exchange of value for both. My point is to welcome all clients but not waste time and resources chasing everyone.

My firm will always take calls from multinational CEOs. We enjoy working with VPs of sales, chief marketing officers, and leaders of multibillion-dollar firms. That's the corporate world where I spent 20 years of my career. However, a demographic fit does not make for a philosophical alignment. If a CEO wants to write an eye-popping check, but that CEO and the executive team are not humble, open, and willing (remember the Will) for radical change, then psychographically, we don't align.

Perfect Client Profiling Process

Who or what is your perfect client profile (PCP)? Your PCP is like the bull's-eye on a target. Hitting that spot is the most rewarding. You still win points landing close to the bull's-eye, but not as many—all revenue is not the best revenue. Your PCP has three distinguishing elements: two sets of attributes, demographic and psychographic, and one set of characteristics, behaviors.

PCP Demographics

Demographics are facts, figures, or statistical data about a company, group, or people. A simple way to remember this concept is the availability and number of *quantitative* facts. For example:

B2B. What is the revenue size of the company, number of employees, location of headquarters, type of industry, speed of growth, business model, public or private, or profit or nonprofit?

B2C. Who are the consumers, according to gender, age, location, worker or nonworker, level of education, household income, living arrangements (single family home or apartment), married or not, married with kids or single with kids?

B2G. Is the government local, state, federal, or armed forces? Do they have budgets? Is there an Approved Vendor List (AVL)? How many employees?

PCP Psychographics

Psychographics are psychological criteria such as attitude, aspirations, emotions, and feelings. These are the triggers, drivers, and final decision motivators in someone's heart and mind. This is sometimes called the "emotional construct" or "hot buttons." A simple way to remember this concept is *qualitative* feelings.

PCP Characteristics

Behaviors are the area that can drive you nuts dealing with clients. Think "type" or quality of customer or client. Think of your clients who are a joy. They do what you ask. They pay on time. They apologize when they make mistakes. If these clients meet the demographic and psychographic attributes, then these are your PCPs, determining your sweet spot. Remember, you win with winners.

Why Use PCP and Targeting Now

Targeting is the first principle in the Market Ready phase. Most entrepreneurs don't need more clients, they need fewer and better clients. Here are reasons to achieve mastery level with targeting.

More Sales, Less Effort

Targeting gives you greater sales, revenue, and profits using the fewest resources, time and money. The fastest and smartest way you and your team become rich is by how fast your business grows *and* how little you spend making it grow. Targeting creates that foundation.

Faster to Sales and Revenue

Most entrepreneurs spend years and the majority of their profits in marketing and sales talking to the wrong prospects or courting inferior clients. For entrepreneurs, time is your enemy, and anything you can do to exploit windows of opportunity or close major contracts before your competitors is money in your bank account.

Better Account Coverage and Penetration

Targeting gains more and better sales from fewer clients. Remember adding more clients means adding more costs from every function—more marketing, more sales, more delivery, and more support. That's growing a business. Revenue growth is fewer (or a perfect number) of clients paying you the most money.

Easier Client Attraction and Retention

Understanding how to attract more prospects is challenging for companies when they don't know their PCP. Buyers want and need to make decisions, and if you can show them how you're the best choice, they will find a way to buy from you. In addition, if buyers come to you for the right reason, unlike low prices, they will stay with you for a long time. Client retention is another powerful way to lower costs and increase profits.

Sense of Urgency

Targeting your PCP encompasses the steps to determine a cluster of perfect clients, your sweet spot. This profiling and pursuit effort will drive every strategic and tactical decision in your business. If you change any details about your targeting, it will ripple effect every downstream decision. If you don't know who your best clients are and how they think and feel, then every business decision carries huge risk.

There is nothing wrong with changing your target as I demonstrated in a personal example. Because of market forces, new technology, or competitive threats, you must change your targeting periodically. Sometimes your PCP changes will be minor or major, that's normal. However, once new variables are introduced in your targeting, new work begins.

Targeting Your Sweet Spot Action Plan

You and your team should develop a list of demographics. I recommend at least 10. Then sort those demographics in order of priority. This can be one of the hardest steps, so make sure there is team agreement. Remember, a minor change in demographics (recall the fish example earlier), such as ranking size of company over industry type, can change every decision you make in each of the subsequent steps you will learn about in the following chapters.

Next, identify the psychographics of your PCP. Why do people buy? What are the feelings driving the change? What emotions do they want that they don't feel today? Once you have a solid list, rank each item from first to last. I recommend including at least five feelings. Use these to sort and filter whom you target.

Create a list of good and bad client qualities. What is it that you like most about the clients you have or want? What do you like least? For example, I don't like leaders who are not engaged in the transformation effort, so I created a set of questions to determine a leader's commitment up front. Create a set of questions like that for your prospects to determine whether they have the qualities you want or don't want.

You've mastered targeting when you progress from these deliverables: PCP, sweet spot, exact number in the sweet spot, and percentage of current portfolio. Most companies have a small percentage of PCPs with whom they work. Build a plan to fill your client portfolio with 80 percent or more who fit your PCP.

Now that you know who you want, how do you get them to want you? The next chapter, "Packaging for Value," will be your client magnet.

CHAPTER 6

Packaging for Value

Don't all buyers want a bundled value of something?

staffing firm located in north Texas had been growing at a steady pace for several years. I met the owner after he hired me to speak to his entrepreneurial group with about 150 members. After my talk he shared with me how happy he was with his company and teams. However, he admitted being frustrated that the growth wasn't close to the potential of his vision.

In an initial meeting I asked the entrepreneur how many competitors were in his space. Without hesitating, he claimed with exasperation, "Anyone using a computer holding a résumé," adding, "That's about 38 million people we compete against every day."

After I had worked with his teams for a few months, the owner, excited but nervous, asked me for a favor: "I'm about to make the most important sales call of my life. Would you consider going with me to the meeting?" Although he felt confident in his selling abilities, he wanted my experience and background helping teams sell billions in new contracts in boardroom meetings.

At first, I was hesitant because we hadn't prepared for the meeting. He twisted my arm by pleading that winning this major brand account could be "business changing" for his firm. If nothing else, I could help make sure we applied the revenue growth principles I was implementing in his company. One of the worst mistakes entrepreneurs and salespeople make in a sales role is *selling*. People in "sales mode" focus so much on signing the contract, they miss the bigger picture. If you want to consistently sign major agreements, you must stop pushing your products and services.

During our company presentation to the prospects, we observed the quizzical look of one of the buyers. She commented, "I like everything I'm hearing. However, I hoped for something different—a more strategic approach." She added, "What you're offering is like the other staffing companies."

Most salespeople would mistakenly treat that comment like an objection to be handled—thus winning the argument but losing the sale.

For the next few hours, the entrepreneur and I led the executives through an exhaustive "wants and needs" brainstorming session. We pivoted from vendor sales presentation to letting the buyer buy, using open-ended, buyer-based questions.

"If you could have your projects staffed and milestones delivered any way you want, with no limits or parameters, what would that model be?" we probed. The "buyers" started sharing unique ways they wanted services provided, with different levels of reports, documentation of project progress, fractional management, and so on.

Following the principles in the phases Revenue Ready and Market Ready, we created a compelling "package" of staffing services. It was not a bundle of typical augmentation offerings like placing more headcount, but now grouped as a comprehensive program, and structure, including external talent.

The result? A massive new agreement. This firm's transactions, of providing people, normally averaged about $100,000 per placement. This new contract was valued at more than $5 million, roughly 15 to 20 times larger than expected. Imagine selling your yearly revenues in one meeting. Not only did this prospect meeting generate amazing top line, it was ridiculously profitable.

To sign $5 million worth of coders and programmers, the staffing firm would have needed about 10 to 15 more salespeople working through about 300 to 400 selling cycles (remember you don't win all pursuits). With each additional salesperson headcount, you add eight categories of expenses, eating your profit.

This story shows the power of customizing a "package" during the selling process. This concept of grouping your offerings for extreme value can transform your company. Packaging is a robust principle to explosive revenue growth with less costs. I've integrated this buyer-friendly idea into many organizations, helping owners and stakeholders become millionaires, in some cases, instantly.

Would you like to increase these performance objectives in your business? Quickly sell more products and services. Use less marketing and sales resources. Make product delivery easier while requiring fewer employees for support. Move more higher margin items all at one time. Create happier, more loyal customers. Did you say, "Sign me up?"

Companies in almost every industry use bundling in some form or fashion, from product companies like automobiles, fast food, and computers to firms offering intangible services. Many of my clients have learned to use this concept, and they're quickly doubling and tripling sales. They're experiencing more demand for their goods and services, cutting their contact to close cycle times by more than half, moving more profitable items, and leaving their competitors frustrated.

Of the hundreds of modules I use helping entrepreneurs become rich, a fan favorite is packaging. This chapter on bundling ideas will help you master the concept, principles, and how to apply them. You will learn the three best times to offering packages. Plus, I will cover the most common mistakes businesspeople make by misapplying this principle.

Warning: Many entrepreneurs and famous CEOs who work to learn bundling still fail in the execution. The right intent with flawed delivery is worse than not doing anything. Packaging works best when you follow the principles of Revenue Ready and Targeting. Those proven sequential steps will make your packaging strategies quick, smart, and potent.

Act Like a Buyer

To become a multimillionaire entrepreneur as fast as possible, you must stop thinking like a business owner or employee and start acting like a buyer. What does that mean? My experience working around the world proves all buyers share the same objective. Prospects measure success in these terms, colloquially stated:

> *Once I know what I want, I want a*
> *real deal getting what I want.*

Buyers, believe it or not, are human beings. Okay, at certain holidays or closeout sales, they can behave like animals. However, prospect goals never change. And shoppers being humans have a deep psychological need to feel or be treated as if they are the only person in the world. Take a minute and absorb this critical mental construct as it is why so many companies fail.

Every buyer wants to feel special.

Here is a tongue-in-cheek example, using a consumer buying a truck in Texas.

"Billy Bob, beautiful new 4×4 pickup truck you just bought!" said Bobby Roy.

"Thanks, Bobby Roy. I couldn't be happier or more excited. The dealer let me pay way over retail. They had several trucks like this lined up at their dealership. They told me to pick any color, then add 20 percent over sticker price and the truck could be mine," exclaimed Billy Bob.

"Wow, Billy Bob. I should take you along next time I buy a new truck," Bobby Roy mumbles sarcastically.

Is that buyer conversation real? No. Here is how an authentic truck buyer's dialogue occurs in the Lone Star state.

"Billy Bob, beautiful new 4×4 pickup truck you just bought!" said Bobby Roy.

"Thanks, Bobby Roy. I couldn't be happier. This new and limited model just arrived at the dealership. I'll be honest, it felt like stealing. I sped off the lot so fast I squealed the tires. Told my wife not to look back. I crushed that 'couldn't stop talking' salesperson and his no-value manager. They offered me a huge rebate, $5,000 cash back, a special model discount, and zero percent interest financing for 72 months, with free extended warranty. Then I told the sales suckers I wasn't buying till they threw in free tires, tire rotation, oil changes, and free car washes for life. They told me if they had to negotiate with more people like me they would go out of business. Ha, that got me thinking. Since they were so easy, I might go back and buy cars for my wife and son," bragged Billy Bob.

"Wow, Billy Bob. You're an amazing negotiator, and it's not even 'Truck Month' in Texas. You rock," Bobby Roy said.

"I know," Billy Bob said, beaming and feeling special as he was validated by his buddy.

Feeling unique or smart to "catch a one of kind deal," is a fundamental part of all consumers' DNA, whether you have two first names or not.

Buyers must emotionally *feel* like they received a genuine deal. The offer must be legitimate and not always available. No gimmicks. The buyer must always receive significant value.

What Is Packaging?

Packaging is combining multiple goods or services into a group. It is sometimes called "bundling" because the idea started last century by grouping products. Packaging for value or demand is what the seller achieves. Bundling for value is what the buyer receives. The words are interchangeable with benefits for both parties. The intent of packaging is twofold: First, make it simpler or cheaper to buy. Second, make offerings easier and faster to sell.

For example, if you market a product like a razor, which needs blades, then bundling the blades and razors together makes sense. Today, it's common practice to package products and services together. Quick, think of what you have purchased recently that was bundled. For example, car dealerships offering their own financing, free car washes, and maintenance services included with the final price of the car.

Keep in mind, services can be packaged alone without products, which is a reason that I believe so few entrepreneurs around the world apply this cash acceleration principle. The US economy is almost 90 percent services, and many strategies that worked to sell products in the last century haven't made the transition. Although I argue most business concepts from last century are stale, bundling is not one of them. The principles for effectively grouping services is exactly the same as clustering products.

Packaging for *value* is quite different from basic grouping or adding products together. To create interest and attraction for your bundle, a unique offer of worth must be presented to the prospect. The most natural packaging value creation method is a lower price than buying the items separately. But don't limit your package to discounting. Smart packaging to create higher demand might include items that have never been available or bundled before, and the price is not lowered since the consumer can't buy the pieces or assistance separately. The holidays are popular times to add those "one of a kind" choices to a bundle and increase the overall pricing and margin.

Before going much deeper into effective "packaging," I want to make sure you and your team own this concept by giving you broad examples. A unique method of grouping is the experience at certain fine dining establishments.

French restaurants are most known for *le serveur*, the waiter, offering a two-page open fold menu with similar foods on both sides. On the left side would be items listed "al a carte," food choices offered separately with their respective individual price.

On the menu's right side might be the "prix fixe" or fixed singular fee at the top or bottom. By design the right side will rarely list all available dishes. The choices on the right will be grouped into courses, created by the chef for a limited time, usually three to five sets of properly paired selections.

There are three differences between the prix fixe and a la carte. First, the prix fixe menu doesn't list every food item available. Second, you must choose only one item from each course. Third, there are no individual prices, only a single charge for all plates combined.

Why would a fine dining institution offer two different menus basically serving the same food choices? The intrigue of packaging. Combining foods in certain clusters can add to the dining experience, making the event special. Courses can allow clientele to experiment in savoring foods they've never eaten before. Fixed price menus can help control what is ordered by clients, which makes preordering supplies easier. Patrons can save money by not buying the choices individually. And restaurants can sell more of their high margin items such as custom desserts and expensive entrées, and their less labor intensive but profitable wine pairings.

Please don't be like the lady in one of my seminars who wrote on the evaluation survey, "We don't run a restaurant, so your concept about packaging doesn't apply to us." I'll bet that lady's business has missed a million dollars or more in the 15 years since she heard me speak but didn't *listen* to understand my point.

When to Offer Packaging

Are you excited and filled with ideas and different ways to group your goods and services for growth? Even if you've packaged in the past, your markets, buyers, and competitors have changed. Bundling must evolve over time to stay "buyer smart." I also find many entrepreneurs who understand packaging, yet mistakenly only use this strategy one way or at one instance. When it comes to effective bundling, there are three times to apply it.

Ongoing

Companies should group their offerings in different forms year-round. That helps consistently attract new prospects and allows clients to continue to engage for longer periods. Whether you have only products or only services, create packages that are "win-win" for you and your PCP. Or offer unique bundles to always have one available that drives demand.

Seasonal

Almost every business has some kind of "seasonality," meaning that in different periods of the calendar sales are higher or lower. Use packaging and the cyclical demand levels to your advantage to increase purchases or manage volume.

One-time Deal

Sometimes you want to move certain products quickly. Or you want to launch new services or sell a larger agreement. For example, you want to craft a customized package like the staffing company story, creating a robust offering to secure a multimillion-dollar contract. Whether your services are transactional, project, or ongoing, how many items can you add to make the bundle better for your client and for you?

Here is an example of our firm using "packaging" services to deliver an event in Asia or Europe. I will bundle our services since an event can take up to 24 hours of flight time one way, like traveling to Singapore. The package might include a keynote, workshop, assessments, and sometimes an executive retreat. That bundle saves the client a lot of travel budget and money and allows me to be more effective at transforming teams faster.

Packaging Mistakes

Obviously, the biggest packaging mistake is simply not grouping your offerings. However, even if you and your team decide to bundle your goods and services, there are still many ways to fail. These include not aligning or realigning value, not providing an authentic deal, not creating motivation to buy now, or crafting pricing options that turn buyers off. Let's make sure you avoid all these mistakes.

First, align your PCP and buyers' perception of value. Those insights are found in the synergy between your FMP and the sweet spot in the market you want to exploit. Both McDonald's and Wendy's discovered a few years back that their kids' meals were out of alignment with the final buyer. The Happy Meals made parents unhappy because this bundled item included overly salted, trans fatted, nutrient-robbed french fries. The smart and quick fix was to provide options, such as sliced apples or yogurt.

Don't make the mistake of marketing bundled items so cheaply that you take a loss. Also, always "discounting" a bundle is not a smart pricing strategy. For example, a baker's dozen isn't packaging, it's giving something up with little in return. And 13 for the price of 12 started because scales were inaccurate hundreds of years ago and buyers were often cheated.

Another packaging mistake is adding in the mix something buyers don't want or need. Occasionally, I see packaging efforts where the selling entrepreneurs were trying to get rid of something. Pushing what has little value to the buyer is always wrong. For example, cable companies offer me a package of 800, 1,200 and 1,500 channels, but my family only watches 3 or 4 stations in total.

Client Case Study

A highly successful entrepreneur was continuing to grow and expand his family's printing and distribution business. The company started decades back and through excellent stewardship became the dominant publisher in its space. Working with their clients of associations and institutions, they print member directories for past and present alumni.

Their end product creates a compelling value proposition for their client institutions, helping them increase outreach, fundraising, marketing, and a host of other member benefits. The enterprise follows a well-designed direct mail and highly professional inbound call model for growth.

The challenge for the publishing firm, like all businesses, was managing the rising costs of operations. Paper and print expenses, production, and the technology investments kept increasing. Hiring and keeping qualified professionals to manage the calls and engage with clients' constituents continued to eat more budget. Fulfillment and delivery expenses kept rising because of limits with automation.

To continue to outpace competitors, this firm would need to spend more money in marketing, sales, and operations. The problem was price sensitivity. Although the company offered a valuable final product, slightly increasing the product fee had a negative impact on sales. Probably like your company, higher costs, but limits on what the company could charge, squeezed profits.

Like most companies, performing in the Go to Market phase for decades, their marketing and selling methods were entrenched. Plus, making changes in how they marketed, or their sales execution, would not give them the game-changing breakthrough they needed. The question they had, and you probably have today, was, how best could they make more money without dramatically raising prices?

Many times, the solution to the problem is not in the department experiencing the issue. I led the team through the Revenue Ready phase and then the principles of Market Ready. After I explained the concepts and principles of Packaging, they were elated. They had been offering a single product for a fixed price. Now the inbound sales agents could offer product options with budget-friendly choices.

After working through the Packaging steps and design, they started offering three different bundles from basic to premium. The three groupings were an instant success, close to doubling sales and margins with very little increase in costs. In addition, an interesting set of side benefits emerged.

The salespeople said that with packaging choices their stress levels were lower. And comparing old and new recorded marketing calls, the buyers sounded more relaxed too. The calls, hundreds a day per salesperson, moved from transactional to more relationship-oriented and conversational. This was far superior to the high pressure, "take it or leave it" approach from the past.

How to Package Effectively

To help clients further understand this packaging for value principle, I have led many teams through this exercise. I ask them to identify three markets or industries and how they use bundling. Here are two examples:

Automobiles originally sold with choices such as colors but few other options. In the latter half of the last century car manufacturers started offering different combination packages, called trim levels. This meant you could purchase different versions of the same model car with set combinations of features. Sometimes, and still today, these are called the "standard package," "luxury package," and "sports package."

Bundling is a smart and effective hedge against commoditization facing entrepreneurs. As the markets try to reduce your offering price and profits to zero, most leaders settle for smaller income. Instead, you can learn a lot from the fast-food industry, where companies survive by fighting for millions of pennies. How do they do it? McDonald's and Wendy's almost simultaneously created their Value Meals, offering a "combo" (combination) of sandwich, fries, and drink. The big benefit to the stores is selling more of their astonishingly high margin (close to 80 percent) drinks.

Counterargument

On occasion I have a client who tried packaging and it didn't work. Or clients argue it isn't applicable in their business. Usually I receive the highest resistance from entrepreneurs and leaders who sell a single product or offering like professional services firms.

Eight out of 10 times, the first issue when packaging doesn't work can be fixed by what I discussed in the mistakes section. However, it is rarely just one mistake like misalignment. In many cases, the bundling problem is threefold: an alignment problem, an incorrect value assumption, and a combining issue. Once those errors are fixed, grouping your goods and services can work embarrassingly well.

"We can't do that in our business." I remember hearing that while delivering an all-day executive workshop to partners of a law firm. The one issue the lawyers had was they had to change how they were creating demand. However, they argued (what attorneys do) that every case and situation was different. They believed their client engagements had too many variables and different needs to package their services.

As we discussed and debated, they agreed they would like to attract more small businesses, especially funded start-ups. This was a sweet spot because growing ventures need all kinds of legal help. As we talked, a clear set of legal needs for small firms emerged. Not realizing it, the law firm already had a wide inventory of "boilerplate" legal documents, templates, and methods to bundle.

Our brainstorming led to these concept bundles: "start-up," "fast growth," and "expansion business" legal packages. Each offering included several options like the groupings of a prix fixe menu. Their solution sets, and yours, can be driven by a client's business maturing or changing and needing new or different assistance.

Why Create and Offer Packages Now

The benefits of Packaging could fill a whole book. Bundling is simply one of the most proven ways to generating more sales, revenue, and profits, while using the fewest resources. The "win-win" for buyer and seller is the biggest reason to take this action right away. Here are additional benefits.

Bigger Transactions

Clients are finding they can achieve two to three times their normal size purchases with effective packaging, and they can achieve those financial goals without any extra work. Sometimes entrepreneurs argue against bundling because they give up margins to win bigger contracts. However, once I show them the marketing, sales, and operations dollars saved, they realize the greater profitability.

Speed to Decision

Tapping into the prospect's emotions is essential for faster buying decisions. Every buyer—consumer to commercial—needs that personal sense of accomplishment. When prospects can see the logic—potentially receiving more than they expected—and they experience earning it themselves, the motivation to act kicks into gear. Nothing motivates someone to buy right now like these two emotions—the excitement of winning and fear of losing out.

Protect Profits

Making money for the company and your teams is the essence of *Entrepreneur to Millionaire*. The key to earning huge profits is to stop spending—or not giving your bottom line away to achieve growth. When buyers decide to buy, usually price is the deciding reason. However, with effective packaging, price can drop to the third or fourth factor in purchasing. Value, exclusivity, and limited time reasons become more important than the cost of an item. Plus, lower expenses from less marketing and selling makes your overall margins bigger.

Sense of Urgency

The principle of packaging on its own can be game-changing. I have used it with many entrepreneurs and employees to make them almost instantly millionaires. But to unleash the full potential of this concept—repeatable and sustainable fast growth—you must follow the sequential steps in this road map before creating the grouping and applying the later phase principles.

We have clients that have used my work to create packages that are still being used 15 and 20 years later. The packages are evolving, yes, but not moving away from the original core concept and proven principles. Follow the sequence from FMP and Revenue Ready strategies through the Market Ready phase. Packaging has generated tens of millions of dollars in sales, revenue, and profits for start-ups and small businesses and billions for large corporations.

One last thought. Everything about the marketplace is changing, and now more rapidly than ever. Just like every principle in this book, your packaging must transform to stay current and remain value adding. If you make even one change in your Revenue Ready or targeting, then you must reevaluate your bundling strategies.

Packaging for Value Action Plan

How do you and your team go about creating smart packaging? The first step is to start at the beginning of my road map and relook at your FMP. Reanalyzing and reframing the marketplace problem will answer many questions about scope, scale, and most important, value for bundling. Those attributes are critical for the prospect experiencing the pain or missing opportunities to become satisfied.

The range of buyer emotions will drive the choices, from providing a basic package to the upper end where you can make embarrassing amounts of money. Remember, bundles must be genuine in offer and fee.

Next, make sure your company can effectively market, sell, deliver, and support your new bundles. During design, use a cross-departmental team to represent the client-facing functions. Include finance for cost and pricing strategies. Further refine your PCP. Does that targeted sweet spot need modifying to better drive income and create more profit?

Before you Go to Market with your new packages, ask current PCPs or future prospects for feedback. Use focus groups to create a "buyer's perspective." And finally, create bundles for all three times mentioned.

Now that you are "packaged" for success, don't let your offerings be the world's best-kept secret. In the next chapter, learn how to craft "Power Messaging Tools" that compel prospects and buyers to take the right and immediate action—buying what you offer right now.

CHAPTER 7

Power Messaging Tools

What we've got here is failure to communicate.
—The Captain, *Cool Hand Luke*

R ight before going on stage to give a speech in Miami, Florida, I was outside the ballroom in the hallway discussing an overview of my presentation with several executives. "My message is *no cost* explosive and profitable growth—to create business wealth," I told them.

Overhearing me, the CEO entrepreneur of a logistics company broke into our small conversation circle. "Of all the topics you're going to present, what's the quickest and smartest way to grow faster—*and not spend any money?*"

"Easy," I told him. "Messaging. Make sure everything you say and everything you show differentiates and motivates your perfect prospect to take the right action."

"Okay, what's the first place to start?" he inquired.

Without time to probe or scan his website, I asked, "Let me see your business card." Pointing with my index finger to words on the front, I said, "You have six different messages on this side. Your logo counts as one of them." Flipping the white textured card over, I saw that the back was blank—hmmm, expensive notepad.

"Tell me how any of these symbols or words separate you from your competitors? Which of these communication pieces motivate me to contact you or start a conversation with your company?" I probed.

Scanning the front and back, he answered, "None," embarrassed.

"You have a 'sleepy' business card with boring information. Not a *tool* creating demand for your offerings. This piece with words and pictures is not doing any work—you are. The first step is crafting compelling language, phrases, and symbols. The second action is turning this assembly of words and graphics into a Power Messaging Tool—a PMT. A card that inspires prospects to make contact and start conversations without you making any effort," I explained.

He asked if I could come to his office and share this thinking with his leaders.

A couple of weeks later, I met with the logistics executive team in their boardroom. They spread their outdated brochures on the table like a blackjack dealer showing all cards. Projected on a monitor were old website screen scrapes. Next, they laid their overhauled marketing materials above the older ones to show before and after. The graphics, the flow, the colors were a major upgrade from the original but outdated glossy documents. Not only did they create all new one pagers, but each page was stagger cut to overlay other pieces in a color-coordinated pocketed folder.

"How much have you invested in your new materials and website?" I asked.

"All in all," responded the VP of marketing, "with web design services, programming, coding, and printing, just under $200,000."

"For a small firm that's a ton of money," I exclaimed. "How well are the new messaging tools and Internet presence working for you?"

"For all that time and effort, it's not meeting our expectations. We were expecting more traffic, more new leads, more clients, and for the materials to assist with closing prospects," the CEO stated disappointedly.

"What motivated you to go through this extensive refresh?" I probed.

"Our public relations firm convinced us we needed a major update and that their marketing makeover would help grow the business. Plus, our salespeople have been demanding new information sheets," replied the VP of marketing.

"Did you tell the PR team that you weren't happy with the results? How did they respond?" I inquired.

"They said it takes time and we'll probably need to put more money into an SEO and digital advertising campaign to get the message out," said the CEO frustratedly.

"Like so many company and situations, I agree you needed to overhaul your brochures and web language. However, time and more media spend will not fix the strategic flaw and root cause of why your materials and site aren't driving client growth," I shared.

I went on, "The problem is not design, graphics, or flow—*it's content and intent*, weak messaging and wrong goals. Who is your perfect client profile, your PCP? Where is there an example of the messages speaking directly to your PCP? How does this engage them? Of all your marketing propaganda, where do you address your PCP's pain and how best to fix it? What specific action should your prospect reader take right now?" I machine-gunned the team with questions to push their thinking.

The group was quiet. The VP of sales responded after gazing over the literature and information created, "We've been thinking about this the wrong way. We thought creating these marketing pieces and having a new site would help drive growth."

The CEO piped in, "We've always thought of our brochures and website as *support* to our marketing and sales teams. We never considered measuring them as *tools* to market and sell *for* us."

How Do You Address Your Audience?

To grow a highly successful business last century you needed a brick-and-mortar site—*a physical address*. Over the past 20 years a cyber location, known as a URL—*a web address*—has been essential. Today, unlike a physical or cyber address, there is a more important form of address, which is less *where*, the location, and more *how*, buyer point of view. How you address—*how you speak to and engage your audience*.

Do you address your prospects with empathy and respect to connect, pulling them into a value-based conversation? Or do you insult and turn them off by blabbering to the point of boredom about your company and your offerings? If you were on a first date at a fine restaurant and you talked about yourself the whole evening, would you be rewarded with a second invite? Probably not. It's the same principle in business.

> *Buyers won't care about what you offer*
> *till they know you care about what they need.*

To help you create the fastest and most successful company possible and make a fortune doing it, this chapter on power messaging must be mastered and applied continuously as communication nuances evolve. This section is not about crafting independent single messages, but a whole toolbox, and making sure the communications methods work off each other and have real energy and thrust.

You will learn how to define messaging content and what gives a tool surprising power. I will cover the multiple forms of communications packaging. You will also read a painful personal story of an authentic "elevator pitch" disaster. In addition, I will cover the mistakes that most entrepreneurs and business leaders make with creating and delivering their communications. To further help, I will give you some tools—methods— to test your existing messaging strategies.

How critical is creating compelling language and symbols into a power toolset? If your messaging and communication strategies are weak, or emotionally neutral, it will sabotage your success. Bad messaging means you and your teams will chew through profits by making more sales calls, presenting more slideshows, delivering more proposals, spending more on marketing, and waiting years to make money. Don't wait, your competitors are radically improving how their language attracts and connects with prospects, and you must too.

But What Is a PMT?

Basic business messaging tools are anything and everything you create, use, or display to communicate information or insights about your company and offerings. They employ symbols, pictures, words, and points. Communication methods can be visible or invisible, tangible or intangible. They either work for you, or you work for them.

Every organization transmits hundreds to thousands of messages. When they are unorganized, these communications create buyer's dissonance. When they are packaged correctly, the synergy creates persuasive prospect motivation.

Messaging has "power" if it creates energy, direction, and thrust for the reader to think differently—even better, to take the steps you recommend or that will help them. I ask a lot of teams: Is your corporate slide presentation informative or persuasive? If they say informative, I tell them never deliver it again. An information-based presentation, with no motivation to think or act differently, has zero value. Did I just render 99 percent of all company slide-shows useless? Yes. Good. What's the *point* if there is no *power* to take action?

If, after reading this, you've transformed your presentation from being boringly informative to shockingly persuasive, then your slideshow is now a power messaging tool working for you to motivate your audience to take *several action steps.*

Let me give you an analogy. Imagine two woodworking shops. Both workplaces create and assemble fine wood cabinets. The first workshop has walls with pegboards filled with hundreds of screwdrivers and wood-handled tools. These screwdrivers have metal shafts that range in length and size with different tips for flat-blade to Phillips screws. There are about a dozen craftspeople working feverishly screwing (installing) and unscrewing (removing) screws in the cabinets. This workshop is noisy, frenetic, with employees arguing over who isn't putting tools back. Basically, the work and environment are chaotic. Does that sound like most sales organizations?

In the second cabinet shop it's quiet, almost serene, with only an occasional hammer tap or drilling noise. There are two people working, both using the same tool, a technologically advanced power device. It's a cordless rechargeable lithium ion fadeless reversible half-inch 24-position keyless clutch with two-speed gear box–controlled, micro spotlight, ergonomic handled electric drill. Whoa, did you get all that? This two-person team is cranking out cabinets as fast as the large crew bumping into each other.

The second team produces solid results and keeps an orderly, creative environment. No one is running around like their heads are cut off. And did you pick up on this point—the ratio of people completing the tasks? Yes, about one to six. But don't think downsizing. Think tripling production using existing headcount.

Those two scenarios are the difference between manual labor and using power tools. For example, you could be going on dozens of sales calls, or you could leverage power messages and only need a few meetings and one-third the sales cycle time. Well-crafted communication strategies allow maximum production (sales and revenue) to be faster, more efficient, with less exertion, and scalable. Weak or nonexistent messaging requires more manual labor (more marketing activities or sales headcount), more energy (calls, meetings, and presentations), and more spend in frequency (digital, SEO, advertising, mailings, and banners).

This impact of power messaging and achieving "more from less" is not theoretical; it's business changing. One client used to send their team to five networking events a week. After we created a PMT, they only attend one event a week while generating the same number and quality of leads. If your competitor starts winning more often, analyze their communication content and methods—did they "power up"?

Bad Elevator Pitch Destroys Nine Months of Work

If you've been in business for any length of time you've heard the terms "company spiel," "pitch," or "elevator pitch." Where did this expression come from, and why is it a "must-have" top-ten PMT?

In my early twenties I was selling multimillion-dollar outsourcing agreements in California. Having won my last five competitive, 9-to-12-month sales cycles, my inflated ego started clouding my judgment.

At the end of an executive meeting in a bank boardroom in California, the president and leadership team had just given me a "verbal"—an oral commitment to sign a contract in the next few weeks. That news was exciting yet somewhat expected after I had soundly knocked out the competitors. I had spent almost three-quarters of a year convincing the institution to transition from in-house processing to letting my company, a third-party nonbank, manage all their mission critical data and customer information.

Walking down the corridor of the top-floor high-rise office, I could see the Pacific Ocean through the 10-foot-high picture windows. Since the headquarters was located near the beach, I decided I was going to need to visit this account at least once a month for the life of the seven-year agreement.

As I stepped into the elevator and turned around to push the close button, a distinguished elderly gentleman angled through the closing doors. While we greeted each other I noticed his attire was different from the standard banking dress protocol of regimented dark suit, white shirt, striped tie, and black laced shoes. He wore a red V-neck sweater and gray slacks with a tweed sport coat with brown suede elbow patches and loafers—quite informal but classy. For him to be strolling on the key locked executive level he must be an affluent customer.

As the doors closed, he turned to me, asking, "What do you do that brings you to the bank?" I smiled, but not wanting to answer as my work was nondisclosure confidential, I needed a non-answer. "I'm here in confidence working with John the president and his leaders."

After sharing his name, he went on, "I'm on the board of this institution, and you need to tell me what you're doing in my bank." His demeanor and tone switched from conversational to interrogative.

In a surreal way, the elevator didn't seem to be going down—it felt more like free-falling.

Nervously, I fumbled, "Well, I've been talking with your bank's team for about nine months. My company takes over all the data management, networks, ATMs, and check processing for financial institutions like yours."

Lights flashing on the door panel. Floor 11, 10, 9 . . .

"I've heard about this project. I'm actually chairman of the board, and I started this bank. We are not transitioning, and no one is 'taking over' all of what we do, especially an outside company—ever."

The elevator stopped at the lobby. My heart was pounding fast and loud, as I had already spent the commissions on a new car. I was just hit by a freight train, and I never saw it coming.

While stepping off he turned back and smiled, "Wonderful meeting you."

The chairman stepped out of the elevator and walked toward the exit with revolving doors. I stood frozen and dazed, feeling numb as if stunned by a taser. Nine months of work destroyed in less than 60 seconds. I had just experienced a real-life and business death "elevator pitch." My verbal messaging bungle took me several stressful months to recover from, but I eventually won the deal. That day, I made a promise to master the art and science of elevator pitches—what to say to the influencer when you have 60 seconds or less. Don't get hung up on the term "pitch"—remember it just means you have a short period to deliver a compelling case to a powerful decision maker or influencer..

The PMT Pathway

The highest form of communicating is linking your PMTs to create a buyer acceleration "path." A path means your messaging tools are connected, leading your reader to more information of value—*for him or her*. When you learn to integrate your content and intent, you can produce millions in sales and revenue and spend almost no effort.

You're holding an example of a PMT and a path. Look at this book title: *Entrepreneur to Millionaire*. Like every product or service, a book must have a name. That naming convention is a message. However, it's only a PMT when it motivates the potential customer to engage and move forward. It becomes a PMT path when it joins with other PMTs and creates a series of proper audience steps to purchase.

For example, the intent of the title was to be evocative—stir feelings in the mind to create two actions. First, of course, buy the book. Second, and more important, is to follow a path to the subtitle. Subtitles, like company tag lines, are longer messages and use more words to *attract* an even bigger audience and *filter* those who don't want to do the work to become rich. In this case I used a subtitle with several emotional trigger phrases and power word combinations: "Highly Profitable," "Fast-Growth," and "Embarrassingly Rich." Which word or phrase resonated with you the most? Most people love "Embarrassingly Rich." Make sure to use these types of techniques in your messaging tools.

If those PMTs did their job, potential buyers and readers will move to the back cover, inside flap, or Contents page, where there is more space to offer additional proof and evidence of the value proposition. This is the exact formula you must use in all your combination message tools—one pagers, website, slide presentations, emails, proposals. Each message should compel your prospects to take more steps.

Where to Begin?

Your corporate Internet site is the "mother of all PMTs." It's your Library of Congress for all message forms you need for contacts, prospects, buyers, clients, partners, and future, new, and existing employees to engage, foster, and retain PCP and working relationships. Your site and digital presence must be designed and maintained properly and must include all three messaging toolsets: visual, written, and oral. These tools must be balanced, integrated, and congruent with persuasive paths.

Quick. What is the single biggest mistake entrepreneurs make with their websites? Poor design, bad flow, incongruent graphics, platform nonresponsiveness, non-value analytics, weak search engine optimization (SEO), or poor focus on long-tail keywords? Did you say, "All of the above"? Yes, all websites could improve in those areas. Yet, entrepreneurs spend tens to hundreds of thousands on improving those things, and they are still disappointed. What's wrong?

There are more than a thousand books, articles, and speakers all preaching better website design and performance optimization. Which is the exact reason websites stink (or are ineffective)? Entrepreneurs and leaders become overconsumed with the look, feel, and flow of their website. Yet they rarely put the right effort into crafting differentiating and compelling messaging strategies.

Why is creating content that attracts and converts PCPs in websites so difficult? Effective, motivating, and persuasive communications in the form of PMTs requires collaborating and integrating several factors: first, intimate knowledge of your FMP and PCP; second, general business and external market acumen and insights; third, the craft and mastery of writing and language; fourth, an intimate understanding of the traits, attributes, and competencies of your enterprise; and fifth, the principles of revenue growth. Every chapter in this book will help you and your team create a more potent money-making website using the design and site structure you already have.

Excuses for Weak Messaging Tools

Why do entrepreneurs and leaders tolerate poor messaging and lack of PMTs and paths? Usually they don't have clear standards to determine effective messaging and compelling communications. Here are the most common excuses for low-octane, ineffective, and lazy language:

▸ We just redid our website or we're currently overhauling our site and we've spent a lot of money on it already, so we don't want to change.
▸ The messaging is good enough.
▸ Our salespeople just need to get out more and make more sales calls.
▸ We hired an expensive PR/ad firm and they created our content.
▸ None of our prospects have commented negatively on our brochures, slideshows, or site.
▸ The salespeople really like the new marketing materials.

Please don't use the "We've spent a lot of time, money, or effort, so it's good enough" rationale. Those comments are excuses, not standards. There is only one measurement for all your messaging tools: What actions did your audience take?

We have many clients who don't have the big brand, low pricing, or superior offerings usually required to win. However, with effective PMTs and paths, they are kicking their competitors' asses and taking more than their fair share of the market.

Reasons to Create PMTs Now

Motivating messaging is a game changer for every entrepreneur, whether starting a new company or running a large mature one. However, having many communication methods is not a solution. If you have a burning desire to create wealth, then you *must* master creating, using, and leveraging PMTs. Here are a few astonishing benefits.

New Client Demand, Less Work

PMTs can create amazing amounts of prospect interest in the form of new leads, repeat business, and client referrals. Every lead that is generated by your communication tools has almost no new costs. Imagine an enthralling corporate video that keeps bringing in new prospects without human intervention.

Recently I asked a new client, while signing our contract, what had him so motivated to reach out and want to join our RAMP® program. I was expecting "So-and-so referred you," he heard me speak, or he enjoyed one of our CEO Knowledge Letters. He stated, "I reviewed and read your website, and it had everything I needed to know." That's a major contract without the time or expense of a sales call, presentation, proposal, or any direct marketing effort. Can your website engage and complete a complex sale with no human touch point?

Speed

PMTs create more demand in days, not months. For you to build a fast-growth business you are going to need to generate more leads faster and close those leads quickly. You don't have the time and shouldn't burn the money to get to every prospect and buyer physically. Let your messaging be your muscle.

Filter Demand

One of our first clients advertised on the radio before joining our program. They created their copy with the help of the station and ran ads for a few weeks, proudly generating hundreds of leads. They spent hours calling back every lead to qualify. Less than 1 percent of the leads met their quality standard, and they only sold two small contracts. The profits didn't come close to covering all the campaign expenses. Great messaging can attract *and* filter your PCP, saving you time and making you money.

Sense of Urgency

If you're like most entrepreneurs reading this, you're more than eager to wake up your dreadful messaging. You now have new insights for transforming your boring language into PMTs. With a fresh and real definition of language tools, understanding different communication forms, you can tap into the path and power to huge profits. With effective communication you're ready to connect and engage your perfect prospects and turn them into new clients faster than ever.

Power Messaging Tools (PMT) Action Plan

Have your team identify three different messaging tools—I recommend visual, oral, and written. In many cases, the first page of a company website might have all of those.

Choose one. For example, what is the first written message a prospect or visitor sees? Does it grab attention? How? What could be done to increase engagement? Can you make it more evocative or provocative?

What technique did you use for your first messaging tool? Did you use a question, statistic, comparison, or other?

How is this messaging tool intriguing or engaging? Does it make the reader want to know more? Or find out the answer?

What is the exact next step you want your PCP to take after reading this message? Why should prospects do that? How does your messaging tool motivate or compel them to take the next step?

Go through this process for the two other forms of messaging tools you identified. Look at your graphics, videos, or symbols. Do those visuals compel anyone to do anything, or are they the standard, ubiquitous, and distracting scrape-and-paste photo gallery?

You have achieved mastery of PMT when you have a minimum of 10 power messaging tools (PMTs) that work for you without you working for them.

Formally assess your messaging tools a minimum of once a year. Like a car, they will lose power if not maintained.

Your team now has their targeting sights on the perfect client profile (PCP), with packages that excite and messages that compel. Let's add one more power principle, "Tiered Pricing Strategies," to attract and engage better clients faster and turn relationships into revenue and prospects into profits.

CHAPTER 8

Tiered Pricing Strategies

*Ninety-five percent of entrepreneurs price
their products and services too low or too
high; the other 5 percent don't care.*

Near the end of the second day of a three-day executive retreat, I couldn't help but stare out the massive conference windows. The leadership team of entrepreneurs were still on break, so there were a few minutes to enjoy the breathtaking golf course scenery. A foursome was playing their second shots on the dogleg uphill par four. Our agenda was to play golf after this session, so I felt pressured to solve their issues and complete the day.

With less than an hour to go, I reviewed the self-sticking flipchart pages of business issues the teams had identified. Working down one large page of crossed-through choices, I came to the last topic of concern at the bottom of one of three easel pad sheets we hadn't addressed. This leadership problem didn't make the high priority list, but quickly resolving it would complete the list of challenges on this one page. Completions are wins.

One of the attendees had scribed *Pricing*, with a capital *P*, using a giant black Sharpie, a hard-pressed question mark punctuating it. Only one executive believed what they were charging was a priority issue, meaning it should be quick to resolve. A good point to end the day and go play team golf.

However, when I asked the team how they felt about their fees, war broke out. The discussion quickly turned from happy debate to holy debacle. Everyone chose a different corner arguing their opposing thoughts on whether their prices were too high or low. Here is how they voted on pricing:

- Sales thought it was way above the competition.
- Operations believed it was about right and didn't want to change. A single price modification meant multiple changes in systems and communications—a high PITA (pain in the ass).
- The CEO argued they needed to increase, dramatically touting new features and services.
- Finance wanted it adjusted up to protect margins.
- Marketing didn't want it increased as higher prices make their job harder.
- HR didn't care but commented they heard rumblings in exit interviews saying it was "messed up"—but couldn't elaborate.

After 45 minutes of no reconciliation, I broke in. "Can we all agree we all disagree, at least?" garnering a few smiles and chuckles while lowering the emotional temperature.

"How do you go about pricing?" I probed.

The responses were punchy: "We throw darts at the colored board hitting different numbers," "We stick a wet finger in the air," "We look and see what the competitors are charging and try to be a little lower."

"Well at least you're scientific about what you charge, like other companies," I said in jest, trying to maintain levity but feeling a bandage had been ripped off an unhealed wound.

Before the CFO chimed in, I proclaimed, "Let me guess how you go about setting numbers. Knowing a little bit about your company, here is what I suspect. You calculate all your fixed and variable costs. Next you categorize what you sell and how many you need to sell. And finally, you add roughly 20 percent to total costs for each offering. You're basically following a cost-plus pricing method."

The team sat with no response.

The CFO, with a half grin, quipped, "That's exactly how we do it."

"How did you know?" asked the marketing director, whispering softly as if not wanting a competitor in another conference room to hear their secret strategy.

"That's how everybody does pricing. Cost plus is why more than 9 out of 10 entrepreneurs offer prices too high or too low. They use a method that is 'all about them,' not about the buyer. In addition, following a common but flawed approach misses out on millions in profits. That formula narrowly focuses on costs and price. Meaning what you charge does not link to the most important ingredient, value. I'm going to also assume you use the basic scheme for everything you market and sell?" I continued.

"Pretty much," said the CFO. "We must maintain our margins."

Everyone knows CFOs and finance play a critical role in companies. Yet comments like "must maintain our spread" should rattle every entrepreneur. Notice the "we" and "our" in the CFO's statement? Right, nothing about "them," the client? Financially driven and one-sided cost-to-profit philosophies can dramatically slow company growth and profitability.

Trying not to rub salt on the wound, I probed deeper: "How does your cost-plus approach attract, engage, expand, and retain new prospects and clients?"

No response. The group stares at me and then replies almost chorus-like, "Now that you mention it, I don't think we know."

"What you're doing is called a basic or simplistic pricing method, meaning the level of sophistication is not using what you charge as a strategic tool. To drive fast growth, with huge profits, you must transition from simple to a tiered set of pricing strategies. Using multiple purchasing price points will attract clients in several ways and help retain them forever," I explained.

At the end of the third day, one of the comments on the event survey confirmed the importance of understanding pricing principles. "The insights on how to charge at different rates will allow my company to generate millions without any more effort. We could have spent the whole retreat mastering that subject. Wow, we almost missed this opportunity."

Unlocking the Power of Pricing

At this point your teams should have learned and be applying the principles from the Revenue Ready phase. How and what you price is driven by the concepts of Market Ready through Targeting, Packaging, and Messaging. I hope you're eager to add another "profit acceleration" methodology to fast-track your path to success.

Implementing tiered pricing, with different margins, seems like a protected secret. I say that because so few entrepreneurs understand this principle, or know how to use it well. Which means there is a window of time for you to outdistance your competition if you and your teams have the will and discipline for mastery.

Before we unpack this concept, you need to know why this is so important to building ridiculous profitability. Teams spend months to years, hundreds of thousands of dollars, and create huge waste trying to entice, convert, and retain PCPs, blindly following "more from more" because the old path still brings in new customers on occasion.

The smarter, but counterintuitive approach is to think about every mundane area in your business, like pricing, and ask the "more from less" question. For example, how can we use what we charge to attract, engage, and expand our prospecting and client retention, while spending a fraction of the time and money doing it?

Thinking through tiered pricing can become a mind-numbing and challenging area in a business. I understand. Which is why most entrepreneurs and leaders default to a "cost-plus," sleepy price structure. But assigning a value to sell is like all the principles I'm sharing with you. Do not simply turn those efforts over to a single department. Work together as a cross-functional team to make sure every department has input in finalizing the market-facing numbers.

This chapter will provide you with the philosophies and concept behind the principle of multiple pricing ideas. Once you understand the "why," I'm confident you will never think about how you price the old way again. In addition, you will learn the correct definition, so you and your team have common strategies for setting numbers. Deciding *what to charge* is not a one-time static task. What you sell your goods and services for must be dynamic. Meaning you might be changing, evolving, or never altering what you want a buyer to pay.

Next, you'll discover a proven approach I've used for decades in how to rank your pricing options and offerings. To help you avoid the over and under catastrophes, I'll share most common mistakes. And because there are people new to business and who need more profit right now, I will share a six-tier approach to help find the right amount to suggest for your offerings.

Basic Pricing Strategy

A basic pricing strategy means choosing a singular approach to decide the price a buyer pays for your offerings, often applying that same methodology to the full line of existing or new products and services. Once the grand scheme to determine prices is settled, leaders feel complete, like they have commandments written on a stone tablet, declaring to all marketing and sales minions, now go forth and sell.

Retailers for about a hundred years used a single pricing approach—marked-up retail. But at glacial speed they finally added a second scheme, the sales price. However, the retail versus sales price is still the same method, with no or low margins. Companies in complex sales do the same, determining what they want to charge and what they will accept.

Too many entrepreneurs use price as a sales conversion strategy by cutting or lowering it to win new accounts, which is basically discounting and buying business, the opposite of winning new clients. Don't do it. If you want to make embarrassing profits immediately and consistently, you need to think differently from everyone else as they sleepwalk their pricing decisions.

You should know that virtually every company uses two variables to price: cost and markup. What has been retail's performance as an industry segment recently? Brick-and-mortar stores are being crushed. One of their fatal mistakes is using Stone Age schemes to decide what customers should pay.

However, some retailers like Walmart continue to gobble up global market share. Why? Because Walmart acted more entrepreneurially. They refused to follow what competitors were doing. They treat pricing as a tool, not a technique, and continuously take customers from others by using different methods to determine their prices. Later, I will provide a pricing strategy example in which Walmart was sued for selling items below its costs.

Tiered Pricing Strategies

Too many entrepreneurs employ basic cost-plus pricing applying two variables. Tiered strategies mean applying a mix of four variables. Moving from two to four options increases your choices exponentially. It's like having a joystick on a supercomputer giving you control over how fast you want to scale sales and profit making. Here are those four choices explained.

Variable 1: Range of Offerings. From a few to many. Or from a tasting sample to the whole buffet. What is the breadth and depth of what you want to market and promote?

Variable 2: Multiple Combinations. Do you want to offer a mix of goods and services in each grouping, or only one type? Such as products on the low end and services on the upper end? Remember to anchor your combinations back to your PCP and FMP.

Variable 3: Profit. Warning: The basic pricing model dictates all clusters follow the same method as cost-plus markup. Don't fall in that trap and join the cemetery of retailers past. The counterintuitive approach to what you charge is twofold. First, offer products or services that don't earn any profit or are zero margin. What, you say? What loose cannon would run a business with no profit? Second, go crazy train off the rails. Offer goods and services where you lose money all the time or your client doesn't pay you anything. Costco's $4.99 roasted chicken loses millions. By design. Can you think of the three reasons they offer it?

Variable 4: Profit Margin for Each Group. This should range from free to extremely expensive. It is critical to stagger your price points across the range of offerings. By design some items will lose money and others will deliver little or no margins. At the high end of your offering spectrum, there must be ridiculous markups. For example, profits 2 to 100 times the normal cost plus. Companies call these "halo" products.

Tiered Pricing Wheel

Shrewd design of what you feel buyers should pay requires integrating and leveraging several different principles. The first is value to your customer and to your company. Second, how best to manage risk for both sides. Third, how the exchange of money for tangible and intangible offerings makes sense for the purchaser and seller.

To ignite the power of pricing, you will need to provide a range of offerings with a mix of products and services. You must offer items individually or clustered (remember Packaging for Value) at different price points. And most important is using a variety of margins from losing money to making extreme profit—yes, selling some items for less than cost.

I understand if the concept of tiered pricing strategies is still a little fuzzy. When I learned this several decades ago, it took me years to master all the layers. Although it's complicated, this might be the one principle that makes you and your team rich the fastest. Let me share a visual to further cement your understanding and application of this powerful profit-producing method.

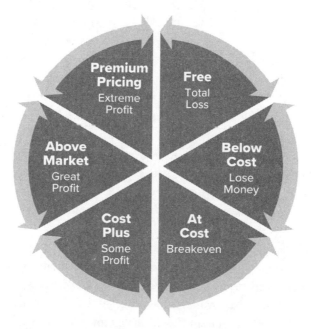

FIGURE 8.1   Tiered Pricing Strategies (Pricing to Profit)

Figure 8.1. is a graphic of tiered pricing strategies as a segmented but continuous cycle. Some clients like to use a line spectrum. If so, use arrows on both ends to represent continuous client engagement.

This pie cycle graph is broken into six parts. Each part is an offering (product or service) category. You could have any number of parts, but I recommend between three and nine. Six is a good "Goldilocks" that can be considered "just right."

The category of offerings is first segmented by the price the buyer pays. What your client is charged must range from free starting at the top right, to extremely expensive around the circle to the top left. Low prices allow prospects to engage faster with little risk. Some companies are paying people to trial their offerings, but be careful with this approach. The opposite category, of extremely high prices, allows your company to earn ridiculous margins.

Categories must include a product, service, or both. A category may have multiple offerings—think stairsteps. Each directional step in fees must be clearly higher or lower than an adjoining category. Your pricing segmented steps are subjective but spread the change in what customers pay equally around the cycle. Offer something for free and go as high as you want: $10,000, $100,000, or a million. Use four to six equal increments in your cycle. It's also critical to make the value to dollars for each category clear to your buyer.

It's normal to have hundreds or thousands of customers engaging on the low end of your fee cycle, yet oppositely, and by design, only a few clients purchasing your highest price offerings. Continuously evolve your offerings and value to achieve the perfect mix and blend of profits and PCPs. I would reward salespeople for how many clients they could have actively buying the most offerings. Those are account engagement and penetration measurement categories, critical to achieving low-cost fast growth and massive profits.

Now let's track in the opposite direction from top left around the circle to top right. Some entrepreneurs believe this is where you would apply the basic cost-plus modeling in each segment. Whatever it costs, you add your margin percentage. They would be wrong—not only incorrect, but that defeats the whole attraction and retention premise, spoiling the art of the chart. As you move from left to right, your margins must descend from high to breakeven to losing money. Yes, losing money.

The "secret sauce" to this tiered *what to charge* strategy wheel is this guiding principle: value.

You must deliver extreme value relative to each pricing segment.

The reason prospects and buyers, your PCP, don't connect quickly, don't engage wholeheartedly, don't buy more, or leave is because of one word: risk.

Number one buyer fear: they don't receive far
greater value than the price they pay.

Value must be greater than risk. Mastering this principle is how I've helped so many clients quickly become millionaires with their businesses. One client, whose company sold for an astounding valuation, reported, "Once we got our heads around presenting laddered pricing, incorporating positive and negative margins, we never went back to last century's cost-plus-model-fits-all-buyers method."

One more key point if you didn't see it: A prospect can engage with your company in many ways. Clients can buy your offerings at low, medium, or the extreme range. Or they can buy everything you offer. Hopefully, they spend all their budgets with your company and not with your competitors—like I hope you do with my firm (it was time for a shameless plug).

Here are the six different pricing segments described in Figure 8.1. Remember these are methods to determine your costs to selling price. Using the wheel, I'm going to apply a different *what to charge* strategy to each category to keep this simple.

Free

Total loss. No charge, no obligation. The prospect pays nothing. Think of any store offering free samples of items. Costco and Sam's Club have no limits for sample snatchers, only shaming from the hungry people standing in line behind them. Every entrepreneur offering products or services *must* offer something for free.

Below Cost

Lose money. Here the prospect pays some amount. However, the price doesn't cover all the cost of production, delivery, or the service. The item needs to be at a price point that creates perception of significant value and low costs. This is also called a "loss leader" or special. However, many loss leaders are not at cost or below costs, but with minimal markup. I want you to always offer a Below Cost item that fits between Free and the next category, At Cost.

Toys 'R' Us knew Walmart's costs and sued them for "predatory pricing," selling toys below what they paid for them. After an expensive court battle, Toys 'R' Us lost. Did Walmart sell below cost to kill Toys 'R' Us?

Who knows? I believe it was a smart attraction and engagement strategy. Kids don't buy toys or drive to stores, so their parents join them, and the parents end up buying stuff too.

At Cost

Breakeven. This is also called a "wash" or breakeven point pricing. You are paid what it cost to make, sell, and deliver. You should have at least one offering, ideally more, in this category because you don't want any huge gaps or wide spaces between the price categories of your offerings. This category is hard to calculate when you're in the services space because you're selling time. One method is to think like you run a law office and create billable hours by experience. Are your services the value of a junior, senior, or partner level? Lawyer rates have profit built in, so make sure to discount to arrive at pure cost.

Cost Plus

Some profit. This is the de facto standard model of *what to charge*. It's costs plus profit equals price. After calculating all costs and expenses, you determine what profit margins are needed to be successful. It's designed for protection of profits, margins, and companies. However, the final price point, with this approach, is usually too low, giving away money while damaging brand.

Above Market

Great profit. This pricing point is above what the market pays and the outside competitive range. For example, your competitor prices their services at $100,000. Because you've methodically implemented the Revenue optimization phases, you're able to price and sell at $150,000 to $200,000. Clients have learned how to price their offerings at 30 to 40 percent or more above their competitors by aligning their strategic value with pricing. However, don't price too far above the competitive pricing range as perceived by your buyers.

Premium Pricing

Extreme profit. Ultra-high-end fees. This is your most expensive offering. Your product or service must offer instant, extreme, or sustainable value as perceived by the buyer. You should offer one or more Premium-priced choices. For example, recently a well-known car company offered a brand-new convertible model with limited production (100 units) to retail for about $120,000. The first one off the assembly line, with the 001 VIN sequence, sold at auction for $2 million.

Pricing Mistakes

The first and biggest pricing mistake I see from our formal assessments is that most entrepreneurs and their teams use one or two *what to charge* strategies, at best, similar to the failing retailers using retail and a sales price. Usually those two prices are cost plus with the sales price barely making any margin. In addition, the sales or discount price strategy is usually seasonal or promotional and not available all the time.

You might be wondering how a retailer could offer something for free and still make money. Don't only think product, like perfume testers. Also think services like instant makeovers. For example, if you're a clothing retailer, pick a day of the week (maybe Saturday) to provide an hour or two of free clothing analysis and consultation. This idea comes from my experience selling high-end men's clothing in college. It was disheartening how many businesspeople couldn't color and pattern coordinate a silk tie, shirt, and suit, and others who couldn't properly tie a necktie. Once I taught them how, they would come back and ask for me. I wish I had been on commissions.

Another mistake is not following the Revenue Ready and Market Ready phases to drive the steps and strategies to setting fees. The concepts of pricing tiers, value, and risk are not what *you* think, feel, or believe. Although price perception can be influenced by the seller, you don't make the final decision. The buyer, over time, is the final judge and jury of proper pricing to value ratio.

You might be thinking, what if everyone buys at the lower tiers with free or low to no margins? A great example is a client of mine who develops mobile apps. They help their customers develop a basic or free app as well as a paid app. The free app must be solid and work great. However, for a few dollars more, the app user can enjoy a much more robust experience.

Almost everyone has used a free mobile app and then paid for a more expensive one. The secret is that the paid app must offer tremendous value: features or functions that provide extreme productivity or joy for the user.

It's critical that you have a clear and discernable value step to each higher price segment. The step can't be simply *"more better."* For example, if your free offering has a value factor of 1, your next segment pricing must have a value factor of 5 or 10, not 2. That paid app could be a gateway to a robust desktop or enterprise solution. If it offers extreme value, the client could buy it through a high-margin enterprise license or subscription service for all employees.

Why Implement Tiered Pricing Now

Offering different price points can entice buyers. But when you turn pricing into a three-dimensional power tool, your new client engagement and profits can explode with no effort. Using the pricing segments from free to premium is one layer. Mixing up your profitability on your offerings provides you additional variables to attack and attract your sweet spot PCP. Here are more reasons to master the principles of tiered pricing immediately.

Fast Attraction and Massive Engagement

The number one challenge for every company is generating enough leads and attraction with high-quality prospects. The Tiered Pricing Strategy is the smartest, fastest, most cost-effective way to kick-start new client relationships. This must become part of your Entrepreneur to Millionaire DNA.

Speed

Many entrepreneurs in the B2B or B2G space know that if you're offering complex services, it can take 6 to 12 months to engage and sign a new client. Imagine if prospects could test-drive or experience your offering with minimal hurdles of time, risk, or money. I've taught many clients how to offer assessments or analysis at low cost points to hasten engagement. That approach can attract and filter your PCPs and allow them to become long-term customers much faster.

More Profit

Creating value for your clients and making money for your business first, and you last, is the prime objective of this book. The right *what to charge* strategies protect, grow, and stimulate the highest margins possible and best client retention. Tiered pricing will make your company money faster, protect your margins, and with lower costs, make your business more profitable.

Fewer Resources

Another profit-producing aspect of tiered pricing strategies is no-cost and no-time prospect engagement. If your company "has the goods"—offers extreme value—leverage it to attract and convert prospects and buyers into clients and cash. Use the wheel to engage customers early and to have them buy more, so your business enjoys better margins. Not only do you need less marketing and sales, but it takes less time, requiring even fewer resources.

Sense of Urgency

Adding a Tiered Pricing Strategy to your growth arsenal can drive your competitors nuts. When applied in the right sequence, phase, and time, it becomes a strategic weapon for creating new demand and quickly converting prospect attraction into customers, clients, and cash.

Sadly, too few entrepreneurs, leaders, and teams use this thinking and these pricing strategies as a way to own a market. This is another reason entrepreneurs struggle to generate serious cash, drive cash flow, and create working capital.

The big excuse for not being creative and crafting a strategy on *what to charge* is that it takes thinking, not action. Yet using mental muscle is where entrepreneurs make money, and manual effort is where they lose profits. As a team you must go through the pricing process periodically.

Follow the process, tie together the data points, and make compelling *what to charge* decisions. Don't worry, no one ever masters creating all strategies and categories of perfect pricing the first few times. You need to develop the categories and structure, and work to validate, calibrate, and constantly realign for maximum results.

Tiered Pricing Strategies Action Plan

I'm sure you're excited, but don't run off changing all your prices right now. Make sure your company is Revenue Ready and has worked through

Targeting, Packaging, and Messaging. Mastering the earlier principles will make Tiered Pricing Strategy decisions so much easier and more engaging. Also, please read the whole book, as pricing strategies must integrate and align with other decisions.

Your team must start with making sure you offer high-value items for free. Look at the Appendix of this book, "Additional Resources." See all the free, no-obligation items we offer? They all cost us money and a lot of time—which is the point. We want people to see, read, and experience the value of my material and my methodology with no risk to them. I believe that to get more, you have to give more.

Use your free services as both a marketing and filtering process. For example, after reading my materials, watching my videos, or having a no-obligation short phone conversation, if someone doesn't like or agree with my philosophy, then that means they're probably not our PCP. I saved them time and my team headaches by not putting up with people who won't do the work to transform and optimize their company. This is a win-win.

Next, do you offer something of extreme price and value? You must. Again, look at the Appendix. Our extreme pricing and value is the high intensity programs. Clients can purchase the rights to our templates, tools, methods, and IP and have their employees certified to use them in their companies. Instead of experimenting and missing millions for decades, they can start using proven tools right now and make millions in one-tenth the time.

Finally, have your team create and offer something for all the segments you choose. I recommend six segments. Assign one of your team members to poke holes in your pricing wheel. Question the offering, value, price, and separation from other segments. Run your value wheel by a few of your PCPs. What do they think? What would they change?

Congratulations, you have just completed the chapters and core principles in the Market Ready phase. You and your team are more prepared to grow and scale sales, revenue, and profits than 99 percent of all companies. Now it's time to put your foot on the gas and accelerate your path to millions. Maybe billions. In the next phase you'll think about marketing and sales differently and add four more core principles to creating scalable, explosive revenue growth.

Go to Market

(WINNING)

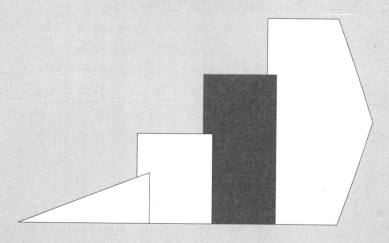

About 98 percent of prospect calls my company receives are from frustrated entrepreneurs and exasperated CEOs struggling in the Go to Market Phase. About a third of those calls are from leaders who are doing well, but are hungry for that next level of sustainable and explosive profitable growth. They want to go from incremental to monumental—now. I message their visions and question this way:

How to achieve tomorrow today.

The other two-thirds of calls are entrepreneurs and leaders experiencing one or more performance area failures. In my Go to Market models, there are four performance areas (also called buckets) you must measure and manage to optimize and sustain high-profit, low-cost growth. Failure in one or any of these areas will block your future and fortune.

1. *Lead generation.* Is your business creating enough in quantity, quality, and easily qualifiable new client demand that is growing or scaling?

2. *Robust PCP pipeline.* Is your prospect funnel filled with high-quality PCPs, with high-margin opportunities bursting the pipeline in all phases, from initial discovery to completion and harvesting?

3. *Prospect to client conversions.* Are your sales opportunities and prospects moving through the pipeline rapidly, saving resources, time, and cash flow, with accurate predictability?

4. *Exceeding targets.* Is your business consistently meeting and driving past sales, revenue, and profit targets through building and leveraging a high-quality PCP portfolio?

Most of the root cause issues that drive poor performance in these four areas are from mistakes made in the Revenue Ready and Market Ready phases. However, even if you perfected those phases, in this phase, you can still shred money faster than the government can print it.

Let's not burn money, time, and resources in your Go to Market phase. Remember, *Entrepreneur to Millionaire* is all about how much money your company can make and keep, not how much it spends. These Go to Market principles will allow your company to keep the millions that other companies waste.

CHAPTER 9

Marketing Demand Creation

Sixty-seven percent of marketing efforts are a complete waste of time, money, effort, and resources.

A t 11:15 a.m. we had reached the midpoint of a formal Revenue Growth® systems assessment. The executive leaders were embarrassedly absorbing the failure points, disconnects, and missing parts discovered in their company. However, it appeared they were stressing about unpacking and analyzing the next important area to successful revenue growth—the design, performance, and production of their marketing organization.

Before I started asking specific questions about their marketing structure, models, and strategies, I opened with a broad request: "Tell me about your marketing."

"It sucks," quipped a leader.

"It's not working," added another.

"We get a lot of leads, but they're not high quality," said the frustrated VP of sales.

"Wow, I'm sensing strong disappointment with how you attract new prospects and clients," I empathized.

The entrepreneur CEO then commented, "That's why you're here and we're going through this process. Over the last couple of years, we fired our PR partner and tried three different advertising firms. We've been spending a fortune every month on digital efforts and SEO, without much success.

We've been thinking about hiring a lead generation firm, but I'm tired of wasting money."

"I understand. Marketing is the most frustrating, underutilized, and least respected function in literally every company. However, when designed, executed, and measured properly marketing can be foundational to generating explosive corporate wealth and ridiculous personal fortunes. However, the misconceptions, flawed philosophies, and outright lies keep it from pulling its weight. I'll help you transform your marketing results if you're willing to execute the function in a radically different way," I explained. "Let's start with the basics. What is marketing?" I asked.

With some hesitation, finally an answer: "It's promoting your business to potential clients," said a team member.

"It's being on social media or advertising to let people know what you offer," said another.

"What is your core marketing philosophy?" I probed.

"Be everywhere we can to promote our message," added the VP of sales.

"How do you measure the success of your marketing?" I pushed.

As a group they answered: web hits, web traffic, people filling out contact forms, when the phone rings.

"One last question. Are marketing and sales different, or the same thing?" I inquired. No answer. "What is your confidence level in your answers about marketing?"

"Crappy," said the CEO.

"Clueless," exclaimed another.

The VP of marketing sat quietly.

The discussion continued with the team sharing more thoughts and concerns, but I finally summarized: "Other than a narrow tactical view, activity-centric model, digitally dominant, with no performance thresholds, you're on a perfect strategic path to generate new prospects *on occasion*."

Thankfully, the group chuckled, as I was trying levity to release the pressure in the room. "That approach wouldn't be a problem if your company were generating more than enough new clients. In addition, it doesn't appear the number and quality are increasing to meet growth needs each month," I added.

"Right now, your efforts to attract new business, like most, are a low production, high expense 'digital activity factory.' But I must add, in today's hypercompetitive, rapidly shifting markets, this is not your marketing leader's fault. All of you, as leaders of departments, are *responsible* for new customer demand, lead creation, and prospect conversion. Marketing is *totally accountable, but only partially responsible*," I asserted.

The VP of marketing approached me at the break. I was prepared to take "incoming" (anger-based comments) from her.

She said, "Thank you." She quietly added, "Ever since being hired, the leaders pushed me and my team to increase our activities on the Internet and spend more time supporting sales efforts. I'm frustrated we are so tactical and not strategic. But I'm tired of fighting, so we just do what we're asked."

Empathizing, I replied, "I understand how you feel. About 94 percent of marketing talent feels undervalued and disrespected. From CMOs to interns, most are driven down to their lowest level of value, such as repetitive activity–based digital campaigns, hours remaking brochures, rebuilding slide presentations, and writing proposals."

Now smiling, she curiously asked, "How can you be so specific that 94 percent of people in marketing feel abused?"

"It's based on the statistic and my experience that only about 6 percent of leaders have extensive marketing backgrounds, broad experience, or advanced degrees. Entrepreneurs are usually overly energized people with expertise in operations, technical, financial, or legal, pushing their ideas. Bless their hearts. Which means they won't see or measure marketing as a holistic demand creation system, but as a 'do more activities' robotic effort," I explained.

Marketing Lacks Strategic Leadership

An entrepreneur of a technology services firm asked for help to redesign and build an in-house, high-powered marketing organization. This CEO wanted more control of growth with an on-site executive leading a full-time team. She asked what title and role was best for her business. Did she need a manager, director, or chief marketing officer (CMO)? I responded that for the size of company, budget, people responsibilities, and sophistication of the deliverables, a director is the right fit, with a development path to CMO. However, before we started interviewing, I warned her to prepare to be somewhat disappointed with the applicants.

Using a solid contingency recruiter network, subscription job boards, and qualified referrals, we gleaned the résumés to identify the top 10 marketing director candidates. The interviewees each spewed knowledge of digital activities and popular optimization trends—platforms, SEO algorithms, clicks, traffic, analytics, impressions, CTRs (click through rates), rankings, engagement, bounce, and web page statistics.

After the first rounds of interviewing, the CEO had signs of worry. She turned to me with a sigh: "You were right. Everyone we interviewed completely focused on tactical and digital marketing activities. Only two of them discussed strategic direction and measurement. Only one interviewee mentioned the key foundational element for all business relationships. Not a single applicant could articulate a clear and concise marketing philosophy. What do we do?"

"Let's hire the best talent most willing to change professionally and develop new thinking. Someone with the will to leave the flawed 'more from more' activities-based marketing path. Then I will help set up a framework to generate the demand generation 'more from less' production you need," I answered.

Sadly, how companies execute marketing, and the role itself, is now a digital playground bursting with commotion and actions. The marketing function, like sales, is now more "busyness" than business results. Internet efforts fulfill a portion of how to attract clients, but they should not be the total focus. Ironically, most web promoting is strategically misguided and tactically mismeasured. Other than those issues, it's a perfect path.

"But shouldn't a director of marketing need to be well versed in all things digital?" she asked.

"Yes and no. Yes, if they are the only resource. However, it's common to use one or more third-party specialists. But that creates another set of problems," I cautioned.

"Stop, I'm getting a headache," she complained.

"Don't worry. I'll take you through a proven framework needed to transform marketing into a powerful demand generation and new client attraction system," I replied.

"Can't you just tell us which platforms, strategies, and the best digital marketing things to do right now?" she wondered.

"Not until we complete some 'readiness' phases and principles and put an operating framework in place. Today's technology and platforms are rapidly changing, aggregating, and morphing—which is another reason demand creation fails. Once you're following the revenue growth road map, making platform, strategy, budgeting, measurement, and hiring decisions will become a hundred times easier. If you don't implement the phases and principles in sequence, you'll just keep guessing, hoping, and burning money," I added.

"What's the first thing required to get on the right path?" she quizzed.

"Stop thinking and saying *marketing*," I said, smiling.

Typical Marketing Fix: "Outsource It"

Want to know the greatest marketing lie being told and sold? "You need to spend more to grow more." To accelerate your business, you must expend more budget, do more activities, more digital efforts, more email campaigns, more advertising, and push more out there to build brand awareness. If you're not getting the results, just increase the budget and numbers, the so-called experts preach.

Often, I'm called by frustrated executive leaders because of new client attraction issues. Their third-party marketing partners, lead generation companies, PR and advertising firms weren't delivering results. Sometimes, it takes entrepreneurs burning through several different types of external business growth programs before they're ready to *change paths*. Sadly, experimenting with "more from more" wastes years and loses millions in sales.

Yet, it's rarely the third party's total fault that enough leads or high-quality demand isn't produced. It's the entrepreneur who has failed for not completing Revenue Ready and Market Ready phases. In addition, lack of clarity and thinking in core business philosophy, directional strategies, and key measurement sabotages marketing results. You might have your third-party partners read this material so they are in alignment with your new philosophies and they are also on the right "more from less" path.

Why Weak Marketing Demand Persists

Is the word "marketing" a noun or a verb? Think carefully and choose one.

Have you ever thought about the difference? Almost no one does.

Your answer will determine whether your company makes millions or wastes millions.

People are taught, told, and sold to think of "marketing" as a verb, even when the intent is a noun. Have you used or heard the following phrases? "If you want to grow your business, you need to do more promoting." "If you want to increase sales, you must do more marketing."

This confusion of marketing being a noun or a verb is where and why entrepreneurs never have enough new leads and prospects for fast growth.

Interestingly, the dictionaries define "marketing" as a noun.

Google search shows this definition:

> *Marketing—noun—* . . . *the action or business of promoting and selling products or services, including market research and advertising* . . .

The American Marketing Association defines and reconfirms its explanation every three years:

> *The activity, set of institutions, and process for creating, communicating, delivering, and exchanging offerings that have value for customers, clients, partners, and society at large.*

Marketing as a noun or verb? Still confused? Why is the difference a *really* big deal? How you think about something determines how you expect it to perform. Here is the three-step slippery slope to not having enough new client demand:

1. When entrepreneurs hear and think of marketing as a verb, they see taking action.
2. When they think of actions, they're thinking tangible and physical results, more traffic, views, and contacts.
3. When entrepreneurs need more contacts to grow, they confusingly think "more emails and campaigns." Yet more contacts may not have any value.

Here is how you *must* rethink your marketing. It is a noun first. A person, place, *and* things.

Use my definition to make sure your marketing is *always* thought of as a noun for fast, scalable, profitable growth. Be sure to think of marketing for what it should be before you focus on what it should do.

Marketing in a business is a core function, executing a mix of strategic decisions, tactics, and processes to leverage the unique value of products and services to achieve the necessary levels of new client demand.

Why does my definition help clients produce astonishing results? My marketing evaluation and measurement is reverse to how most entrepreneurs are taught.

If you want your results to be different, then see and do things *differently*. My focus is not what needs to be done—*activities*—but what needs to be achieved—*creating client demand*. Remember, your company can do everything the way marketing is defined and never make a dollar. Oppositely, applying my counterintuitive path and standards can add millions to your business in a short time. Our approach is "more from less," when typical marketing is hoping for "more from more."

Transforming Your Marketing for Results

Want to know how I transform, turbocharge, and scale marketing results? It's easy to understand, but hard to master. First, understand that *optimized*, scalable, repeatable, predictable, profitable, high-quality new customer demand doesn't come from:

- ▸ A single function (department), or
- ▸ Employees, or
- ▸ Digital efforts, and
- ▸ Will never be achieved from *more activities*

Creating enough new client demand to fuel the explosive growth you need only comes from a well-designed and executed strategic marketing system—an enterprise marketing structure and culture crafted and managed to attract enough high-quality new prospects (PCPs) for higher levels of sales and revenue growth.

To be able to squeeze "marketing systems thinking and design" into a single chapter, I will boil down what needs to be done into a four-part Marketing Demand System framework. The four parts include Marketing Function Roles, Marketing Activities, Marketing Production, and Marketing

Performance Management with three principles each. The first part is Marketing Function Roles, which range from strategic to tactical to support. The second part is Marketing Activities or "executables," from digital to traditional to physical. These are sometimes called marketing strategies or methods. Third is Marketing Production, which is the results of your marketing efforts (activities). This includes leads, database, and brand. Fourth is Marketing Performance Management, which covers measurement, metrics, and thresholds.

Marketing Function Roles

Optimized and effective marketing functions range from strategic to tactical to support. Unfortunately, most companies have voids and disconnects in the strategic area. Without well-crafted strategies, any digital activity might do.

Strategic Marketing Role

This sets the direction and path for your whole company. When effectively executed, strategic marketing provides the answers to the overarching growth questions—who, what, where, when, and how. Well-thought-out strategies help you know when to say yes, but more important, when to say no.

An entrepreneur recently came to me, confused as to which social media platform to use. He said his advertising firm wanted to use a blend of several platforms. I asked him, which one does his PCP follow? Once he responded, I asked why he would consider any other choices. He responded with a "duh." That was too easy.

If you struggle to make simple and quick decisions, that usually means a lack of strategy.

Have you heard of the marketing Four Ps from last century? That model represents the marketing mix of Product, Price, Place, and Promotion. It's a good strategic checklist, but a limited guide to this century's demand creation needs.

In this book, the discussion of "Product" or offering started in the chapter on Modeling (Chapter 3). Pricing Strategies (Chapter 8) were covered after Packaging (Chapter 6). Place or position conversations, regarding scope and scale, were discussed in the first chapter on FMP (Chapter 2) and in Modeling (Chapter 3). Promotion, the fourth and final P, is explained in this chapter on Marketing.

Are you wondering why I didn't put the 4 Ps in this marketing chapter, like most companies do and how it's taught in academia? It is because clients prove my four optimization phases, using a cross-functional engagement model, produce the strongest demand utilizing the fewest resources. Elevating the marketing "Ps" out of the marketing department creates amazing "more from less" results producing highly profitable fast growth.

Tactical Marketing Role

Tactical marketing is where marketing teams and entrepreneurs spend most of their time, energy, and budgets. That's good and bad. Good because this is how you can generate massive amounts of demand and high-quality leads. Bad because being too activity driven without a validated framework guarantees less than optimal results. Which is the biggest marketing mistake most companies make?

Marketing campaigns. These initiatives involve advertising, promoting, and pushing your products and services. These efforts usually have a specific end date. Perhaps you are executing an "email campaign" announcing your new offering, or a digital campaign promoting the next event.

Marketing projects. These are efforts at fixing or creating something to grow the company. For instance, building a more robust website, or designing an e-commerce capability. Projects, like campaigns, have a clear starting and ending point.

Marketing programs. Where campaigns and projects start and stop, a program might go on forever. Let's say your team created a new client referral program, which is a project. The ongoing management, tracking, and measurement could be a "forever program."

Marketing Sales Support Role

Marketing people support selling efforts. When they provide sales support, it's usually around creating or customizing proposals or presentations. It might include creating new marketing materials, like brochures (a project). Many times, marketing resources can be used as "on-demand" sales support. Maybe you must respond to a major request for proposal (RFP).

Marketing can and should provide support for sales activities. However, don't allow your marketing resources to become subservient to or be abused by salespeople. Otherwise being at the beck and call of overbearing salespeople can feel like a career graveyard.

Marketing Activities

Within the "Tactical Marketing Role" I just discussed. are three options: digital, traditional, and physical. Too many entrepreneurs now focus on marketing's tactical role and a single Internet-based approach for creating new customer demand.

There are two major problems with "putting all your spider eggs in one web basket." First, every company "has gone all digital" for broadcasting and promoting, making the ocean of noise on the Internet deeper. Second, executing only one marketing role option never optimizes new client attraction.

Digital Marketing

This is your web presence, e-commerce platforms, and anything else performed over the Internet. This form of promotion is using the IoT (Internet of Things) as places and channels to broadcast. The intent is to increase connects, drive interest, and promote offerings. The good part of the net is the cost of exposure. The "reach is cheap." The bad, when overdone, like too many email blasts, turns prospects off and damages brand.

Traditional Marketing

Traditional marketing means promoting with different mediums, beside digital, to literally broadcast your offerings and company information. Those forms may include any or all of newspaper, radio, TV, print, billboard, and mailers. Traditional advertising is not dead. However, this option is either expensive or ineffective if a methodical Readiness road map isn't followed. Clients who implement and abide by the integrated principles, creating multistep campaigns, have enjoyed amazing numbers of new leads.

Physical Marketing

This is a "human talking to humans" approach. Think "one to many." I know it sounds old-school, but this is how to create *high-quality* client demand. This is you the entrepreneur, or another employee, presenting the content—for example, being on expert panels, delivering speeches, or taking part in interviews. First, few entrepreneurs are willing to master the art and craft of public speaking. Second, it puts you and your company's expertise on a pedestal, above your competition.

My recommendation is this: to achieve fast and low-cost profitable growth, you should implement a balanced, integrated combination of digital, traditional, and physical marketing. Think and execute well "integrated" campaigns.

Marketing Production

What's another reason marketing struggles? Entrepreneurs and leaders track and overmanage daily or weekly activities. They fail to measure production over periods of time. Big mistake. Full disclosure: I too enjoy watching my Google and YouTube analytics with dancing bar charts and hourly increasing subscriber stats.

However, sustainable next-level success requires concentrating on the destination, not the daily dashboard. Before you read any further, write out what you believe are the three essential production milestones to effective marketing. Short *monthly*, mid-term *quarterly*, and long-term *yearly*?

Short-Term Production: New Sales and Sales Leads

Marketing results are not the same as activities. Don't be satisfied with actions. Marketing production must be measured by new demand—*sales leads*. Always assess your leads with these three measurements: quantity, quality, and level of qualification. In addition, for fast growth, your quality new client attraction numbers must increase in size and value every month.

Mid-Term Production: Marketable Database

Once your organization is hitting its lead generation threshold and scaling the demand needs, you must focus on the next most important production measurement—the number in your *marketable database*. The operative word is "marketable." It's imperative you don't measure the size or number of contacts, names, or companies in your lists as value. The only characteristic that matters is the specific quantity of PCP "suspects or prospects" who might or can buy.

Long-Term Production: Brand

Brand is a critical measurement of overall marketing effectiveness. Entrepreneurs think brand happens naturally. Don't let it. You should think about how your company and offerings are positioned from the very beginning.

Start with design elements, parameters, and protection. However, make sure you don't waste time and money on ineffective efforts. Be careful of wasteful "brand awareness campaigns" when you're starting.

Also, make sure to know how "brand" is perceived. There is much confusion. This is the definition I use when doing assessment or transformation work: brand is "how people think and feel about your product, services, and company."

Marketing Performance Management

The fourth part of your strategic demand creation framework is marketing performance management, which includes measurement, metrics, and thresholds. Maximizing marketing performance is achieved through having these three areas predetermined. To keep marketing production and marketing performance management clear, the former (leads, database, and brand) are the lagging indicators that are achieved over weeks to years. This section, marketing performance management, represents the leading indicators tracked by hours, days, or weeks. You must oversee both.

Measurement

This is deciding on a category or area to track and analyze the number or ratios of activities, production, or results. For example, in marketing, there are hundreds of things you can measure. The key is identifying the critical categories having real revenue growth impact. In the last section I covered three you can use: leads, database, and brand.

Metrics

These are the details of the numbers inside the categories you are analyzing. Let's use sales leads as a measurement category. To manage performance, you must track quantity and quality. The quality element is subjective unless you assign an attribute creating a metric. For instance, how many leads have formal budgets, a motivated buyer, or specific decision date?

Thresholds

These are the exact numbers expected of a metric that must be achieved or exceeded. Let's say your company needs, as a goal, to generate 50 qualified leads this month. If your enterprise (notice I didn't say marketing) doesn't meet or beat the target for new prospects, your revenue growth goals will most likely be missed. Effective use of metric targets is your gold standard for high performance and rapid growth. Also, think of thresholds as minimum or must-have requirements. Using the example above, 50 leads might be the threshold, but the marketing team is not bonused unless it meets or exceeds a target of 75 leads.

Creating Demand Responsibility

Who should be most responsible for lead generation? Marketing or sales? Neither, if you want an optimized growth model. Too many entrepreneurs and leaders rely on salespeople, one function, or a third party to create the bulk of new prospects. This is a terrible mistake. You can become a millionaire three to four times faster if you move away from that last century unbalanced model.

Every area of your enterprise, from leadership to marketing, sales, operations, and external partners, must play a role in generating more prospects. Everyone and every part of your firm must take *responsibility* for producing new client demand. However, that does not mean "everyone is in sales." Yuck. That approach, like having engineers or technicians carry quota or be bonused, turns everyone off and creates stress and tension on employees *and* consumers. I've fired my last two HVAC companies that used that cheesy, conflict-of-interest-producing philosophy.

The marketing department is *accountable* for all leads. Marketing must act as the collection point, the clearinghouse for prospect demand from all sources. They must also work with every area to facilitate customer attraction. If lead numbers surpass the "threshold" or targets for quantity and quality, marketing should be rewarded. If the number of qualified prospects doesn't meet the goals for a period, marketing is at fault. Where your new customer demand originates is not important.

Biggest Marketing Mistake: Relying on Word of Mouth for Fast Company Growth

Want to keep your small business small and your profits unpredictable? Use word-of-mouth marketing, which I call "fool's gold," when your goal is fast company growth. Over the decades I've had people champion word of mouth as a way to grow their small business. What's ironic is that I agree with them in the case of ordinary growth. However, for fast growth and quickly becoming embarrassingly rich, it has too many flaws.

At a Las Vegas Business Growth Conference (I didn't name it), after delivering a day of speeches and breakout sessions I was still on stage at 7:30 p.m. My speech had ended an hour earlier, but I wanted to answer every question from those who queued. Being hungry, exhausted. and feet aching, I started cutting my answers short.

The next person in line asked, "I heard what you said about different lead sources. But what do you think about building a business based on word-of-mouth leads?"

Before I could answer, the attendee in line right behind this person jutted forward, exclaiming proudly, "I built my whole business through word of mouth." Blatantly undermining what I had presented about using multiple lead generation methods to manage risk and create explosive growth, he continued, "Word of mouth works well for me, and I highly recommend it."

If I hadn't been so cranky, or that person wasn't so obnoxious, I would have responded more diplomatically. Instead, I said, "I'm sorry to hear that, as word of mouth can be one of the most inconsistent and high-risk ways to build a *fast revenue growth company.*"

Mister peacock strutted away in disgust before he gave me a chance to explain. Here is how word-of-mouth leads can keep a small business small.

When someone contacts your business, from someone who knows you or has used your offerings, its commonly called "word of mouth"—meaning the prospect interest could have come from any number of people.

There is nothing wrong with leads coming from out of the blue. I receive many and love them. Yet there are numerous risks in relying on this nebulous demand source to build your company fortune.

If you're happy running a small business, you might be able to rely on word of mouth for leads. However, if you want to make millions from your business success as fast as possible, relying on that form of leads will never optimize your growth. Here is why:

> ▶ *No control.* You have literally no influence or power over "word-of-mouth" leads. You're reactive to what or if the market delivers.

- *Unpredictable.* "Word-of-mouth" new prospects can be extremely inconsistent, and that may never improve.
- *Doesn't quickly scale.* If you need 5 or 50 quality prospects a week (pick a number), will that number go up in the future? It might go down—and your firm with it.
- *Inferior quality.* "Word-of-mouth" leads will rarely be superior, the biggest size, your PCP, or the company-changing growth in demand you need to achieve faster, more profitable growth.

Why Change Your Marketing Thinking Now

Are you inspired to transition from activity-based "more from more" marketing and experience the lower-cost higher-production-demand-based "more from less"? When you start following the superior path, new client attraction can rocket—but only if your marketing performs as a complete, integrated, and balanced system. Here are more reasons to transform your marketing thinking, execution, and measurement.

Speed to Sales, Revenue, and Profits

Creating superior demand in the form of PCP high-quality leads is one of the greatest accelerators to success. Superior new client demand sails through sales cycles (a visual pun). When your client attraction is weak and lead quality is low, it takes an army of salespeople burning tons of resources to wrestle a contact to close.

More Earnings

The higher the quality of demand, the greater the profits—from not spending more on marketing and sales and from higher-margin contracts. In addition, more profit can be made from clients staying longer or using your services for years. Higher-quality clients require less management and support, saving money and improving the bottom line.

Quality of Clients

Just as you lose with losers, you win with winners. Any company that has the best clients is usually the best positioned for superior financial numbers.

Nothing makes a company more valuable for purchase than a first-class customer portfolio. And nothing makes a business more miserable than dealing with clowns for clients.

Control of Success

If you are truly entrepreneurial and want to create a fast or explosive growth company making ridiculous profits, then the more factors you can control the better. Effective marketing can both attract and filter the amount, quality, and size of client spend from the marketplace.

Sense of Urgency

Unfortunately, marketing is one of the least effective, most frustrating, and most undervalued functions inside companies. That lowly position is validated when the marketing department is the first area cut when times get tough.

The "keep shooting till you hit something" approach is *not* how to optimize your new client demand production or results. Only marketing that follows a proven framework, field-tested strategies, and measurement create fast and profitable growth. Some clients religiously following these principles have generated more leads than their sales teams could manage, without spending more time, money, or adding headcount.

This chapter wasn't designed to share the latest on digital platforms, new technologies, or SEO algorithms, as they will change tomorrow. Its content by design is systems-based, strategic, and philosophical to guide superior fast-growth decision making and execution for years to decades. Stop thinking marketing and start—*creating demand*.

Marketing Action Plan

Although marketing teams are extremely busy, there are a lot of holes in most marketing systems and organizations. I recommend starting by having your whole leadership team assess your marketing philosophy. What is your core marketing belief? Is it strategic, systems-based, and transformational, or is it tactical, activity based, and short focused?

Next, assess your marketing goals. Are they activity based or production based? Identify your core marketing strategy. What is the one thing your team can do to generate all the leads and client demand you need? You might have many strategies, but what is the primary one? We have one core marketing strategy in our company, and it can fill our prospect client pipeline for years. What is the one strategy that will take your company to the next level?

After creating your marketing demand creation system, strategic marketing plan, and goals, what categories and metrics will you use for performance management?

You've achieved mastery when your marketing is leveraging your enterprise to create sustainable, growing, high-quality demand that meets and exceeds prospect and lead targets every month. Let's move from creating demand to converting it into the most clients and cash possible. The next chapter, "Sales Conversion System," will put the wind behind massive sales (pun intended) for many entrepreneurs.

CHAPTER 10

Sales Conversion System

Consistent and explosive sales growth doesn't come from salespeople—it comes from a well designed and executed strategic sales system.

An entrepreneur of a multimillion-dollar services company called me at 8 a.m. on a Monday morning and asked—*more like demanded*—"When this week can we meet for coffee?" I chuckled and said, "Wow, what's the problem?" He said, "I've burned through so many salespeople I'm waving the white flag."

Sipping a large java, I listened for what seemed like hours, finally interjecting, "How many people from sales have you hired and fired?"

He mumbled, "About 50."

"Wow," I choked. "Over what period of time?"

"The last three years," he said sheepishly.

"From what you've shared regarding size of sales team, quotas, team targets, accounts, and coverage, this is my rough calculation. You've missed, or lost out on, about $10 to $15 million in revenue and profits." Ouch.

"What have you tried to fix your problem with sales?" I probed.

He said, "Everything. I added more sales management. Raised the base salaries to sign better salespeople. Started using recruiters to source people with proven selling backgrounds and have a guaranteed replacement if they didn't work out."

He went on, "Oh yeah, a year ago I brought in a popular sales training company. My managers promised more people trained would fix the problem. We put all our people through their classes. After two of my best salespeople completed the programs, they were stolen by my competitors offering bigger salaries. And my other top people aren't using what they were taught. Training was a waste of time and budget."

I explained, "Don't feel bad. Sales, selling, and salespeople are the number one frustration and headache for entrepreneurs and small business owners. The inability to manage salespeople and control sales performance brings even seasoned entrepreneurs and senior leaders to tears.

"From what you've shared, and without a deep diagnostic evaluation, there are several failure points we need to address. First, it sounds like you're out of sync. Right now, you're executing in the Go to Market phase trying to sell as much as possible. However, it doesn't appear the Revenue Ready or Market Ready phases were completed. Skipping those steps will create many of the challenges you're facing.

"Second, from your comments about your employees in sales, you're operating with last century's salespeople-based model. Meaning you're counting on the most unpredictable, inconsistent, never-sure-what-they're-going-to-achieve device—humans—to meet growth targets. Your company isn't set up for success—it's designed for inconsistency and underperformance. But there's a bigger danger. The future success of your business is most likely resting on the shoulders of salespeople who are most likely incompetent," I explained.

"Wow, things are worse than I thought," he responded. "But I'm not an expert in sales, I'm an entrepreneur. I had no idea there were so many things wrong. But I know I'm responsible. How do we fix this? Should I blow everything up and start from scratch?" he pondered.

"No, you can't," I cautioned. "If you want to solve the root cause of all your sales performance issues, then you're going to have to change your path. Your business success, your overarching strategy, and your profit-making are all too dependent upon people and a "more from more" model. As long as salespeople are the 'heartbeat' of your growth engine, you will never optimize making money or performance," I warned.

"Are you saying get rid of all my salespeople? Using automation or outsourcing?" he asked.

"No, you can't. Your market is B2B and B2G, meaning long, complex selling cycles. Those markets require multiple human touch points and competent salespeople for prospect to contract conversions," I explained.

"What are you suggesting?" he asked.

"We need to transform your salespeople and management into a strategic system." Your focus is people-centric activities and transactions. For optimized performance you must do the opposite. You need a design where people play a role in production and conversions, but they are not the cornerstone of the system," I explained.

"Should we get a new CRM? We have been talking to a company that has a 'sales system' they want us to buy. Is that what you mean?" he asked.

Laughing politely, I responded, "You can't buy a strategic sales system—it has to be custom designed, built, and implemented into your model. Besides, most companies selling 'systems' are providing tactical training steps or digital marketing. They market what they do as a system, but they really want 'butts in seats' training, and they're delivering old or stale selling techniques. Also, 99 percent of the popular sales training is for simple sales pursuits. Your company competes in the B2B and B2G markets engaging in enterprise type sales," I cautioned.

"I will lead you through a more transformational and holistic revenue growth architecture. As I mentioned earlier, many of your salespeople's performance challenges are caused by factors outside the sales department. The next thing we must do is change many of the sales and selling philosophies you and your team are following. Then we will focus on the three major areas of a strategic sales system, including the hard and soft parts, the people components, and sales support areas," I continued.

"Here is the bottom line. More training, more sales management, more salary games, and more hiring and firing to win more business will only achieve incremental growth at best. 'More from more' will never maximize sales production using minimum resources because 99 percent of sales performance interventions are 'salespeople fix it' solutions, when only 1 percent of sales issues are the salesperson. We need to solve the cause, not the symptom," I explained.

The Weakest Link

In what department in a business can an employee be successful roughly 3 or 4 out of 10 times and be considered a hero? Operations? Finance? Support? Quality control?

If you said sales, you win. Can you imagine if your product only worked 30 percent or 40 percent of the time? Or your service offering failed 7 out of every 10 attempts? Your company would instantly go out of business and probably be sued. Winning one out of three or four times, a horrific performance statistic, is why sales is dysfunctional and burns the most profit. Yet many entrepreneurs and leaders are too accepting of these mediocre results.

Why are sales organizations, not only the people, so inconsistent, unpredictable, unscalable, and shred more money than any other department? It starts with stale philosophies. Why does the sales area remain a quicksand of inefficiency, mediocrity, and waste? Flawed design.

Selling, salespeople, and sales organizations have barely evolved. They operate more like tribes than sophisticated societies based on systems-thinking. Why is that? Over 95 percent of sales information is tips, tricks, and techniques for simple sales from last century. These stale tactical methods are what make selling cheesy, greasy, and sleazy—which is why most entrepreneurs hate sales and selling and so do their prospects.

Furthermore, adding and using more technology does not bring sales organizations and salespeople to higher levels of competency or proficiency. In most cases, more technology creates a false belief that the salespeople are leading edge in their thinking and execution. Technology can create and show more sales activities; however, there is little correlation between sales efforts and sales production. One does not guarantee the other. I have dozens of case studies of our prospects spending a fortune on technology, with no discernable increase in sales growth—another "more from more" failure.

Why Hiring Salespeople Is an Entrepreneur's Worst Nightmare

When entrepreneurs start their businesses, they might be the only salesperson. Over time, however, being the solo sales generator will bottleneck success. You must add salespeople and build a strategic sales system focused on conversions. For fast growth, someone other than the entrepreneurial leader must be dedicated to selling full time. But remember, hiring a group of salespeople does not make a team. A team is not an organization, and an organization is not the holistic system you need to optimize success.

Your company will only grow as fast and make as much in profit as the weakest part of your sales system.

Salespeople are often viewed as the weakest part. They're not. The system that hired them, developed them, and is leading them is usually weaker.

Bringing on your first salesperson can range from daunting to disastrous. Every entrepreneur has a story of hiring the first person for sales being frustrating, scary, high risk, and their most nervous growth step. Here is the frightening statistic from thousands of entrepreneurs who join our workshops and programs:

Ninety-eight percent of first sales hires fail.

Without effective, strategic sales system design, the odds of your first hire dedicated to selling, producing results, covering all expenses, and generating a profit is like scoring a hole in one on the golf course. It happens, but seldom. Quick—how many golfers do you know personally who have scored a hole in one? Even worse, every time you hire a salesperson, you add eight additional ways to chew up profits. Yet, to grow quickly, you must continuously increase new sales revenue.

Typical Sales Results

Whether you're hiring your first salesperson or have an army, here are some business-killing sales statistics. This data comes from work inside sales organizations, ranging from first hire to clients with thousands of salespeople—from teams selling small contracts to signing billion-dollar multiyear complex major agreements. Below are a few of the reasons why a "salespeople-dependent model" can be so damaging:

- ▶ Ninety-five percent of entrepreneurs and salespeople are delusional about their "gift of selling." In reality they sign new business by giving things away, lowering price, or negotiating weaker terms. That is not winning business—it's buying it.
- ▶ Eight out of 10 sales calls fail—the prospect relationship does not move forward. Most move backward, but the salesperson still delivers a proposal that will be used against them.
- ▶ Sales win ratios—if salespeople believe they close at 40 to 50 percent, the true and scrubbed figure is really half that, 20 to 25 percent.
- ▶ Fifty to 75 percent of proposals in pipelines are unwinnable or become a nondecision.
- ▶ Less than 1 percent of sales managers can explain the concepts and philosophies of simple selling versus complex selling.

- ► More than 95 percent of sales philosophies that entrepreneurs and leaders use are from last century.
- ► Salespeople wrongly count on product, price, or personality to close (win) sales.
- ► Ninety-eight percent of long sales cycle contracts become smaller, less profitable, or weaker when signed.

Common Sales Fixes and Why They Don't Work

If sales performance is critical for success, yet sales is often the weakest link for companies, how do most entrepreneurs try to fix it? Here are some popular "attack the salesperson" methods.

More Hires, More Fires

This is called the "burn and turn" approach. Like the story that opened this chapter, the premise is to grind through salespeople till you find a few worth keeping. Think "boiler room" sales. The real burn is damaging brand and destroying customer relationships.

More Training

Billions are spent (not invested) in sales torture programs (whoops, training programs) because it feels like the right thing to do. However, the "classes for the masses" show little return for dozens of reasons. Many clients who spent big budgets on selling skills turn around and pay us to deprogram and then reprogram their people.

More Managers

"Helicoptering," suffocating, and cattle prodding will make anyone jump a few times. However, more management adds more layers of profit-eating costs. And proven sales talent leave once they find their new superior (boss) to be inferior and not adding value. The weaker your sales system, the more sales management is required.

Failing to Understand the Two Selling Environments

From my experience physically building and transforming all parts of over a thousand sales organizations in 36 countries, would you like to know *the* number one reason sales fails? The bulk of all sales, selling, and salespeople performance issues start with a worldwide misunderstanding and severe confusion about selling. There are two unique and distinct sales environments that must never be commingled.

One of my entrepreneur CEO clients running a $30 million company recently told me, "Learning and understanding the two different types of sales situations was the biggest game-changing insight from your program. Splitting my organization to align with these different sales environments helps generate an extra *and more profitable* $5 million a year."

There are two unique and radically different selling situations where your salespeople might compete. Simple and complex. Simple selling has been around for hundreds of years and is still applicable today. Complex sales evolved post–World War II when corporations—*committees and teams, not an individual*—started making major purchase decisions. Warning: Your company, like many clients, might be competing in two sales environments within the same sweet spot and PCP. This confusion about sales and selling *kills* entrepreneurial growth and small businesses. Do not get this wrong.

Simple Sales

Simple sales, also known as "transaction" selling or "product sales," is when the buyer evaluation and decision are completed in a short time, typically at point of sale (POS). The consumer "sees it and buys it." What makes simple sales unique is these six factors: low number of buyers involved, quick cycle time, few decision steps, low levels of risk, low price, and few people affected by the decision.

Examples of simple sales include retail purchases or Internet sales in B2C models. Selling environments become murky for some high-end decisions like buying an expensive automobile. That process could start as a simple sale, yet morph into a complex decision situation. That shifting of buyer characteristics is why I sometimes create two different divisions within a sales department to align with the two sales environments.

For example, selling Toyotas is often thought of as transaction selling. Sell them cheap and move them out, "high turns and low margins." Selling a Lexus, however, involves a slower sales process, multiple meetings, and higher margins. But do not make the mistake of thinking one is relationship selling and the other isn't. I have spent decades deprogramming salespeople who've lost billions of dollars in sales by wrongly applying simple sales techniques in complex sales environments and vice versa.

Complex Sales

Complex selling is longer and more complicated, with more decision makers (buyers) than transaction selling. It is also known as "enterprise" or corporate sales. This more sophisticated buying process and selling cycle always requires several meetings—unless your first sales call fails. Where simple sales can be characterized as "single step, single buyer," the complex sale is "multiple steps, multiple buyers."

Several buyers and many steps can mean sales cycles taking months to years. Long complex sales cycles consume resources, have huge sales expenses, and can burn the profits of the contract even if you win it. This is why focusing on sales *conversions*, not *activities*, is the transformational key to making ridiculous profits.

The complex sale can include extreme levels of decision risk, 7- to 11-figure-plus prices (yes, multi-billion) to buy, and enormous costs to use. The number of people or departments affected dictate how complex a sale becomes. Think of your business buying an enterprise CRM. A companywide decision is a complex sale with several evaluators and many users. If you are in the B2B or B2G markets, you and your teams will die relying on simple sales skills. Team members must develop clusters of advanced and complex selling skills, or *competencies*.

For a few years during my corporate career I worked to provide all the sales strategies for sales pursuits that averaged $1 billion in size. The cost of the sales process and expenses could sometimes be more than a million dollars with up to a thousand people working on the sales side. Those are ultra-high-stakes complex sales where winning or losing could create millionaires or destroy careers.

High Costs of Each Salesperson

Adding sales talent to your business inside a well-designed system is a critical and essential step to ridiculously profitable growth. However, as mentioned earlier "simply adding bodies to sell" is high risk and wastes profits.

Few entrepreneurs or CEOs realize the entirety of expenditures for sales and salespeople. You might want to make sure your sales team reads this book, so they know the massive investment your company makes to have them. Here are eight hard and soft areas of sales costs you must plan for and budget.

Recruiting Time and Money

Whether you use recruiters or not to source your sales headcount, there are dozens of costs associated with hiring one salesperson: attraction strategies development, advertisements, job board fees, interviewing time, background checks, personality tests, and skills testing. And multiply those costs by however many are needed to develop a pool of qualified candidates.

Onboarding

Most entrepreneurs and companies cut corners by skipping effective acclimation, and it costs them massive sales in the future. In addition, it increases turnover and increases risk. A well-crafted and executed onboarding program can tell a talent from a turkey in weeks, not 9 to 12 months.

Base Salary

This is a fixed or hard cost whether the salesperson produces or doesn't. This monthly expense can be crushing for a small business. If you are in complex sales, base salaries can range from about $65,000 to $350,000. Yes, you can hire for less, but your costs will go way up in other areas. Even if you try a "100 percent commission structure" (which only works in a few models), your expenditures will come from higher variable pay.

Variable Pay

This includes commissions and bonuses. To attract and retain proven sales talent, you must provide a rich reward program. Again, you can be cheap in this area like a lot of entrepreneurs, but you will pay in a different way. You will not attract or retain top talent and will end up hiring candidates who are shiny on paper and dull on results.

Benefits

Nonmonetary rewards are becoming a larger part of pay packages and a bigger cost to companies—from healthcare to time off, from car allowances to technology tools, from childcare to paid vacations, from sick leave to insurance.

Infrastructure

Every salesperson needs space and tools. A trend had been making salespeople work remotely even when local. However, the "on-site off-site" fad comes and goes due to lack of camaraderie and efficiencies. Still, without a well-designed sales system, it's impossible to optimize salespeople, even if they sit next to you in the office.

Management Time

Salespeople, sales, and selling requires a tremendous amount of on-demand interaction. Selling cycles are fluid and can eat a large portion of time from entrepreneurs and department leaders. All this time requires profit-eating costs, which you need to track and measure. Plus, don't think there are economies of scale adding salespeople.

Costs of Sales and Selling

Chasing a potential sale has many levels of outlays. Some pursuit expenses are covered under salespeople time. However, additional costs of sales include these categories: sales support, engineering, proposal development, presentations by experts, and use of functional resources.

Are you in shock or choking right now? Perfect. Entrepreneurs, CEOs, and leaders far underestimate how much money, profit, earnings, and dollars marketing and sales burn. This is how and why my road map and methods have made thousands of entrepreneurs and employees millionaires. They save, protect, and avoid wasting millions of these unnecessary dollars. Become embarrassingly rich from your business not by how fast you grow, but by how much you don't waste growing.

Sales Transactions Versus Sales Conversions

To make the most money as fast as possible, you and your team must own the difference between sales "numbers" and sales "ratios." Transactions are thought of or measured in "numbers." How many sales pursuits can you work through? Conversions should be tracked in "ratios." How many sales cycles can you win? And how fast?

This might sound like semantics, a different way of saying the same thing, but don't make that mistake. High transactions *can* win sales but burn profit. High conversions *will* make you sales with smaller costs and huge profits, faster. Applying this subtlety is what turns a good business into a fast growth, embarrassingly profitable venture. And it's the path of converting "more from less" that creates no-cost sales growth. This thinking and counterintuitive philosophies are how I've made many salespeople millionaires in less than 12 months. If you're a salesperson, did you underline that last sentence? These principles are designed to make salespeople embarrassingly wealthy if they make the company rich first and their clients happy.

To anchor the difference between transaction versus conversion, I'll use a metaphor from the rapidly evolving auto industry. For the last hundred years cars were powered by gas. However, the future is electric. BMW recently stated that within the next 15 years they will only manufacture electric engines.

There are many reasons to switch from gas to electric power. One reason, core to my philosophy of fast revenue growth and profits, is how the two engines differ in conversion ratios. Both engines convert energy to thrust. Sales conversion is the energy moving a "contact to a client." And this is where the two models, gas powered versus electric powered, are like a turtle to a hare.

The gas-powered engine typically "converts" about 33 percent of its energy into thrust moving the car. Similarly, most "salespeople-based" models typically convert prospects about 20 to 30 percent of the time. This means about 70 percent of the effort (gas energy) doesn't create movement for a car, but produces mostly heat and noise. Like salespeople? Stop laughing.

The electric car is far superior, converting energy to thrust by almost 98 percent. That performance is three to four times greater than gas engines—without the clamor, clatter, or pollution. Clients switching to a "systems-based" model, more like an electric engine, have achieved three to four times their past sales win rates. In some cases, achieving 80 to 90 percent prospect conversions for years at a time.

Building Your Strategic Sales Conversion System

Now you know to achieve the most sales using the fewest resources, you need a strategic sales system designed to maximize contact-to-client conversions. And your salespeople will operate within that system. Let me unpack strategic sales systems design.

A generic system is something composed of key parts, functioning together, to consistently produce something of value. Your basic "strategic sales system" design will include four areas: soft, hard, talent, and support.

Don't be concerned about the word "basic" as I've implemented this framework in multibillion-dollar companies. Plus, once you have all four areas and parts working as an integrated, balanced, and adaptive system, your sales organization will be in the top one-tenth of 1 percent of designs in the world. This powerful framework is how I have personally run public and private companies, enjoying low-cost explosive growth and 90-percent-plus sales win rates for years. A later chapter will discuss more sophisticated methods and adaptive modeling for sales and other departments.

Soft Areas

This part includes philosophy, culture, and strategies. These are three of the most powerful guiding forces that dictate sales direction and success. Although these areas are soft, meaning not always visible, they are the beginning and essential elements to dominating sales and optimization. These forces guide every sales decision.

Here are a few stale beliefs that damage sales organizations and kill careers:

"Sales is sales." Mistakenly meaning all sales are the same. No. As discussed, there are two distinct types.

"Sales is a numbers game." Meaning you have to lose a lot to win a lot. Perfect if you like burning through people, time, and money.

"If we could hire one or two top salespeople things would be great." That model is still "people-dependent" and full of risks.

"We really need more leads." False. Sales teams need better and higher-quality leads.

"You need to hear a lot of nos to hear a yes." That is the same as the numbers game. Real relationships are built on "yeses" not "nos."

"Sales is all about prospecting and closing." If salespeople are doing all the prospecting, the leads won't be optimized. And closing is transactional, simple sales language.

Please run from anyone preaching those stale platitudes. They're focused on action and activities, not ratios and conversions, and they don't understand optimized sales production.

Hard Areas

These are the parts of organizational design that are more visible, including such areas as reporting structure, methodologies, templates, and tools. Before designing these components, you must be confident in sales philosophies, cultural reinforcement, and directional strategies.

Organizational charting is critical for decision making, allocating resources, and deploying talent. Sales methodologies are how formulas and competencies will be applied to manage simple to complex pursuit cycles. Sales methods and up-to-date techniques for speeding prospect conversion must be proven. And finally, you must implement the right set of subprocesses to support your methodology. For example, these are some sales subprocesses: physical steps in a sales call, proposal development, financial modeling, and presentation creation.

Talent Areas

Now that you have decided or completed two major sales areas, it must be time to hire your first or another salesperson, right? Wrong. A major reason the first and subsequent sales hires fail is lack of effective sales leadership. As the entrepreneur, are you qualified to lead the sales organization? If not, you won't attract or keep top sales talent. But don't think running the company will make you a strong sales leader—it won't. However, mastering the principles in this book can hyper-accelerate your leadership development for sales and growth.

Now, by this point in the book it must be time to attract and hire a salesperson? Not so fast. If you want to create a fast-growth, ridiculously profitable company, helping every employee to become rich, then you must only hire proven sales talent. Understanding who and how to hire a sales talent, versus a salesperson, is game-changing. In Chapter 15 I explain my talent optimization framework, which you should use for every person you ever hire—especially salespeople.

Once you've hired a salesperson, don't let them try to survive on an island. They must be supported and kept on the right path. They will need sales support, experts, engineers, and sometimes resources from delivery or operations. In the past, the philosophy was to make salespeople product experts. We have hundreds of case studies showing superior knowledge of goods and services can turn off influential buyers and sabotage sales. Major decision makers think and speak business (value, risk, return), not features and functions. Product geeks are rarely dealmakers who make millions.

Support Tools Areas

At this point you have about three-quarters of your strategic sales system either designed or in place. The last major section is called the support tools area. Every company has some form of customer relationship management (CRM) platform or contact type automation and pipeline software today. That's an important part of technology for support.

However, an area that is extremely weak or missing for high performance is effective job aids and tools. Most salespeople are not using proven formulas, current methods, or power templates and tools. So, they wing it. Winging it is neither a strategy, hope, nor system. Take this quiz: Name the major phases of a complex sale. List the major steps in an effective physical sales call. What are the five parts of a compelling elevator pitch? Name the formula for a basic three-point value proposition. If you and your salespeople don't know the answers, you're winging it.

And finally, measurement and metrics. This area of a sales system is always broken for two reasons. Corporations measure too much, from the important to the meaningless. Small companies measure too little. Here is a must-know sales measurement. Your sales win-to-loss (conversion) ratio. This percentage (when validated) provides critical insights to solving sales performance issues.

Counterargument

I totally understand if you might be saying to yourself, "Wow, as an entrepreneur I have to worry about building and leading a strategic sales system, with all these parts, people, and areas?" No, you don't. You can join the thousands of entrepreneurs wasting millions in profits, missing revenues, and spending years on the small business treadmill.

Mastering, implementing, and continuously adapting the four areas of your strategic sales system are only important if you want to create a fast-growth company and become embarrassingly rich.

Remember the chapter about the *will* to take a different path? This is the fork in the road. You must have the mental strength and discipline to follow this proven way. Every entrepreneur wants to be wealthy from their business, but few have the *will* and the *way* to achieve it. And their weak sales organizations and poor sales performance prove that lack of will.

Why Focus on Sales System Conversions Now

Transforming a sales department into a "strategic sales system" by itself can add millions to tens of millions of dollars of value to a small company. This sales system–based approach is so powerful it can wake up sleepy businesses and turn them into dynamic forces. Here are more reasons to put a system in place now.

More From Less

A strategic sales system is the purest path to optimized growth. We have hundreds of sales system case studies of either one salesperson selling 10 to 20 times more or sales teams doubling to quadrupling sales growth without spending another dollar.

Speed to New Sales and Revenue

Making money is all about speed. Most sales organizations are an army of salespeople creating thousands of activities hoping for results. A well-crafted system focused on conversions is the fastest path to go from contacts to cash.

Attract and Retain the Best Sales Talent

If you don't have the best talent on your team, then you are at a competitive disadvantage. If your competition has high performers working in a powerful strategic sales system, then your company is at major risk. In addition, talent is attracted to a great system and won't necessarily leave for more money, helping eliminate the sales turnover crisis in most companies.

Triple Profits

Not giving up margins to win. Earning more profit faster from quicker conversions. Spending less expense earning that profit. Those are some of the ways to make and keep more money. Most entrepreneurs fight to win more to make more. Instead spend less and make more.

Extreme Valuation

There is nothing that will increase the value of your company faster than a robust sales production and conversion engine. The ability to consistently generate volumes of sales, cash, and profits makes investors drool.

One of my clients told me, "I drive a brand-new Porsche convertible as a fun car to take my daughter out for ice cream. She giggles every time we go. I was able to afford this sports car splurge because my sales team stopped being individuals and started working in a system. My company's sales grew so fast, excited buyers created a bidding war. My company sold for a valuation number tens of millions above my wildest dreams."

Sense of Urgency

Sales in most companies is broken on many levels. But it doesn't need to be, and now that you've read this chapter, you won't settle for mediocrity. Don't stay on the path of "more from more" thinking. Don't follow the myths of "transaction selling" and focus on sales activities. Stop putting your salespeople at the center of your growth engine.

Demand superior and optimized sales organization performance. Remember, scalable, predictable, sustainable, fast growth, and extremely profitable sales do not come from salespeople. Maximized sales growth, using minimum resources, comes from the intelligent design, integration, and execution of a strategic sales system focused on conversion. Sales is the most critical area to company growth and personal wealth.

Sales Conversion System Action Plan

First, determine if your sales organization is people based or systems based. Are you dependent on individuals or heroes to make your numbers? What is your transformation plan to go from people to system?

What are your existing sales conversion rates? If 40 percent or less, do you have a plan to double it within the next year or two?

How consistent, predictable, and high quality are your wins? Is your sales team consistently winning bigger and better contracts every quarter or year? Are you signing what you can find, or are you building a portfolio of PCPs? Do not hire another salesperson until you and your leaders go through the Revenue Ready, Market Ready, and Own the Market phases.

Do you have sales managers or sales leaders? If you have managers, what is your plan to transform them into leaders? Too many sales managers are either glorified salespeople or redundant sales process police.

Create a plan to double or triple sales growth with existing headcount. What are the goals, and in what time frame will they be achieved?

Remember this key point: Many of the prospects I talk to have terrible win rates on larger, more complex sales pursuits. Your win ratios should not drop off too much for major contracts.

Sales conversion rates, when fully scrubbed (everything included), should be at least 75 percent consistently. That's a good sales win rate standard to meet or exceed.

You are now thinking about marketing and sales in the right way to move closer to optimization, balancing efficiency and effectiveness. The next chapter, "Partnering for Demand," will take your explosive revenue growth to an even higher level of performance—in some cases, for free, with no effort.

CHAPTER 11

Partnering for Demand

*Why grow sales and revenues yourself
when someone else can do it better,
faster, and for less money?*

During a break in my speech at an Entrepreneur CEO Growth Summit in Asia, one of the attendees approached and asked, "Besides what you shared about how creating power messaging tools can instantly transform a business, what other principles can quickly create explosive profitable growth without having to spend a dollar?"

"When we come back from break, you will learn the key principle that helped a company skyrocket from $2 million to $36 million in two and a half years without spending more on marketing or building a sales army."

Once the audience was back in the room, I continued. "We've discussed the sequential principles and phases of Revenue Ready and Market Ready. In addition, I shared key Go to Market concepts to help you crush your lead generation, sales, and profit targets. Now let's continue with this third phase of optimization and examine another no-cost, hyper-accelerating revenue growth and profit production strategy. If you're not excited about this next set of ideas, you're not being entrepreneurial. And you're not serious-minded about no-cost, fast-track success and becoming embarrassingly rich.

"The third principle, which has made many clients wealthy in the Go to Market phase, is Partnering. I'm not referring to an internal business associate or equity sharing, but external affiliations. Strategic teaming is working together with other individuals to synergize and leverage the strengths of both companies.

"I want you to think of partnering as 1 + 1 = 3. Mutual teaming, when executed in the right sequence of phases and steps, can produce jaw-dropping results. The earlier phases and order of mastering and applying my road map principles is critical to effective partnering. Leveraging others is a business acceleration 'more from less' strategy. Smart affiliations can rapidly accelerate your company's growth while you spend little to no money, time, or effort."

"However, with the enormous benefits of creating affiliations, comes bad news. Few entrepreneurs are willing to *mutually* engage with others and team up effectively. Even fewer are suitable for working with external teams. Many entrepreneurs have tried this strategy and failed. Sadly, they confess they never want to work with other companies again. But *their* failures mean more opportunity for *your* company to team for differentiation and market space domination."

> *To have what others want,*
> *you have to do what others won't—partner.*

"Why do so few entrepreneurs partner well?" an audience member asked.

"Because partnering is outside many entrepreneurs' comfort zone. Engaging with another firm takes willpower and discipline to make the sharing successful. Effective affiliating means first being positioned to be a fantastic partner. You need to become 'partner ready.'

"You and your teams need to set up a mutually beneficial teaming model. Plus, you have to continue to nurture and optimize these sharing strategies forever." I further added, "It's the same two reasons that personal relationships fall apart. First, if one party doesn't know how to be a solid partner, the teaming construct dies. Second, if either side is too lazy to put in the effort, the engagement collapses."

Partnering for Explosive Profits and Growth

This chapter will provide the key ingredients, concepts, and measurement to effective partnering, offering ideas on affiliations from strategic to tactical and from formal to informal. After receiving the clear definition with scope and scale, you will learn the right way to frame teaming and how to make it succeed. I will also share with you the common reasons teaming up fails to gain traction and how your team can avoid those mistakes.

External value-based partnering can be satisfied in unlimited forms, range, size, and levels of engagement. It's really up to you and your future partners. Choices include working with an individual or as companies. Be creative. The overarching and driving philosophy for perfect teaming is shared benefits.

Start by asking these engagement questions: How could a potential affiliation solve an FMP better and create more value for your PCPs? Can both companies experience a net advantage in a business relationship? A three-way win will create the sustainability for your teaming model. If you and your partners can't answer those questions, working together might not make sense.

To help make this teaming for growth and profitability concept clearer, keep this in mind: You can team up to do anything in business. However, the way I want you to use partnering is in creating demand, which means sharing or opening doors to better contacts, leads, and prospects for your respective business, then exchanging something of value like money or contacts.

I'm not talking about teaming up for production or delivery. For example, to write, produce, and publish this book, I worked with an extensive team: a publishing consultant, literary agent, editors, and book publisher. That is not teaming up in the definition I want you to follow. That is how creation, production, and distribution works. The relationship I just described is a business association because the experts were paid or will be compensated for their work, not for creating leads, prospects, and PCP demand. Yes, we "partnered" in the sense of wanting to achieve shared goals, but that success is measured or compensated financially not by trading or sharing. On the other hand, if my literary agent and I discussed helping our two firms grow by trading potential client leads, that would be engaging for revenue growth. That form of partnering can last a lifetime.

Demand-based affiliations work by leveraging relationships with those working in or around your business ecosystem sweet spot representing PCPs, suppliers, distributors, customers, agencies, and yes, even competitors who are in the space you want to dominate.

Did you catch that point about competitors? Sometimes it's shrewd to work with those you compete against. The word for this collaborative competitive approach is "coopetition." This teaming alongside your adversary is a time-tested principle for winning. This is not new. This adage has been around for thousands of years: "The enemy of your enemy is your friend."

Effective partnering expedites your salespeople covering, scaling, connecting, and exploiting your market sweet spot. Teaming with key influencers can achieve that territory coverage and account penetration hundreds of times faster. In addition, if you help your partners do the same, those objectives are no cost for both. Many clients have experienced shock at how fast doors opened to strategic accounts through connected affiliates. The right external allies can easily overcome the barriers, obstacles, and walls keeping you out.

> *Without a connected partner on the inside*
> *you will remain stuck on the outside—looking in.*

The Perfect Partner Profile (PPP)

Partnering for mutual growth by creating "more from less" means to pair up with individuals or companies to achieve a specific business goal. The concept of teaming can offer many choices in scope and scale. Partnerships can be created for strategic intent or tactical purposes. Also called affiliations, these can be contractual, with structure and definitive actions, or can be loosely managed with no guarantees of compensation or exchange.

This demand-based partnering for revenue growth is optional. You don't need to team up to be successful. We have entrepreneur clients who have not executed teaming with anyone and have still become ridiculously rich. However, effective teaming is an accelerator to wealth because of scalability, minimal effort, and a no-cost structure.

You've learned about the Fundamental Marketplace Problem (FMP) and your Perfect Client Profile (PCP). This is your Perfect Partner Profile (PPP). The attributes of a teaming model include any person, company, association, or institution that can help you create more demand for your business. There is no shortage of your contacts who will talk a good "partnering" game, but how well do your associates and you meet three requirements: ready, willing, and able to help each other? If one requisite of partnering is missing, teaming in an optimized model won't occur.

Ready

Are you ready to be a stellar partner? Have you and your teams worked through the Revenue Ready and Market Ready phases? Can you clearly explain to a potential partner the FMP you are working to solve? Can you provide the demographic and psychographic characteristics of the PCP you're targeting? And how do those create a specific shared sweet spot of geography, accounts, customers, or industry segments? Can your potential associates answer the same questions? If you can't articulate who exactly you want and need as clients with clarity and specificity, then how can anyone help you?

Willing

Are your company and team willing to do the work to be a perfect partner? Do you have the discipline, focus, and determination to work with external teams for mutual benefit? Is there a structure designed to accommodate a formal or informal affiliate relationship? As an entrepreneur, know this: until a team member is assigned and accountable for teaming success, big accomplishments will never happen. Someone in your company must live and die, career-wise, for external relationships, meaning that person's goals, targets, and compensation are tied to successful partnerships.

Able

Interestingly, your team can be ready and willing, but not be a fantastic partner. First, if you don't have the connections and relationships to open doors for your partners, you might not bring value to them. If you're not able to pay for or exchange leads or other items of value, outsiders may not want to team with you. If you can't deliver compelling value with your goods or services, then you may not have the ability to help your partners strengthen their brands.

Quick point: Giving referrals is not a form of demand-based partnership since there is no expectation of reciprocity. You or your contact are simply being polite and helpful. Teaming, by definition, has some level, structure, or intent of mutuality. Please, always share referrals, introductions, and leads, but don't expect anything in return. Don't force anyone to team up.

Types of Partnerships

Partnership models can take two forms. One is formal and the other is informal. You can have one or the other or a combination of both. To quickly become rich, I recommend a combination of both. Plus, learning how to partner through informal relationships can help you be much more successful when you create structured teaming agreements.

Formal Partnerships

Formal partnering is when you capture the terms and conditions in a binding contract. Teaming agreements may include many parts. For example, reporting structure, processes, framework of responsibilities, deliverables, and compensation. Formal affiliations to increase demand can also take many shapes, including strategic alliances, channels, or value-added relationships (VARs). In addition, well-designed partner structures spell out roles, tasks, and due dates. There will be lines of work demarcation (where a team starts or stops) and when efforts will overlap.

Effective partnering requires a motivating compensation plan. Sadly, payouts make participants yawn in many teaming agreements. If the reward system is not designed properly and administered effectively, relationships for growth will sputter. Quite often affiliate engagements start off with a bang and die with a whimper. Besides poorly designed compensation, inconsistent communications is another reason for relationship breakdowns that you must avoid.

Informal Partnerships

An attractive element of teaming is the flexibility in creativity, choices, and execution. I recommend that every entrepreneur create and maintain three to five well-structured, strategic, formal partnerships. In addition, you should have numerous informal engagement pairings to create more demand and scale growth.

The difference between formal and informal partnerships is timing and deliverables. In a structured partnership, commitments must be delivered by a date, with specific quality or volume. These contracted associations have balance of exchange by design. Unstructured partnerships are the opposite where there are usually no requirements of time or effort. Matter of fact, some of your most effective engagements will be out of balance, meaning your partners might do more for you, or you for them, and it is never reciprocated evenly. That isn't a problem. Relationship sharing never stays in balance.

Building organizations around the world, I use hundreds of contingency and executive retained recruiters to source the talent. Some headhunters pay a referral fee, and some don't. I've helped a few placement companies make ridiculous amounts of money as an informal partner by hiring hundreds of candidates through their firms.

Recently one such recruiter, who had never reciprocated early on, sent me a slew of referrals. Years back, I was flipping a lot of leads to this partner with little in return. However, lately they've been excellent at sending me well-qualified PCP leads. This demonstrates the ebb and flow of how unstructured teaming can balance out in value over time.

The Power of Partnering

To quickly convert your goods and services into cash crops, you must respect the potential and scale of formal and informal partnerships. To grow your revenues, you must produce contacts, conversations, leads, and prospects. You can do all that heavy lifting yourself through expensive and intensive marketing and sales. But why? You don't need to.

Instead use formal and informal associates to augment your Go to Market efforts. To understand the difference between direct sales and indirect partnering, let's start from the ground up. Literally. It's the similarities and dissimilarities between farmers and orchard owners, each trying to turn their produce (products) into money using different approaches. Both are focused on yield. As a farmer, you go through the same grueling four-phase cycle every year, which is similar to sales cycles:

- ▶ First, your teams "plow the earth." They research, prepare, learn, practice, apply, and test your accounts and territory.
- ▶ Second, they "plant seeds." For marketing and selling, that means spreading your "fertilizer," I mean propaganda, to attract PCP prospects.
- ▶ Third, they "nurture." They grind through the short or long sales cycles, deliver presentations, craft proposals, provide

demonstrations, and watch out for pesky bugs and critters—the competition.

> ▶ Finally, if the first three phases worked, it's "harvest time." This includes final presentations, negotiating price, and working through terms and conditions to sign a client. Rinse and repeat. Some crop cycles (sales efforts) create cash, but many don't.

Now imagine skipping the first three most challenging and costly phases of farming (marketing and sales) work and still creating a massive yield of new clients by using informal partnerships. Hmm—that's like sitting on your back porch watching friends pick all your new prospects from the orchard of growth trees for you.

I receive more calls like the following today than I did when I was starting my business. A CEO rings and says, "I've been told to hire your company." Without needing three-quarters of a sales cycle, we can harvest a new high-quality client who usually isn't focused on price. Wow. Doesn't this help you see how teaming can make business more fun and lucrative?

Warning: As beautiful as partnerships are, like orchard groves, they can take years of cultivating, pruning, and nurturing. But once those fruit trees start bearing fruit—partners sharing leads—these exchanges can run for decades. When I was building strategic corporate partnerships and channels with IBM, Cisco, HP, and Accenture, it could take 18 months to two years to successfully navigate their matrixed enterprise labyrinths. But once teaming agreements were in place, tens of millions of dollars fell out of the trees with no new farming needed.

Partnering Mistakes

Partnering for entrepreneurs can be feast or famine. Skipping any principle or step in Revenue Ready, Market Ready, or Marketing and Sales principles can doom your "business marriage." Other teaming failures include not even trying to engage, or trying a little and giving up. Not compensating properly is another roadblock to creating sustainable affiliations.

I am in shock at how many entrepreneurs and companies don't partner for growth. They network and they refer, but they never take it to the next level of a formal commitment or reciprocity. Why don't more entre-preneurs engage in mutually beneficial affiliations? Because our Western culture values self-reliance versus working together. Some entrepreneurs believe relying on others shows weakness. The real weakness is not leverag-ing another company's strengths. For you and your teams to make fortunes quickly, associating with others is an accelerator.

After not even wanting to try, here is another pushback I often hear: "Oh, we tried teaming up, but it never seems to work out." OK. Would you or did you marry the first person you dated? Probably not. But following that logic, would you say, I tried dating and it didn't work, so I don't see ever being married?

My advice to entrepreneurs who have failed at creating mutual affiliate relationships is this: Don't stop. Get back up on the teaming horse, know-ing you might fall off many times. Do this until you learn how to ride. Partnering is a proficiency, taking years to achieve mastery.

Partnering Mastery Examples

As an entrepreneur, you must always be looking outside your industry to find examples of how other companies find innovative ways to make margin. Fast-food or quick service restaurants (QSRs) are a laboratory for testing ideas to earn a new penny of profit. Affiliations is one of those principles that help corporations like McDonald's hedge against profit-eating competition. Look at their success winning with razor-thin margins in commoditized markets.

As discussed in earlier chapters, there are pricing strategies and other concepts to attract business and create traffic through the door. However, discounting, packaging, and other practices have limitations, or floors and ceilings to effectiveness. This is where teaming can create a stronger profit level.

Take a second and write down how McDonald's partners with external companies. In what ways, not necessarily in their space, but aligned to their PCP, do they generate more traffic and convert that demand faster? How many can you list?

One affiliation example McDonald's uses to elevate their same store sales is how they partner with Hollywood by adding soon-to-be-released movie figurines or toys to a Happy Meal. What kid doesn't want the action figure from the new Star Wars picture they are about to see? I remember driving to different Wendy's, burning hours, to find every color of a toy for my son who was four at the time. He was convinced he would die if he didn't have all the colors. I was convinced I might die trying to find them. Darn those effective fast-food partnerships.

Why You Must Partner Now

The partnering principles of "more for less" should have you ready to knock down doors because of how quickly it can help transform your good business into a fast-growth company. But let's look at more advantages so your stakeholders fully engage in making partnerships work. All employees must play a supportive role in sustaining your teaming capabilities. Your investors can also make introductions to potential associates they know.

Speed
Entrepreneur to Millionaire is not about someday. Becoming embarrassingly rich from a profit-generating business must start now and be executed every day. Time is not your friend. Why spend years being a farmer working the plowing, planting, and nurturing cycles when you could have orchard trees producing fruitful relationships? I know many clients who have spent years trying to connect with an influential CEO when a partner can facilitate a warm meeting in days.

Profits
You will not become a millionaire quickly if you burn money on marketing and selling like 9 out of 10 entrepreneurs. This whole book is about teaching you how to make more sales, revenue, and profits using the fewest resources necessary. Partnering is the epitome of being able to generate loads of cash with little to no effort.

Bigger, Better, and Higher-Quality New Business
Partnering is the gateway to the most perfect PCPs and sweet spot. Imagine your current crème de la crème clients and having external associates bring you more of them. Effective teaming can allow you to say yes or no to only the highest-quality customers and clients.

With affiliates you can have a client database of those who pay on time, don't buy on price, and handle all their responsibilities, as well as a portfolio of customers who are fanatical about providing you with referrals and references and who keep buying from you for years. Did that vision bring tears of joy to your eyes? Sadly, because entrepreneurs don't partner, most of their clients are the opposite of every quality attribute I described.

Sense of Urgency

Excited about partnering? Sold on working diligently to create external teams to leverage success? Great! Because if your competitors are teaming and you're not, you don't have a chance, as they will own the market and determine your future for you. But where do you start, or how do you begin to build affiliations? It couldn't be easier.

Identify a list of companies and people in your business ecosystem who could be partners. Brainstorm every individual or firm; don't leave anyone out. There are natural associates who simply make sense because they are positioned where your team needs to be.

Here are three places to look for partners: Analyze your PCP. Who are their suppliers, vendors, and distributors? Assess your competition and their relationships. Are they working or teaming with those who might be wonderful allies for your firm? Look at everyone who interacts with your company. Would any be suitable partners?

Just because you're perfect marriage material doesn't mean other people and businesses are ready to engage. As one of my clients frustratingly said to me, "You are so right, the majority of people are terrible at teaming up." One reason entrepreneurs are terrible at partnering is because they are so proud of their incremental success following last century's paradigms. If they do not have the will to radically change, they won't make a wonderful team.

Once you find someone and decide to partner, start at the beginning of this book and discuss Revenue Ready, Market Ready, and Go to Market phases. If you and your associates just want to trade leads, then go through each principle and share with them what you are doing. If you want to make a formal joint partnership, in which you work side by side to share the work and the rewards, then go through each phase as a single team.

Meaning, start with the FMP you're both trying to solve. Are there synergies and mutual value? Are there vertical roles or horizontal duties you can each execute? Go from there.

Teaming successfully takes a long-term commitment and long-term effort. Partnering is a competency of hundreds of skills applied throughout both organizations. Effective affiliations are rarely successful unless someone in each firm is accountable, measured, and rewarded for partnership success. Some entrepreneurs have a person in marketing or sales departments who manage partnerships. But partnering is so important that I recommend creating a role dedicated to partnership such as channel director or channel manager. In a larger enterprise, it might be a director of strategic alliances reporting to the CEO.

Partnering has many levels, structures, and benefits. As an entrepreneur you need to be strategic and creative in your affiliations. Like serious personal relationships, partnerships take effort to set up and stay mutually beneficial. Communicating and compensating properly are part of the ongoing management and maintenance essential to effective associations. Once your orchard grove of partners start producing, your profits will soar, and you and your team can become embarrassingly rich.

Partnering for Demand Action Plan

There are already many to-do items in this chapter, but here are a few more to do right now. Make sure you and your team are partner ready. Next, assign someone to be responsible for Partnering for Demand. Does that person own building partners full or part time? How will you compensate and reward the person for this effort?

Develop a plan that sets a deadline for you to have both a formal and an informal partnership working. Once you reach this milestone of one of each partner type, focus on the next 12 months. How many partnerships can you create in a year's time?

Your teams are now marketing, selling, and partnering on levels that most CEOs of large firms could never imagine. However, ultimate entrepreneur to millionaire success isn't about contacts. It's about contracts. The next chapter, "Pipeline Acceleration," focuses on quickly putting the "r" in contact—speed to revenue.

CHAPTER 12

Pipeline Acceleration

*Ninety-eight percent of information in
prospect sales pipelines is stale,
false, historical, or of no value.*

An entrepreneur running a commercial duplication business with a few hundred employees calls and shares his frustration with his sales team's inability to close new deals. He called out their slow progress and inconsistent prospect conversions. He talked bitterly about his high-salaried sales team spending a fortune of time and money on selling activities and chasing opportunities.

In addition, he's perplexed by the prospect funnel bursting with short close dates that always seem to slip. He feels their sales cycles move at the gradual speed of an ostrich egg through a skinny snake. Plus, he seemed angry and exhausted by "reviewing the same darn deals every month." He said, "We've trained till I'm blue in the face and added an expensive sales manager." His belief in his teams is slipping, "because they don't know how to *close*." He declared, "If we don't start converting these opportunities faster, I'm going to get rid of all my salespeople." Don't laugh, many entrepreneurs say that under their breath.

In our sales pipeline analysis and review meeting, the entrepreneur wanted to accomplish two objectives. First, he wanted to understand why the snail pace conversion problem existed. Second, he wanted to implement an immediate solution to sign more contracts in 30 days. A few minutes after he projected their latest prospect pipeline data on the giant screen monitor in the room, I shared with him some statistics: "Fifty percent of

179

your funnel is filled with business you will never win. And 98 percent of what is in your sales funnel is based on information that is stale, flawed, historical, or of no value. Also, your team's selling win rate of 40 percent, when scrubbed, will be more around 20 percent.

"And your forecast accuracy is less than 10 percent, meaning you'll sign contracts not forecasted and lose some you're predicted to win. Also, not only will 9 out of 10 deals you sign not happen on the dates in the report, but many will never sign on the predicted actual days listed, unless you start opening your business on Saturdays, Sundays, and holidays," I predicted.

The CEO's faced turned red. He glared at me with astonishment and disbelief. "How do you know those things? You're seeing our funnel for the first time. How can you make those statements about our sales force?" he questioned.

Smiling, I gave him two reasons. "First, I've reviewed thousands of pipelines and analyzed sales cycle pursuits, from small opportunities to multibillion-dollar contracts. After reviewing sales funnels for 40 years, the stats are sadly the same. Second, prospect management is one of the weakest competencies in every organization. Managing complex selling cycles is a relatively new proficiency and requires clusters of competencies that few have mastered.

"Which means information in pipelines has three major flaws: In most cases the funnel data is gathered from contacts who don't have accurate information, filled out by salespeople who don't understand, and forecasted by managers who can't ascertain true probability. Other than those three issues, the typical sales pipeline and forecast are quite believable," I told him.

He finally laughed. Defensive of his company but being hyper-competitive, he bet my statistics were off. He argued that their funnel was solid for three reasons: the hours his salespeople spent inputting data, the management time probing for accuracy, and their intensive internal sales prospect review meetings, during which they updated their numbers.

I replied, "Amount of time has no correlation to accuracy in reports or predictions. In addition, having more data has little to no value and might be the main reason your opportunities aren't progressing."

After "scrubbing" the pipeline together with his team, here were the actual and specific statistics: Two-thirds (67 percent) of current pursuits were unwinnable using several criteria. There were massive amounts of no-value data: who, what, or where filled 90 percent of the pipeline. The remaining information was correspondence tracking (phone and emailhistory and content exchanges). The sales funnel content and reports provided no insight into "why" or "how." And their win rate was determined to be about 22 percent based on three years of wins, losses, and "no decision made."

Why were the pipeline data poor and the insights weak? The majority of the funnel information was about the salespeople's activities and pursuit process. Their sales cycle phases showed no correlation or alignment to the six stages of the buying process. As an entrepreneur, don't try to fix a weak pipeline by believing, "More accuracy will come from spending more time inputting data." It's the opposite. In addition, their sales methodology and process steps were quite dated, even though they bought it from a brand-name firm.

The Sales Pipeline

If you're a new entrepreneur, or learning to lead a sales organization, let's make sure you're using the correct definition of sales pipeline, also called a "prospect funnel." It is a method for tracking and reporting sales activities and the progress of opportunities in different phases (stages), from initial contact to final contract or signing.

More than 95 percent of our clients use some form of customer relationship management (CRM) for their sales opportunity pursuit management and reporting. CRM also provides different levels of sales forecasting, which is the ability to predict, with weighted probabilities, how much new revenue will come into a company during a specific time period. Robust and well-managed prospect funnels answer five critical questions of a potential sale: who, what, when, where, and how.

Sales pipeline management involves tracking pursuit progress and predicting the revenue results. A prospect funnel splits into multiple progressive stages, ranging from initial contact or meeting to closing (instead of closing, my firm uses the term "completion" in our trademarked complex sales methodology). Different stages, typically from three to nine, are assigned higher percentages based on the probability of winning.

Mistakenly, salespeople, entrepreneurs, and corporate leaders predict sales win probability based on the number of sales activities completed or time spent on an account. Don't make that rookie leadership projection mistake.

Forecasting is the ability to predict the exact date when a new client will convert from being a prospect to customer and the value of the sale. Unlike accounting and finance that focus on historical data, a well-designed and executed sales funnel methodology should provide insights into the future. Sadly, more data does not drive more accurate results. Less data and more *insight* will. Here again, "more from less." Although complex selling is fluid, it's possible to achieve about 95 percent accuracy within 60 to 90 days, but almost impossible to determine high probabilities of amount of closing revenue past three months or a quarter.

Sales pipeline competency can make or break you and your company's ability to create wealth. Without visibility to predict future contracts and cash with accuracy, bad things can happen. First, you can't manage cash flow. You won't know if you have enough working capital or discretionary income. Plus, it's impossible to "manage a bench" (experts on hand for delivery or support) if you're not sure when you will have new clients and the scope and scale of work.

Death by CRM

On a plane flying to Atlanta where I was to deliver a speech, sitting next to me was an Armani-dressed man in his early forties. I guessed this person to be a CEO or a job interviewee. It was the latter. He shared his role as a senior salesperson, at the top of his game, pulling down about $700,000 a year in salary and commissions. Why would someone making close to seven figures want to leave his job?

He offered several reasons that seemed plausible, but I wasn't buying. After we both had a round of drinks, he appeared ready to share the real story.

I probed, "Why are you *really* quitting?"

He confided, "I'm exhausted with management." He went on to say how he spends hours a day inputting every account and sales pursuit detail into their CRM. He added, "My meeting notes, conversations, my phone history, any emails, and on and on." He complained, "I have to look through the CRM reports daily and scrub them a half a dozen times before they go up to executives." He continued, "What's pissing me off was still having to play 21 Questions with superiors and sometimes the CEO. I feel tortured by everyone."

He grumbled, "Every week I'm forced to spend more time on reports, inputting data, answering questions, and explaining my notes. I burn a lot of hours in team sales meetings, pipeline reviews, and end-of-quarter emergency forecasting calls. I spend more time with my management than with prospects. Not only is this hurting my commissions, but selling isn't fun anymore. I hate working for these leaders, so I'm getting out."

I empathized and shared, "Yes, we used to joke about death by Power-Point—bad presentations. Now I'm seeing death by CRM."

He laughed and motioned for the flight attendant. "I need another drink." Turning back to me, he asked, "Why are CRMs killing salespeople and taking the fun out of selling?"

I smiled and replied, "It's not the tool. It's poor management and weak leadership. Also, a big gap in understanding and mastering complex selling competencies. As you know, a CRM is a platform technology designed to automate and manage prospect and client relationships. And that's where the problem begins. Nine out of 10 entrepreneurs and executives use the tool in the wrong way. To *manage* prospect relationships. That's why companies suffer from what I call the 'pregnant pipeline' filled with opportunities that are slow to close."

I continued, "Mistakenly, maximum sales, using minimum time and resources, can never come from focusing on *managing* relationships. Sales optimization will only be achieved through quickly creating and swiftly *converting* relationships. Sales is about speed and ratios—how fast you can get a potential client in and out of the pipeline. Which means leaders and salespeople must learn to use the CRM features as a tool for 'contact to prospect acceleration and rapid cycle conversion.'" He turned his head to the side as if not sure what I had said. I reiterated in "sales speak": "Meaning win bigger, better contracts twice as fast." He smiled.

I added, "Sadly, CRMs have become disablers not enablers. CRMs, used incorrectly, suck the joy out of selling and the life out of salespeople, costing companies millions and billions."

"Yep, that's what my company is doing, and it's killing our whole team," he muttered.

Pipeline Management to Conversion Acceleration Thinking

Three major sales challenges occurred after the 1960s. First, sales split into simple and complex. Second, a single salesperson struggled to manage the massive information, resources, and moving parts of sizeable and lengthy multistep, multibuyer pursuit cycles. Third, it became more difficult to accurately predict new sales, cash flow, and contract signings with cycles taking six months to years.

Entrepreneurs, leaders, and salespeople view the pipeline as a "funnel" with a wide opening on top to let prospects in and narrower at the bottom to show net new sales. This is a decent visual for seeing progress and understanding that not all pursuits become clients. But thinking and using a pipeline as a funnel has extreme limitations and never harnesses the power to hyper-accelerate relationships to revenue.

To tap the real potential of your sales pipeline as a power tool, stop thinking of it as a funnel, tracking system, or report generator. You must design and construct your prospect pipeline to work as a "crystal ball"—not like a fake fortune-teller telling you what you want to see and hear, but more like the Wicked Witch of the West from *The Wizard of Oz*, who used a crystal ball to track Dorothy's movements, predict her gang's future decisions, and strategize to defeat her.

In other words, don't use your pipeline report for historical reporting nonsense. Use your funnel to provide game-changing insights. Learn to develop competitor-destroying strategies and accelerate buyers' actions. Start to determine the probability of sales revenue based on buyers' behavior rather than pursuit progress. Clients who have transitioned from pipeline management to prospect acceleration thinking using their funnel are doubling and tripling sales and reducing selling cycle time by 50 percent or more. That's effective sales leadership versus last century sales management—more sales, using less time, less effort, and less expense.

Why Is Pipeline Management Broken

When you hear the words "waste, fraud, and abuse," what do you think of? The government? Bloated institutions? Inefficient giant corporations?

Would you believe every company, small to large, suffers these issues with their sales pipeline and how they use it?

This waste, fraud, and abuse is not about your employees, but how your team tracks and (mis)manages sales pursuits and contacts. A prospect funnel reflects the future health of your company. Effective pipeline acceleration determines whether you remain a struggling business or you and your employees become wealthy. Sales pursuits are where money is made or lost (and profits wasted). Transitioning from pipeline management to prospect acceleration is the smartest way to allocate precious resources, reduce risk, and protect profits—your future fortune.

Pipeline Waste

Sales pipeline mismanagement burns many resources. Wasting support expertise, eating time, distracting management focus, and squandering prospects' time. Are you thinking the waste is not the pipeline, but the wrong selling activities?

Intelligent pipelines will clarify which are right or wrong efforts and decisions. Please don't count on salespeople to tell you what is good or bad. Effective pipeline leadership should operate like a three-color traffic signal for pursuit decision making. Green is go. Yellow is caution. And red is dead (stop).

What exactly is waste in sales? Waste is where or when resources are used with little or no *proven* chance of return. For example, in one client situation a new sales manager was stressed trying to increase sales. He, of course, pressured the salespeople to make more calls and produce more proposals. Can you guess the results?

The flurry of production won a few new contracts. The "more from more" thinking sadly reinforced the idea that more activities can mean winning more. However, they soon realized they had added four levels of waste—or profit-eating expenses—with only a small return.

As we helped the entrepreneur and leadership team buy into "more from less," they decided to take the opposite approach. By using a "contingency filter," meaning all proposals must include a mutually developed three-point value proposition, we cut about 50 percent of their outgoing proposals. Their win rate went way up, and overall new revenues skyrocketed. Support costs went way down, driving up overall profits. The sales manager stated, "The results from using our pipeline differently, 'doing less and winning more,' have reduced 90 percent of the stress I was experiencing."

Pipeline Fraud

Close to 100 percent of the information in sales pipelines is bad or outright fraudulent. Yes, it's almost criminal how stale, flawed, inaccurate, or worthless the data that populates prospect funnels is. Too often this faulty information drives bad decisions. Sometimes pipeline data is crap by mistake, other times it's garbage by intent.

What many contacts tell your salesperson is simply inaccurate. On occasion account contacts lie, but many times they simply don't know. Prospects in accounts (especially lower-level employees) don't want to appear stupid, so they make up answers. However, the biggest reason for garbage in pipelines is this key point: your salespeople are not gathering and corroborating information from the most influential leaders at your prospective account.

Sitting in a manager's office listening to a conference call with her national sales team, it was shocking what she requested (with me in the room). While reviewing each salesperson's pipeline, she called out one of the senior account leaders: "You need more prospects in your pipeline to make it bigger," she demanded.

Boasting with confidence, he replied, "I don't need more prospects. As you know, my close rates are high enough to more than exceed quota. Besides, I have all the opportunities one can handle."

"I understand, but the executives need to know how busy we are, so please add some more potential buyer names and how much you think they will purchase over the next 90 days," she reiterated.

There was an uncomfortable pause of silence in the room and on the phone.

"OK," the salesperson murmured. He knew the leaders only looked at sales numbers and sales activities, but didn't understand sales ratios and production. Plus, arguing with her would be of no use. He bristled, "How many new prospects would you like on my report?"

Pipeline Abuse

Abusing resources is a common and accepted Machiavellian practice in sales. Far too many entrepreneurs and salespeople follow the "throw spaghetti against the wall to see what sticks" theory of selling. (Notice the Italian connection?) And there is no greater example of abuse than how sales support resources are treated like servants, from engineers, proposal creators, and financial modelers to presentation support. These expert resources are cajoled into producing items of extensive work but of no value to winning the sale. Maybe worse, this practice robs resources from other salespeople who could win important business. I have hundreds of personal stories of sales peers sucking up all the resources and bragging about all the deals they won, but never mentioning all the carnage left behind.

Sales teams that do not follow my principles have a perverse incentive to achieve success at the expense of profits. Too many sales professionals march to a "scorched earth" approach of burning through every resource to try to win a contract. That "more from more" philosophy will prevent the company from generating huge profits and you and the team from quickly becoming rich.

Effective Prospect Pipeline Acceleration and Conversion

Sales pipelines are typically measured and managed using three flawed standards. First, *quantity of information*, pressuring salespeople to input mountains of data and facts daily. Second, pipeline *bloating*, demanding account teams manage a large number of opportunities. And finally, being able to create a *massive number of reports*.

Prospect conversion cycle time should be your focus, measurement, and standard. Here are three proven ways to speed up *contact-to-client* conversions.

Pipeline Inputs

Why is most prospect pipeline information useless? Because there is no crap filter. Everything goes in. There is a phrase in a popular rock song by Aerosmith describing what's in most sales pipelines—Steven Tyler sings about keeping the right ones out and how he lets the wrong ones in. Although the song is about personal relationships, your sales pipeline is about filtering the right or wrong business relationships.

Many entrepreneurs and sales teams are working the wrong deals because they never completed Revenue Ready and Market Ready phases. However, even if you have followed those principles to mastery level, you still must create validation and proof of what belongs in a pipeline versus what stays in your contact database. One simple way to filter is to use qualifiers agreed on by the team, such as buyer's need, dedicated budgets, influencer relationships, or timing. Don't invest more sales resources unless those parameters are checked.

Pipeline Outputs

Would you like to know how I've saved thousands of entrepreneurs millions with only one actionable piece of advice? Read and take this action right now: The two essential outputs of the sales pipeline are pursuit status and accurate forecasting probability. Those are critical, but here is the acid test question to stop burning profits immediately. How many non-deals, dead pursuits, or zombie deals did your sales team walk away from or disengage from this month or year?

"None" is the most common answer. Zero walkaways mean every opportunity in a pipeline is alive and well. Which is impossible. Every month, even in small companies, there are listings for sales pursuits that become "no decision" projects, no budget pursuits, or prospects not moving in months. Salespeople always say, "It might come back to life . . . someday." Remove them now. Or allow 30 days to "move it or lose it." Salespeople become emotionally attached, and leaders logically justify working prospects who are not going anywhere, wasting their time and your money.

Prospect Pipeline Insights

Here is another super accelerator for your sales pipeline. Stop focusing on "when" questions, such as: When will the contract close? When will the deal be completed? Will they sign by the end of the month? Unfortunately, those types of inquiries generate made-up answers since the salesperson wants out from under the police interrogation lamp.

This *no value* question-and-answer routine reflects about 85 percent of most sales meetings and pipeline reviews. Instead, focus on more powerful questions for better answers. What phase of the *buying cycle* is your prospect in? Why do you think the buyers are not in a different phase? How will you move the account forward (listen for strategy, not tactics)? What has your top competitor *achieved* in the last 30 days? How were they able to accomplish those moves?

About every week for five years I've met with a client and their sales team, and we spend two hours focused on pipeline acceleration and conversion. I rarely ask "when" questions but focus on "why" and "how." These latter questions make the salespeople think and execute strategically, helping this team generate millions in sales three times faster and tripling win rates without increasing headcount.

Biggest Pipeline Management Mistakes

Halfway through a public workshop on revenue growth, an entrepreneur said, "The sales forecasting I receive from my sales team is terrible, and it's affecting my investors' confidence in my ability to run my business and predict contracts. Why are sales forecasts unreliable?"

Instead of answering her question, I turned to the whole group and asked, "How many of you run companies and are able to forecast with 90-percent-plus accuracy?" Of the hundred attendees, two people near each other in the front row raised their hands. Almost in unison, two guys near the back of the room loudly grumbled, "Liars." The whole room broke into laughter.

The top reason sales pipelines are flawed, inaccurate, and useless is this: to achieve forecast accuracy, you must predict the amount of sales revenue, not the actual sale, with above 95 percent accuracy. To accomplish this, you must integrate two strategic processes.

First, you need to follow a sophisticated sales methodology measuring progress by sales phase deliverables, not by *sales activities* or *final sales results*. Second, your sales methodology needs to align with the correct phase of the *buying process*, and the salesperson must prove it. We've ripped out many so-called sales processes and sales systems because they are bundled tips and tricks or based on last century's sales methods and can't answer the above questions. If you're serious about making a fortune with your business, you must implement and follow a sophisticated sales methodology.

Why You Must Master Pipeline Acceleration Now

I hope you're thinking about how Sales Pipeline Acceleration will eliminate waste, speed conversions, and produce more profit, increasing size, margin, and return, by crushing the principle of "more sales from less efforts."

Increased Bandwidth

When your salespeople can work opportunities up to 50 percent faster, they can win twice as many pursuits, doubling your team production without adding eight more cost categories for each new headcount. Plus, your salespeople can increase their commissions and not work harder.

High Ratio Sales Conversions

Imagine your sales team improving from winning once or twice out of five times to four out of five times? Or instead of losing 70 to 80 percent of the time, winning 8 out of 10 pursuits. Dramatically improving your win-to-loss ratios scales revenue and profit and earns salespeople more commissions.

Brand Power

In Chapter 4, "Competitive Dominance," I share a story of a team discovering 10 different ways losing a sale damages a company, teams, and a brand. Sales wins are the antidote. In addition, winning accelerates winning. Quickly attracting better clients increases morale, confidence, and brand equity.

Bigger Contracts

Don't settle and "buy" new business. Use your pipeline management acceleration concepts and the other phases and principles in this book to make your contracts bigger. When your average contract size doubles, so do your profits because you are not wasting expenses with marketing and selling.

Sense of Urgency

Want to quickly find millions in new revenue or avoid wasting that much in profit-eating costs? The answers are in your sales pipeline. Your prospect funnel is your crystal ball of how well your overall revenue growth system is working. Your pipeline shows the competency of your firm to create demand and how fast it can convert demand into contracts.

However, most entrepreneurs can't find those answers in their prospect funnel. Their sales pipelines are bloated CRMs filled with non-deals, bad pursuits, and no-win opportunities. To solve those problems and turn your sales pipeline into a power tool, you must use it like a crystal ball, not a funnel. In almost all cases you don't need more pursuits, more selling cycles, or more reports. You need to understand how to generate clients faster with less effort.

More growth from fewer resources will not come from managing your pipeline but by "accelerating" what goes through it, meaning moving sales production along more efficiently and converting potential customers more effectively. Stop thinking how much you can get into your selling funnel and focus on how fast you can get quality opportunities to completion. Radical changes in focus and path will quickly make you and your team embarrassingly rich from bigger, faster sales with less effort.

Pipeline Acceleration Action Plan

The first step to pipeline acceleration is to determine your sales pipeline goals. Yes, that's right, not your sales goals but the quality, quantity, and speed of your pipeline production.

You and your team must determine the size of the revenues and the number of opportunities. Also, what are the quality parameters? Remember PCP? Use that as a profile filter.

Next, decide what triggers inputs to your pipeline. Too many companies add everything to their pipeline, which is a big mistake. Protect what goes in. Determine at what point opportunities should be taken out. What are the rules and terms of engagement? Don't be emotional; be disciplined.

Complex selling and pursuits will require multiple strategies, but start with this one: What is your win strategy for a particular deal? Make sure it is a strategy and not tasks, steps, or actions.

Make sure there is a rhyme and reason behind closing dates. Be able to back each date up with at least three data points. Most salespeople make up the date an opportunity will convert. The closing (or, as I want you to start thinking, "completion") date is one of the most important data points in accelerating opportunities.

You have just completed the Go to Market phase and learned four powerful growth- and profit-producing principles. Excellent work. While your competitors are burning cash, you are burning rubber down the road to creating a high valuation company. But don't stop at having a high-performance marketing and sales engine. The excitement and fun are just beginning. In the next phase, Own the Market, you will learn how to leave your competitors in the dust. This phase IV will allow you and your teams to control your business destiny and theirs.

Own the Market

(DOMINATING)

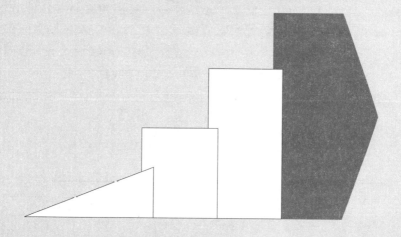

Now it's time to learn how to achieve the highest level of competitive proficiency by winning bigger and better clients—*all the time*.

Remember back in Chapter 5, "Targeting Your Sweet Spot," how I talked about segments of markets? A segment can be millions or billions in revenue and customer spend. A segment can be sized by type of product, service, geography, or combination. You and your team need to choose a segment that makes sense to dominate in some period of time.

To be successful in this phase you must change your thinking and standards from incremental success to monumental results. This phase is where you should be making ridiculous profits consistently.

Stop thinking of fair share and compounded growth goals. Instead, focus on gobbling up new PCP accounts and retaining the best clients forever.

For some of my clients, domination means to own the most market share; to others, it's to make enough money to buy the competition. To others still, it's simply to knock the competitors out of business. That will only happen if you learn from this chapter how to design your organization to quickly adapt, consistently win against ruthless competitors, and have the best talent working only for you.

A client once said after I helped the team learn these Own the Market principles, "Not only will we eat our competitor's breakfast, but we'll eat their lunch and dinner, too." That made me smile. I don't know if a statement like that makes you cringe or stirs your competitive juices, but I will say this. I'm confident you have competitors who think this way and get up every day looking for ways to put your company out of business. Will you dominate or be dominated?

CHAPTER 13

Blueprinting Optimization

Even if you're on the right track, you will
get run over if you just sit there.
—Will Rogers

"The reason I'm calling," said the entrepreneur CEO, "is because we've run into a problem in the last few years, and I'm running out of ideas. We've been in business about two decades and have enjoyed fast growth. We provide services to other businesses, so we are in the B2B market.

"My leaders and I attended one of your speeches on the East Coast about 15 years ago. We worked hard to put in place many of the Readiness concepts and principles you presented. Those ideas helped kick-start our business, and we grew quickly for a long time. Sales and success were almost easy."

He continued, "However, recently, sales have become too inconsistent, making overall growth flat. But worse, we're earning less profit. What's driving us nuts is no matter what we try, we've hit a plateau and we're stuck. Our firm is close to $50 million a year in revenues."

After reviewing a standard checklist of "fix its" with him—hiring more, marketing more, trying to sell more, manipulating prices, and other things he said they'd tried—I asked him about external issues.

"What about your overall market growth, has it slowed?" I quizzed.

"No, it's still growing at a steady pace," he replied.

"Any changes with competition, or competitors being more aggressive?" I probed.

"To some degree. We are seeing some new players and the 'keeping it all in-house' option is becoming harder to overcome. Our sales cycles are longer, too," he said.

"I assume your services and offerings are still the best available. No problems with capacity or bandwidth to deliver?" I asked. "What else can you tell me?" I probed further.

"Well, the stress levels are rising. We've had more team arguments and people issues than ever before. I'm seeing more finger-pointing between departments who used to get along so well. I've fired a couple of leaders and several employees lately. But I'm keeping those willing to grind it out and make numbers," he added.

"Wow, it sounds like things have transitioned from terrific to terrible," I confirmed.

"Yes, you could say that is exactly what's happening, and the business is wearing me down. It's gone from fun to exhausting," he admitted.

"The symptoms you described are quite common. Let me explain. Entrepreneurs who experience fast growth and make obscene profits, even for a short period, become lulled into a coma of comfort. Last century's popular saying, 'If it's not broken, don't fix it' was clever then, but out of touch with this century's pandemics, terrorist attacks, financial crises, and global challenges.

"Resting on your laurels for quarters or years will lead to quick business death. I argue that the unwillingness to change is the top reason a recent census analysis claimed more companies are closing than starting.

"Flat, inconsistent, or low-margin growth is damaging to any size firm. Underperformance eats at a business in several ways. First, unpredictable financial results create tremendous stress on leadership, shrinking their planning horizon, driving more tactical 'put out the fire today' decisions. If financials become strained where the leaders start playing games of who to pay, who not to pay, things turn ugly. Second, the employees sense the executive tension, affecting their focus and commitment. High-talented performers know they can quickly find a home and prepare their exit plans. The mediocre staff has nowhere to go. Employee morale, confidence, attention, and engagement all fall when numbers decline. Third, valuation of the firm is lowered. Investors want return, not risk.

"Entrepreneurs unable to predict or miss targets add more layers of confusion and poor control. Periods of drought and doubt shut off access to capital. Lack of funding chokes growth. Plus, the venture carries a recorded history of missing numbers forever. Fourth, there is an inability to attract new talent. Most business leaders whine about the shortage of high performers. Talent is available. However, proven and gifted employees are only attracted to top-performing, vibrant, and growing organizations," I added.

There was no response. The call seemed too quiet. I worried my phone had dropped the signal somewhere in my story, and I hoped I wouldn't have to repeat it.

"Can you hear me?" I asked.

"I'm here," he responded sheepishly. "Sorry I went silent. You described what I've been experiencing, feeling, and worrying about, but didn't know how to explain. How do we fix all this?"

I laughed politely, "Well, those are only the symptoms and lagging indicators, which is why none of your solutions have worked. You weren't solving the cause. Without being on-site and leading your team through an extensive MRI type assessment and system analysis, here are at least three of the root issues instigating poor performance results: First, you're a victim of success. As a smart businessperson, you understand the challenges of compounding. Adding 40 percent growth to a million-dollar firm is $400,000. This is fairly difficult for some entrepreneurs. However, 40 percent growth to a $50 million company is $20 million—almost 50 times more demanding. The former is like running up a hill versus the latter, free climbing a vertical mountain.

"Your second, maybe bigger challenge is the astonishing rates of external market changes. The outside forces working to slow, destroy, and commoditize your offering's value are increasing in size, intensity, and destructiveness. Here is what I find with entrepreneurs and how I frame the flat to slow growth dilemma in speeches today:

> *Everything on the outside of companies is changing*
> *at rates no one has ever experienced or imagined.*
> *Yet, little is changing on the inside of companies.*

"The third challenge is how you bragged about your teams grinding their marketing and selling like never before. For most entrepreneurs, that means their people are consumed by *getting bigger*, but they're not—"

He interrupted, "Getting better?"

"Actually, getting better was last century. Evolving. Your enterprise is not transforming and adapting fast enough to stay ahead of the tsunami of company-crushing marketplace forces. It appears your growth stalled because your firm hasn't been continuously adapting to changes in the market, competition, buyers, regulations, society, and so on," I explained.

He interjected, "That's not true; we are constantly changing. We've spent a fortune on technology, digital marketing, SEO, new platforms, and training."

"I know that feels like change, but it doesn't mean your company is evolving or adapting to blast through growth hurdles. First of all, every leader is exploiting technology, like you. Meaning you are only keeping pace. Second, if you added functions like GPS, IC chips, digital cameras, and self-driving capabilities to a Model T Ford, would that make it perform like a Ferrari?" I asked rhetorically.

"OK. I get it. You're saying we've focused on growth and getting bigger but not staying competitive for the world today. What should my employees be doing to change?" he asked.

"Nothing. They can't or won't be able to sustain any transformation on their own. Matter of fact, you'll have leaders and subordinates who will act passive-aggressive and resist anything new. Some will be silent saboteurs of success, behind the scenes," I warned.

"If I catch anyone blocking our progress, I will fire them in a heartbeat," he pronounced.

"Slow down, Sheriff. In many cases the entrepreneur leader is the biggest barrier of all," I cautioned.

"To break through a stall and to prevent plateauing in the future, we need to design your enterprise to behave differently. By nature, companies are designed to create, make, sell, and deliver a product or service—a perfect model for the last hundred years.

"Today, your company also needs to be *designed* to change and evolve to continue to achieve more from less. The principle is 'continuous adaptability'—meaning that every part of your company, all hard and soft areas, must work as an integrated system and never stop *evolving* to produce maximum results with minimal costs. I call this transformational performance thinking, *blueprinting optimization*," I explained. "Tell me, what major initiative do you have active right now to make sure your company is continuously adapting for sustainable revenue growth?"

Slow to respond, he said, "We don't have any active efforts like you mention. And it's my fault."

Your New Goal: Continuous Transformation

I hope you and your team have been aggressively implementing the "more from less" principles from the earlier chapters. If so, like the CEO in the story, you and your team are now leading a faster-growth, more profitable company. Isn't running a business easier and more fun?

Warning: At some point your revenues, like for every venture, will slow or stop. Profit and margins will start shrinking. Or worse, new contract size and quality will be more erratic and unpredictable. The highs will become higher and the lows lower.

You can still have good quarters, but then followed by a bad quarter and the roller coaster begins. But overall, your growth trend line will be flat and expense line going up, squeezing profits. If you're willing to start preparing now, your teams can avoid that performance nightmare and not have to flood your company with new products or resort to high-risk acquisitions.

If you're thinking like a true CEO, this chapter on blueprinting will be critical information you and your teams should read every year. Companies all over the world have proven you must adapt or die, but transformational success only happens if you make this strategy part of your DNA.

Entrepreneurs in start-up mode and surviving by the week might not think these principles are important right now. Don't make that mistake. You must be making smart changes early and often. Prospects have told me, "If we would have started the idea of continuous evolution and not driven to be bigger, we wouldn't be on life support today, living with so much stress."

A quick clarifying point: Blueprinting is different from the Japanese practice of "kaizen" or *continuous improvement*. That manufacturing principle is foundational for process and superior quality. Blueprinting optimization is *continuous enterprise adaption for maximum profitable revenue growth*. However, like kaizen, it's a philosophy that must go on for the life of your organization.

Root Problem: The World Changed but You Didn't

Working fractionally inside a dozen different companies each week, this is what I typically observe: When entrepreneurs hit a growth or performance challenge, their first reaction is to put their head in the sand or think "we'll get through it," but they eventually realize they need to take action. Most often the cause is being stuck on a "more from more" path. Here are the classic "fix its" they attempt, unsuccessfully:

First, they spend more money. They listen to outside voices telling them to splurge, buy, hire, add, do more, and so on. Investing in some areas can provide a nice return. However, spending more is almost never transformational. How does what you bought make you more adaptable?

After spending fails, cost cutting is next—not hiring more, not reinvesting, not refreshing technology, and so forth. It starts with stopping bonuses and freezing yearly salaries, followed by downsizing work cubicles to the size of an airplane bathroom and creating pods of desks where teams face each other and are so close they can hear other's bodily noises. This "more from less" attack-the-employee approach is the worst solution. When times are difficult, employees are usually on the front line of being abused. It never fixes what's broken but turns people off.

Entrepreneurs are conscious of how fast everything around them is changing. The shifts in technology, culture, government rules, and social norms are a constant swirl. Add to that whirlwind the natural and man-made disasters over the past 20 years—hurricanes, earthquakes, 9/11, the 2008 financial meltdown, multitrillion-dollar wars in Afghanistan and Iraq, and pandemics crippling the US economy—and it's head snapping.

But those world changes are not the biggest problem killing entrepreneurial dreams. As fast as forces are changing externally, entrepreneurs are making few significant changes to stay ahead of the curve inside businesses. Many of the models, paradigms, and philosophies entrepreneurs and leaders follow were best practices in the 1980s and 1990s. The way executives are trying to make stale ideas work is to double down on the flawed philosophies of squeezing expenses or grinding staff.

Of all the ideas and strategies you learn from this book, put this at the top of your list: The changes in the world will not stop or slow down. External factors, good and bad, are accelerating. You must design and build for that in your company. There will be more calamities, disasters, terrorist activities, countries falling, financial crises, and so on. And more opportunities as well. Stop reacting and start preparing.

Too many leaders believe they are super smart and at the edge of thought leadership. The reality is they've mastered the bleeding edge of burning resources to grow. I call this entrepreneurial paradox "delusions of competency," in which entrepreneurs believe using more technology, more digital marketing, and more social media is transformative.

Here is some good news: Following the concepts in the preceding chapters, in sequence, can give your organization an "almost *not even fair*" competitive advantage. And you might already have implemented a few ideas so you are making millions more. Now for the bad news:

> *Your competitors are reading this book*
> *and using these principles too.*
> *An advantage for you last year can*
> *become a disadvantage this year.*

Here's what some clients do periodically. They use the four phases and principles that are now in this book as a checklist every year. They have their teams make a presentation at their annual company event showing how they changed, adapted, or evolved each chapter concept to stay at mastery level and ahead of all competitors. Employees love seeing things improving.

Flaws in the Basic Block Growth Model

Now that you understand that *continuous adaptability* is the only path to sustainable, explosive, highly profitable revenue growth, let me show you how to apply it. Let's use the classic business block layout from Chapter 3, "Business Modeling" (Figure 13.1). This model seems basic, but too few entrepreneurs and even large corporations run this scheme well.

Client-facing functional activity flow:

▸ M—Marketing labors to create contacts or leads and flips them to sales.
▸ S—Sales sweats to close as many prospects as possible and throws the new contracts over the wall to operations.
▸ D—Delivery/operations toils to satisfy the new clients' expectations and hands off problems to support.
▸ S—Support cleans up as many customer messes as possible.

FIGURE 13.1   Four-Function, Client-Facing Basic Model

I'm confident your company is following a model quite like this scheme. This workflow or linear process has been around for more than 100 years, with marketing and support being the newest blocks. Sadly, there are many design flaws with this silo-based design, and I spend about 99 percent of my time fixing the thousands of disconnects and failure points. Here are a few:

▸ The process is designed to flow one way, which deters adaptability.
▸ It is managed for efficiency, not effectiveness—to achieve more, you have to do more.
▸ It is focused on quantity, not quality. From marketing to sales to operations there are severe handoff issues and drops.
▸ It creates internal conflict. For example, for sales to hit higher quotas each quarter, they will probably have to sign some inferior contracts occasionally, or make client promises that are difficult to keep.
▸ There is no enterprise leverage, only departmental efforts.

This model is perfect for start-ups and small businesses to produce solid incremental results. However, nothing about this design, flow, or intent will ever continuously optimize wealth creation. Never. It can't because it is not designed to drive transformation or effective adaption to changes holistically.

Another fault with this linear and functionally driven process is that it doesn't scale well. You are almost forced to add more employees, especially salespeople, for complex sales. Additionally, departments start focusing on their success first, creating the "silo effect."

The Superior Approach: Dynamic Transformation

Full disclosure: I've helped many entrepreneurs and employees become millionaires using the basic four-part flow model I shared above. However, if you want explosive *sustainable* fast and highly profitable revenue growth, for decades, that design does not have enough *change muscle*. If the classic marketing to sales to delivery to support is stale and flawed, what should you do instead?

You need to design your enterprise and departments as an "adaptive, integrated, holistic, high-performance *system*." How do you achieve that goal? Blueprinting optimization. This is my concept of creating an organization or functional architecture that reactively and proactively transforms for greater performance and production. This sustainability is achieved through feedback loops, cross and reverse flows, and departmental relationship mapping.

When properly executed, blueprinting delivers three powerful characteristics for revenue growth: it provides a dynamic and fluid model by focusing on knowledge looping; production, not activities, as outputs; and optimized results. The key design attribute of effective blueprinting is not a structure for handoffs, but integration for leverage and adaptability.

Don't confuse blueprinting optimization with strategic planning, performance management, or classic organizational design (OD). Blueprinting is different from those disciplines. Imagine that you own a skyscraper. Strategy, planning, and managing performance would be how you earn rent or yield from leasing your tower. Design and organization would be how the floors and rooms would be laid out and connected.

Blueprinting a skyscraper would be creating a design that proactively adapts to changing factors. As the marketplace trended toward more retail space or penthouses, your tower could dynamically morph itself to meet those needs. Your basic structure or offerings might not change, but internal aspects would operate differently, all designed to continuously optimize results by being "ahead of the demand curve."

Here's another example: Let's say your company manufactured gas-powered cars. Now you must switch to electric engines to stay relevant. Your company still produces automobiles. However, how you market, sell, deliver, and support will be radically different. Blueprinting allows you to change proactively versus reacting and being left behind.

Blueprinting an Adaptive System

Blueprinting optimization is creating a living, breathing, and adaptive architecture for revenue growth. It should be used at the enterprise, function, and department levels. Without the space of a whole book to show more sophisticated and customized blueprints, here is a next-level layout (Figure 13.2). Your company will always need these basic client-facing functions. However, how they operate within each department and with other departments is what must constantly change or improve.

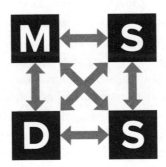

FIGURE 13.2   Integrated Adaptive Revenue Growth Model

This is an enterprise "adaptive revenue growth model," integrating client-facing functions. At first blush this might appear like the linear model simply stacked. In reality, there is more integration, more validation loops, more combinations of information and workflow. Most important is how this layout creates greater speed for continuously adapting to new data. Here are some key design attributes.

Performance Adaptability

This model achieves that objective through cross-functional inputs and outputs. In the linear or basic block model, the inputs and outputs flow basically downstream. For example, marketing outputs to sales, which outputs to delivery, which outputs to support. Three flows. This model has 12 flows, including reverse and cross flows—four times more.

Reverse Flow

These are the lines going to and from each function. It's when one department provides tangible inputs back to the department upstream. Like the sales function recalibrating marketing's lead generation quality to consistently meet a higher threshold. Or the support group engaging sales to modify the client strategic value propositions being created. Or delivery and operations changing client quality control attributes for sales pursuits.

Cross Flow

These are the middle lines where information goes between the nonconnected functions, such as operations to marketing or sales to support.

Systems Thinking

In the classic block model, each function is independent and accountable and responsible for its own production. This is commonly called the "silo." It's a weak model because of so little leverage of production. In a "systems approach," many responsibilities shift to all client-facing departments playing a role.

For example, instead of marketing being responsible and accountable for leads, in this "adaptive model" the whole enterprise plays a role. Leads—high-quality and qualified new prospects—must come from all parts of the company. This means that these four functions don't work for marketing, but they do operate together to create more and superior new client attraction. The enterprise parts are responsible, for helping create more demand, and marketing is accountable.

Counterargument

On occasion, after explaining the concept of blueprinting optimization, I will hear, "We're already pretty much doing what you described. Our sales team and marketing department are really close. Our operations and sales group work well together too." Or, "Our delivery and salespeople are on the same floor."

Working together is expected. Communicating between departments is required. Joint or cross-functional meetings are standard for every company. But when probed, what exactly are the outputs from the functions? Are the inputs and outputs balanced between the groups? How do you track operating as an adaptive system? How has the overall performance improved? How does the current design increase "more from less" each year? How many shared responsibilities can you list? Who is accountable for performance and production?

I've known many entrepreneurs who were cocky, arrogant, and peacock-like "know-it-alls" when their companies were growing and successful. However, when the business goes south, these same entrepreneurs quickly blame external factors, competitors, markets, or employees. Some have even called prospects who didn't buy from them stupid or idiots. Here are excuses leaders use when they can't break through a growth and profit hurdle.

Slow Market Growth

This is sometimes referred to as market space maturity. The excuse becomes, "Our results are a reflection of the market," or, "As it slows, we slow down too." Reality: There are fortunes to be made in every market space, even when the "size of the pie" is shrinking.

Competitor Intensity

When an entrepreneur first starts a venture, there are mountains of "fruit on the ground." The teams don't need to reach up for the "low-hanging fruit." However, the curse with growth is that your team has to climb the tree to eat the bigger, better fruit (larger, sweeter, and better contracts). Yet as you climb higher, the competition intensifies exponentially. The next chapter, "Competitive Dominance" will shatter that excuse.

Lack of Working Capital

"If we could find more money to invest and expand, we could get this stalled business going." That is the cry of many entrepreneurs who find themselves stuck. Yes, there are times when lack of funding is the root cause of struggling. However, in many cases, more money never solves what's broken and can make things worse.

Why Start Blueprinting for Optimization Now

As I hope you are an entrepreneur who never wants to face slow or flat growth, blueprinting optimization is that next level of sophistication for maximized performance. This concept is not only transformational, but when your enterprise is better designed and executing properly, it can continuously tap all your business potential. Which means maximizing faster revenue growth, using minimum resources, and producing the most profit every year.

Being able to adapt and continue to perform at the highest optimized levels is the only way you will come close to dominating your sweet spot. However, if you do achieve that goal, you will find that staying on top becomes more difficult than getting there.

When you are the number one company in your space, everyone is coming for you. There is a huge target on your back. However, too many leaders and employees lose their edge. Blueprinting is how you will maintain and sustain your competitive distance. Continuously becoming smarter, better, faster, and more proficient is how you earn the most money possible.

Sense of Urgency

I understand if reading this chapter might have you rolling your eyes or thinking this is way more complicated then you need as an entrepreneur right now. Understood. You might be starting your first business and still looking for that first check. Or your venture is growing and you're trying to catch your breath. But remember, time is your enemy. The earlier you integrate continuously transforming your future enterprise for revenue growth into your culture, the better.

Please don't be naive and think this is something for 5 or 10 years out. Many entrepreneurs contact us after their first year or two. They started off with a bang, but they are now in a mild fizzle. They didn't fail to launch;

they failed to gain traction—they didn't adapt. Where you are in your business this moment is based on ideas, strategies, and decisions you made months or years ago. In today's superfast transitional world, if you haven't prepared in advance, you might already be behind.

Entrepreneurs need more sophisticated solutions and strategies to continue to accelerate growth and maintain competitive advantage. Blueprinting optimization is a continuous and sustainable "more from less" approach to growth. Living this philosophy will make every stakeholder, client, employee, and investor happy. The only ones who will be unhappy are your competitors who will be losing market share and their clients to you.

Blueprinting Optimization Action Plan

Start your blueprinting effort by talking with your team about the ideas and concepts in this chapter. Share examples of other companies and discuss how they have adapted. What and where in those companies did leaders see or prepare for major changes? What about companies that didn't adapt?

Have each department share feedback loops or cross-flow communications that have triggered major adaption. Discuss what areas of your business need to adapt faster. For example, if marketing is not generating all the leads necessary for explosive growth, talk about how that department must change.

Sales should also present how they have adapted or are doing things differently than in the past. There are multiple stories in this book about how so many sales and other business paradigms are from last century. One example for sales is how marketing and operations are engaged at different points of the sales cycle. When should they be engaged?

What about operations, delivery, or support? Have those groups share how they have or are adapting to transformations in the marketplace. Were those changes planned, or did they occur as a result of competitors or markets changing?

I know this chapter is intense and could easily be a book in itself. But the earlier you understand and develop higher levels of thinking, the greater the leader you will become and the more money your company and your teams will earn. The next chapter, "Competitive Dominance," focuses on the highest standard of competing: never losing.

CHAPTER 14

Competitive Dominance

*Every dollar you lose to a competitor is a dollar
they will spend putting you out of business.*

As an entrepreneurial team, seeking explosive revenue growth, you must compete in "David versus Goliath" engagements early and often. But competing and winning are different. In sports it's win or lose. In business it's cash or crash. David, as you know, wins in the story by attacking the giant's weakness. However, many big-name successful companies don't have glaring flaws to exploit, which means you'll need an effective and powerful win strategy. But remember this: most of the time entrepreneurs taking on elephants get squashed, chewing through precious profits.

*If your company can't win against elephants,
it will stay the size of a mouse.*

Competing for a major multimillion-dollar contract against a massive software company, a small upstart technology firm was struggling to gain traction with the prospect account, with only one salesperson and two sales engineers on its small team. In contrast, the big-name enterprise swarmed the account with an army of engineers, brand resources, and executive relationships. This aggressive international software death star would fill potential accounts with stormtrooper-like programmers, making it impossible for small- to medium-size firms to gain a foothold. Their ruthless "beat or eat" scorched-earth sales strategy was effective and dominant. In this situation, the large firm embedded eight engineers on the prospect's site for several months. The team of power coders had an unlimited budget to develop a customized solution.

Day and night the large competitor's technical experts, supported by corporate, were meeting and relationship building with the prospect's operations team. Weekly they were having executive meetings further refining the computer programs to help this prospect create competitive advantage. It wasn't a fair sales fight for the start-up firm, being outgunned on all levels.

After analyzing the situation, it was obvious the small firm didn't have the budget or could not outcode this apex competitor. But they couldn't walk away either. Winning would change the new venture's revenue trajectory. In addition, this particular client's brand and logos would be eye candy to future prospects and investors.

After months of aggressively pushing and presenting their product's features and functions, the start-up team was solidly in second place. *Out of two*. Unfortunately, in sales, any finish besides first doesn't pay.

During a strategy session with the new venture's salesperson and engineers, we agreed to continue playing offense. This small team's value proposition was compelling, but it was being overshadowed by the big-budget behemoth. For that reason, we decided to compete differently and start playing offense *and* defense at the same time. After a few more months of evaluations and intense negotiations, the small company eventually won the massive contract.

The VP of sales of the giant software company found out I was the architect and strategist behind the start-up winning this major contract. He asked for a meeting. Over coffee, he grumbled about the costs of the losing sales pursuit. His sales expenses exceeded $500,000. He added how he flew in their best developers to guarantee this "must win" deal. Adding insult to injury, he said they forecasted the win to corporate at 90 percent probability.

He politely demanded, almost begging, "How in the heck did your small team win?"

Without going into specific strategies and tactics, I told him, "I believe we won when we changed our goal. You know the old story about the two guys that come up against a tiger? How when they both started running away one of them stops—"

He interjected, "Yes, he puts on track shoes. Explaining to his friend that he doesn't have to outrun the tiger; he only has to outrun *him*."

"That's what we did. We stopped trying to win the account and focused on helping your team lose. That shift made winning easier," I replied.

He half-smiled, processing what he had heard.

Winning *All the Time*

This chapter isn't about winning sometimes or most of the time. It's about winning all the time. It's impossible to "Own the Market" if you're not dominating your competition. Too many entrepreneurs have goals and are satisfied winning slightly more often than they lose. They need to learn how to compete against perfection—and *stop losing at all*. Don't be naive and think the best company, product, or service wins the majority of the time. It doesn't. Also, remember that if you and your team are not hyper-competitive then you're not being entrepreneurial.

When learned and applied, the concepts in this chapter should quickly move you and your teams up the ladder to competitive mastery in your sweet spot. They should prepare you to win over traditional and nontradi-tional competitive choices. To achieve those objectives and generate more sales from less effort, you must master and apply the principles from earlier chapters. Those concepts, such as Targeting, sequentially implemented, are critical to putting you in position to win.

An executive team in Silicon Valley flew me in to their headquarters to deliver a strategic workshop focused on helping them "get in more deals," which is how they described their objective. They wanted help growing their company faster by engaging in more pursuits to increase the number of contracts they won. Their premise, like many entrepreneurial teams, was that more wins come from competing more often. Didn't you used to think that way before reading this material?

Optimizing and scaling sales growth is one of my favorite program agendas because it's easy to find dozens of areas to fix or accelerate. And 9 out of 10 times, the leaders can avoid spending more on marketing or selling and achieve that goal. In addition, because most teams follow "more from more," it's easy to help them see the more profitable value proposition, more from less.

During the session, I led the team through assessing and analyzing their existing enterprise design, marketing organization, sales model, and statistics—for example, lead costs, expenses of pursuits, and selling bandwidth. This included understanding the average expense of physical sales meetings for a typical pursuit cycle. The expenses and calculations showed that each prospect on-site meeting cost the company about $2,000 in time and money (some buyer visits required plane travel). Each sales call represented about $15,000 in potential revenue. Adding the number of salespeople with the eight categories of costs and expenses, the rough dollar estimate was more than a million.

The executives sat in shock at the numbers. Even the CFO had never added up all aggregate selling costs. This group, like most, had only tracked sales, general, and administrative (SG&A) expenses. After eight hours of analysis the leaders had no energy. But I had to tease them with an easily identifiable value proposition.

"How would you like to double or triple your new sales and avoid an extra one to two million dollars in costs?" I repeated, "Double sales with existing headcount and maybe half the current expenses?"

The VP of sales chuckled and said, "Absolutely. What do you propose?"

I explained how the sales growth path they were following was flawed. "'More from more' never creates maximum profitability. Whether you achieve your revenue targets or not, you still eat too much expense.

"Tomorrow I'll teach you the 'more from less' for scaling sales," I said. I purposely laid that concept out at the close of the day to pique their interest in tomorrow's session. They bit too hard.

"Okay, we're not going anywhere until you tell us exactly what you're thinking," demanded the CEO.

"If you guys want to sell this company in a few years and earn higher valuations, you'll need to grow faster and stop wasting money. Your current objective and path must change. Engaging in additional sales cycles to win more contracts will eat huge profits and waste too much time. You should do the opposite. You don't need to work more sales opportunities to win more; *you need to learn to lose less*," I professed.

"What do you mean lose less?" asked the COO.

"From what I've observed, you guys can double or triple your sales, but you're working the win-to-loss ratio wrong. You must stop working the numerator *and* denominator of winning and losing. You need to focus on increasing the top number, the wins, and leave the bottom figure, total pursuits, alone. You don't need to pursue, work, or even compete for more sales. You're working too many pursuits you won't win right now."

The VP of sales glared at me like I had just spoken heresy. She then argued, "We win more bids than we lose, and our winning ratio is better than our competitors."

"If your standards and measurement are to be better than your competition, then you don't need me. You've achieved your goal," I stated.

"What do we do right now?" probed the CEO.

"Stop playing against the competition and start comparing your results against *perfect*. You have to add defense to offense in how you market, sell, deliver, and support your clients. Let me characterize your sales win ratio another way: 'You eat often, but you're also being eaten too much,'" I told the group.

There was still one leader who hadn't converted, who stated, "Losses are part of the game of business."

"I agree. Losing on *rare* occasion. I've run public and private companies for years with over 90 percent win rates on multimillion-dollar contracts, in cutthroat industries. Losing must become so uncommon and uncomfortable that everyone in your organization feels pain," I avowed.

Still sensing I didn't have disciples ready to live my beliefs, I explained the damage of losing sales from another angle. "Have you ever looked at the negative impact a sales loss has on a firm?" I asked.

With no one nodding, I moved to the whiteboard, probing, "In addition to the costs of sales, can you name other expenses or harm?" The group quickly listed several examples. Here are 10 from their list:

- ▸ Missed new revenues
- ▸ Lost profits from new contract we didn't win
- ▸ Damaged team and employee morale
- ▸ Profits going to competitor
- ▸ Damage to the corporate brand
- ▸ Poisoning of the account—can't sell to them for years
- ▸ Competitor can advertise beating our company in a fair evaluation
- ▸ Lost opportunity costs of other contracts we couldn't pursue
- ▸ Competitor earns a leverageable testimonial and reference in the marketplace
- ▸ Lost time of months of effort with no return

The team sat speechless. They had never seen the true "impact of losing." In unison they expressed their eagerness to learn how to play defense along with offense, knowing this new path would achieve "more from less."

Seeing from Your Opponent's Perspective

My son and I were playing a round of chess one evening. Although I was teaching him the basics of the game, I wanted him to learn a more important lesson: the difference between competing, winning, and dominating. However, like most kids, too many entrepreneurs never set goals to dominate, but only to win. which is a reason many businesses stay small.

If the word or thought of *dominating* felt uncomfortable or uneasy, I understand. But keep in mind that you have competitors waking up every day with one directive: completely conquering the space you're in and putting you and everyone like you out of business. CEOs pay me to come into their companies to redesign their models and transform their organizations to conquer markets. Should I tell them they are wrong and that we should all work to get along and split a fair share? My phone might never ring.

My son was enjoying learning how the chess pieces move differently, but he was getting frustrated by not winning the games. During one exchange, I closely watched his eyes to see how he was reading the board. Slowly moving a rook to a new position, he would quickly move it back.

After he repeated these forth and backs, I intervened. Standing up, I suggested, "Come over here and sit in my chair." After a few minutes on my side of the board, I asked him, "What do you see?"

"Wow, Dad, I see everything differently from your side," he said excitedly.

"Yes, you now see the game through your opponent's eyes," I confirmed. "What else do you see?" I probed.

He smiled, "I see the perfect move."

"Yet, when you sat on your side, you were so unsure about which piece to put where. It's because you were using a single perspective. As you sit in my seat, you now have two perspectives. You have twice as much information to make your decision. Not only will your advancement be smarter and more strategic, but look how fast you chose the best option. You have now learned one of the most important concepts and principles to advance from playing, to competing, to winning, to dominating," I said proudly.

I will never forget that night playing chess and the "aha" moment when my boy learned how to compete differently. Hopefully, he always has fun playing games, but knows how to see the world through his competitor's eyes when he has to win.

What Is Competitive Dominance?

The simple answer is someone or something overwhelming and controlling the space or competition. In business it's a company or product that dwarfs the sales of other choices.

During my early corporate career, at age 21, I managed a division of PepsiCo, Frito-Lay. I was responsible for all sales in east Texas, with salespeople in different cities reporting to me. Through hard work and strong relationship development our team held a market share of 87 percent. Fifteen competitors made up the other 13 percent. Would you like dominating ratios like that for your company?

How do you gain competitive dominance, and how do you keep it? Unfortunately, most entrepreneurs believe they will win "by being." In other words, they feel that "because they offer this great product, or that amazing service, people will buy their stuff." That is delusional. You might achieve incremental growth, but the more dominant brands, or smarter entrepreneurs will work to smother you.

To own a market, and keep the number one position, your teams must work to gather competitive insights and apply that information to win in three areas of your business. The first area is your marketing where you must win the fight for *position*. Second, sales is where you must win the fight of *elimination*. Third, your operations or delivery, whoever maintains or supports the client, must constantly win the fight for *protection*.

Competitive Data

Competitive information and insight can come from many sources—from vendors, third-party experts, or new employees, and it can even be purchased from data-gathering companies. Three areas for which you must gather and use competitive insights is in your marketing, sales, and operations. Besides the information being free, it is usually fresh and has high levels of accuracy.

When new salespeople joined one of the public companies I helped run, they had to complete an exhaustive acclimation. One of the assignments was spending two or three days reading, learning, and applying the material from the extensive competitive playbook the team had compiled. This thick binder provided several years of details of win-loss reviews, sales summaries, deal construction analysis, and comprehensive competitor assessments. Before new salespeople were allowed to meet with prospects, they had to prove understanding of offense and defense.

This competitor playbook was not online or sitting on someone's desk like other ubiquitous white binders. This information, painstakingly collected and validated over years, was on a firewall-protected server and available as a hard copy in a three-ring binder. Each new salesperson had to check it out like a one-of-a-kind rare book from a library. Making copies or removing it from the office would end employment. Sound a little over-the-top? Maybe, but not if achieving and preserving competitor dominance is the objective. After a couple of days of study, a new hire came to me to present.

"What was the biggest 'aha' you learned reading the materials about our adversaries?" I probed.

He said with an astonished look, "I worked for my last company for over two years and sold a ton for them. I'm shocked." He went on, "I learned more in two days reading this playbook about them than I did in all the years working at that corporation. I now have insights into the flaws in their model, their preferred sales strategies, proven counter tactics, and information I didn't know existed. It's obvious why your salespeople have been beating everybody so easily. It's almost not fair how you guys use competitive intelligence to dominate."

I smiled. He got it.

Marketing Example

One of my first entrepreneurial clients was struggling with his business and had a critical quarterly board meeting in two weeks. These oversight meetings had changed from collegial to finger-pointing and argumentative. He asked if I would review his slide deck and help him craft a compelling story to reduce the stress from these new "beatings from meetings." He shared that there were two new board members the chairman had added, whom he didn't know well.

Reviewing his presentation, it appeared basic and factual. I told him, "There is nothing wrong with what you have as it appears typical to most general company slide shows."

"Great, so you feel it's rock solid with no changes?" he quizzed.

"No, I don't see anything to alter, but there is a big hole in your story," I cautioned.

"What do you mean a hole?" he asked.

"Don't get upset. It's the same hole in every typical corporate overview. If I were a new board member, one of my key questions that I don't see answered is regarding your competitors. Where do you fit?" I asked.

He looked puzzled. "Do you mean market space and growth rates?"

"No, by fit I mean show me where you're positioned in the competitive landscape," I pushed.

"You mean by pricing, features, functions, or quality?" he wondered.

"Yes, but in comparison to competitor choices. You must show how you've *positioned* your company and offerings against others. As a board member, I'm a buyer, a buyer of your story, your offering, and your value proposition. If you can't specifically position where you fit, then I don't know how best to advise. I wouldn't know whether you're a good investment or not. Or if your pro forma and expected financial projections have truth," I explained.

We spent the rest of the day building a quadrant-based competitive landscape, providing comparisons of major players, boutiques, and in-house choices. I told him, "When you present this, you have to show advantages and disadvantages or pros and cons. But you must show both for each choice." No company has a perfect model. There are always strengths and weaknesses in every business.

He called a few weeks later, the day after the board meeting. I was eager to hear if he presented the positioning slide. He sounded giddy over the phone.

"Not only did I present the competitive landscape we created [aw, he gave me credit], but of the four-hour meeting we spent almost an hour discussing our fit. One member said, in the last two years, she never saw how we could gobble market share from competitors, until that presentation." He added, "It was my best board meeting ever!"

"That is awesome," I complimented his success. "As we confirm the insights, we will add that information on your website, marketing materials, sales pursuits, and in all your business conversations. That information is extremely valuable for your buyers and will accelerate your march to dominating your space," I suggested.

Sales Example

Early in my corporate sales career, after months of hard work, I barely made the final cut to win an enterprise contract valued at more than $10 million. Thankfully, there was some good news. The prospect account sent me the presentation calendar, and for some reason, we had the last slot. Last is best, first is worst, in presenting.

However, my group president unexpectedly "stole" my expert presenter and brought him to the East Coast for a more "strategic win." This left me with second-tier presentation support *over the phone*. And my VP of sales, with years of experience, was also unavailable.

This final round of executive presentations was best and final, win or go home. My internal coach at the account warned me that my position was still third place, out of three, for two reasons: my company had little presence in the state, and we were several million dollars more expensive.

After 45 minutes of a standard company cut-and-paste slideshow, I let the support person present features and functions. He kept the executives awake for a while, but then silence. If you've ever given an executive boardroom presentation where the buyers suddenly run out of questions, that's a bad sign.

The CEO of the company looked at me and said, "Thank you." That's buyer committee code for "We're done here, go away." He paused, "Anything else to add?"

At that point, facing failure, a different gear shifted in my head. Remember the story of teaching my son chess? How I taught him to take your opponent's point of view? That's what I did, except not my competitor's position, but the buyer's.

I wasn't an expert in their industry or a product whiz, but I do understand complex procurements. I started speaking from their point of view.

"Throughout this buying process you and the procurement committee have focused heavily on presence, features, functions, and price. You've negotiated me down to where there isn't much margin left for us. But price is one of the worst reasons on which to base a decision, especially when outsourcing your operations," I suggested.

For the first time in the whole presentation, all the executives were actively listening.

The CFO said, "What are you saying, as budget and capabilities are critical and are helping us decide between the three companies?"

I retorted politely, "Tactically, yes, but strategically, maybe not. Of your choices, two are following the same model with high risk and costs. Those two firms execute multipoint vendor relationships where you will be managing three to four different providers. Our model is pure integration, offering all services under one umbrella, with a single point of contact."

"There is tremendous risk and higher internal costs when depending on a multiple vendor mix for your mission critical work. If something goes wrong, how do you stop your operations while all the parties figure out who is at fault?" I pushed. I shared a few actual case studies.

"Second, our price is higher, but as my team calculated this morning, your overall costs will be much lower. You will need the same size staff to manage three nonintegrated companies. With our model, you can redeploy about two-thirds of your staff to higher-value work. After a few years into the agreement, you should break even on the difference," I stated with nothing to lose. The meeting went on for two and a half more hours.

My manager called that evening to discuss the presentation. He spent the first part of the conversation apologizing for pulling resources and not being available. He knew he was leaving me to die as this pursuit forecasted less than 40 percent. I let him swim in apologies.

Finally, he asked, "So how did it go?"

"Not bad," I said misleadingly. "To be honest . . . they gave me a verbal commitment."

"What? I thought we were losing. How the heck did you sell them?" he asked, shocked.

"I didn't sell them. I played defense and worked with the buyers to help the other vendors lose."

Operations Example

Competitive dominance isn't a sales or marketing only focus, it has to be an operational—*modus operandi*—effort too. With marketing, you're fighting for position. With sales, you're fighting to eliminate other options. However, once you have a client, your relationship is vulnerable to theft. This is why entrepreneurs must learn to maintain competitive immunity at all times and with all account levels.

A services company that sold 10-year contracts discovered a shocking statistic about their client relationships. The actual and average term of their decade-long agreements was only three years. This was disappointing because, decades back, after agreeing, the buyers and sellers would faithfully carry out contract terms and conditions for the life of an agreement. Sadly, today, many executives find it shrewd and cost effective to renegotiate or break contracts, leaving for better conditions or better terms.

A force driving agreement breakage is competitors who have the method or money to disrupt or steal business relationships. Your competitors' salespeople are taught to ask about remaining contract length and terms or options to break a relationship. To Own the Market and achieve competitive dominance, you must remain vigilant in protecting your client relationships. Your account owners must identify, gather specific information, and present competitive threats to leadership on a monthly or quarterly basis.

Why Master Competitive Dominance Now

There are many "more from less" reasons you and your team should be excited about accelerating your journey to competitive dominance, such as controlling your future success, winning with fewer resources, and keeping money away from your adversaries. Here are additional benefits.

Free Additional Sales

Every prospect pursuit you have lost you paid for in several ways. Imagine going to a restaurant and paying for an amazing four-course meal but not being served the "included" wine or dessert. You leave frustrated and hungry, but the money is gone. That is how you should feel about losing. Stop paying full price for all your prospect pursuits and receiving half or a quarter of the results.

Two-Way Profit Impact

When you start dominating your competitors and winning more often, your firm will make more profit in two ways. First, you will stop wasting dollars in lost sales expenses and costs. Second, you will be making money from new contracts and clients.

Speed to Winning

You're not reading this book to become a millionaire in many years. I'm hoping you want to become embarrassingly rich as fast as possible—maybe like some clients and employees, within 12 months. Nine out of 10 times buyers delay because they are overwhelmed with too many choices, too much information, or conflicting data. Once you help your buyers see your company's offerings as a clear or sole choice, *they buy.*

Sense of Urgency

Competitor dominance and controlling the competition is another pillar in your march toward Owning the Market. Many entrepreneurs try to win more sales by competing in more pursuits. You now know that approach is expensive and flawed. You simply need to lose less.

When your business is starting out, playing offense and defense may not seem important. However, once your business achieves a certain size in revenue, you will hit a production wall playing only one side of the ball. Without playing defense too, even if growth continues, you'll be wasting millions in profits and never become embarrassingly rich.

Becoming proficient in dominating your space starts with awareness to play both offense and defense. Remember, your competitors who follow what I'm sharing aren't only working to get bigger and better—they're working to put you out of business, too.

Competitive Dominance Action Plan

Before you start working on your competitive dominance, it's important to remember this chapter is not saying to work every sales engagement. If you or your team thought that, you missed the points in Chapters 5 and 12, "Targeting Your Sweet Spot" and "Pipeline Acceleration." If there is not a fit or won't be a fit—*mutual value*—then disengage. Be careful with crossing the line from competing to manipulation by putting your goals or needs above your prospects.

Competitive dominance starts with gathering competitor data. That can come from hundreds of sources. Some of the best information is just a few clicks away on the Internet. Simply by reading a website you can see how to gather a competitor's model, strengths, weaknesses, and many different business strategies they are using to grow. Another treasure chest of competitive information is formal win-loss reviews. I led an analysis team on a $4 billion win review in Australia. The insights and data from that six-month research helped generate billions in future revenues and save millions in sales costs. Every dollar not wasted in marketing or sales becomes profit, making your company more successful.

Create a competitive positioning map or landscape. What are the major competitive buckets or categories? In most cases, an in-house solution or do it yourself (DIY) is a major competitor. Marketing should create competitive positioning information using matrixes, quadrants, or column sheets. Sales should gather and present competitive information from pursuits, whether that information is collected in an online knowledge library or a three-ring binder. After the end of each major win or loss, have the sales team present their findings.

Every entrepreneur running a company should ask for competitive input from all employees. What are they seeing, and what have they heard? When you and your team work to create competitive dominance, you will never be surprised by your adversaries.

Some of you will be struck by this chapter's hypercompetitive nature. Others will realize why they've been losing so often and how to stop getting beaten. Remember, radical results only come from radical expectations. The next chapter, "Talent Optimization," will change how you interview, hire, and lead people and teams for the rest of your career.

CHAPTER 15

Talent Optimization

*If you're hiring employees and your
competitor is hiring talent,
then your company is at a severe
competitive disadvantage.*

The entrepreneur CEO and leaders sat perplexed, reviewing the results of an extensive employee "talent mapping" session. This is a methodology I've created to help company executives see and visualize what level of performers they have and where they are positioned in different departments. The team chooses colors to put in the boxes of their organizational chart, based on specific performance categories.

The intent is not to "slash and burn" the nonperformers like some philosophies from last century recommend. It is more about providing company leaders a baseline of the percentage of nontalent to high performers making up their departments, with the goal of building a transformation and development plan to transition and populate their teams with proven performers by a certain date.

Performance analysis sessions by their nature are intense; however, they can be outright painful when leaders discover a major talent void exists, potentially sabotaging revenue growth. Although assessing team members is an emotionally and politically sensitive exercise, not understanding and having clear insight into the employee areas creates bigger issues. Too often, entrepreneurs will try to fix employee symptoms instead of the cause of underperformance.

The morning started by projecting the firm's departmental charts, with boxes for all employees, on a giant screen. Four different colors were shown in the legend: green, yellow, red, and white, reflecting performance or longevity. Each employee box had vertical lines connecting subordinates to their manager. Some boxes had dotted lines routed to show indirect reporting to provide a second perspective of evaluation.

From where I stood at the back of the boardroom, you couldn't read the specific names and titles in the boxes. But that lack of detail didn't minimize the obvious performance "aha" problem. The number of red boxes far outnumbered all other colors combined. A red box meant underperformer. This chart was bleeding. Could this be the reason for the high turnover and burn rate (chewing through cash too fast)?

The leadership's astonishment came from the huge gap in their hiring confidence and their scoring reality. Each department head was positive they had been attracting and onboarding top performers. However, applying clear performance criteria, they categorized 75 percent of line and staff as underperformers.

"Why the shock?" I asked.

The CEO muttered, "This is frustrating. We've spent a fortune of time and money recruiting, interviewing, and using outside recruiters. Two years ago, we set up a grueling hiring process, with five individual and team interviews. I've personally interviewed people for three to four hours.

"We go through extensive background checks, social media assessments, and require third-party personality tests. How did we hire all these nonperformers? Should we fire people, pay higher salaries, or become better managers?" he asked.

"I think we need to double or triple our training efforts," interjected the director of HR.

"None of those solutions or interventions will solve what is broken," I professed.

"First of all, your hiring practices are just like those of every other company. Other than social media background checks, you're following best practices from last century. Did you hear yourself? The fixes you mentioned will never achieve optimization because they're 'more from more.' That's the wrong path. And you don't need to fire anyone, as *willing* team members can develop into performers. Second, paying more money can make things worse. And no company needs more management, as I'll explain later. More training? Typical classroom efforts of 'one size fits all,' or butts in seats for weeks, is good for skilling, but is not transformational.

Plus, there is no case study of extensive training optimizing departmental results," I explained.

"Where are we messing up hiring?" asked the head of the company.

"First of all, don't feel too bad. These results are fairly typical as entrepreneurs and leaders struggle with understanding talent and performance management. Second, you have wonderful people, but you're not setting them up for success. Third, you have solid hiring processes and tools, a best practice from the 1980s, but you don't have a strategic framework for sustaining and optimizing talent performance," I added.

"What's the first thing we should do?" asked the COO.

"Forget everything you've been taught about hiring and building teams. Stop bringing employees on board. Never believe what you see or hear in interviews. Eliminate nonproven training. Stop managing your people. And above all, quit paying for work, and start rewarding performance. Other than those things, everything else you're doing regarding people performance is perfect," I shared.

The group nodded and smiled with acceptance.

A Strategic Talent Framework

Entrepreneurs and teams who want to make millions quickly must learn how to attract, retain, and maximize top talent at all levels. You must make talent optimization a core competency. However, creating a company filled with high performers is not only a process. It requires a strategic framework with four parts.

The first part is how to Attract talent. Never forget: if you can't attract the best, you can't optimize them. Second is Acclimation. Most people think of onboarding, which is far too limiting. Third is Development. This is beyond training; it's robust and ongoing transformation to achieve next-level production. Finally, Care, which involves compensation. Many entrepreneurs fumble this area as they are cheap and underpay or worse, overpay, believing they can buy loyalty.

In this chapter you will learn the key principles, philosophy, and steps to maximize the talent you have or need. Many clients have come to us because they've faced employee nightmares that you might experience as you grow your enterprise. For example, compensation, especially for salespeople, is an area always out of alignment, broken, or that fails to motivate effectively. Notice I said "always"? Yes, I have fixed, changed, or reengineered every client's compensation program once they learned what you are reading.

Do you wonder why this Talent chapter is in the Own the Market phase? Shouldn't it be in the Market Ready or Go to Market phase when you first start hiring? Yes and no. You should start following these principles immediately. However, Own the Market is the phase in which clients might start hiring hundreds to thousands of new employees. And mass hiring before your company has successfully learned and implemented the earlier Ready phases is why hiring fails.

I'll never forget an entrepreneur in the mission critical hosting space, who came to me after implementing the Ready phases and their sales win rates tripled. He half-jokingly said, "I'm not sure how we can deliver on all these new contracts. We're going to have to hire like never before."

"Isn't slow growth the problem you said you wanted to solve a few months back? Now that your team has completed the first three phases, you are ready to attract and retain the appropriate top talent necessary to fulfill all those new contracts," I replied.

He nodded, confirming the importance of following the phases and sequence.

What Is Talent?

The word "talent" is typically used to refer to a special skill or ability. For example: She has a talent for piano. He is a real soccer talent. Our employees who fix third-level support issues have a distinct talent.

Take a minute and write down how you would define "talent."

This is the definition I want you and your teams to use to refer to someone who consistently achieves high performance:

A talent can see and do what others can't.

I'll bet as soon as you read that, a person or employee you know came to mind. Write down three people you know who you work with or have known who fit that performance category. What did they do to meet the definition?

A true talent has the ability to make a difficult result appear simple. A proven outperformer can achieve success virtually every time, in different situations, and against challenging odds.

Nature or nurture? Ah, the classic human resources (HR) question. Are business talents born, or can they develop? I have transformed thousands of employees around the world to become leaders and individual high performers, so yes, in my experience, people in business can develop talents to perform at high levels for sustained periods of time, which is considered a proficiency.

Regarding naturally gifted talent, I believe that someone who can do exceptional things with little to no training is a prodigy. But please don't hire to clichés like, "He's a natural-born salesperson." There is no such thing. Or "You're born an entrepreneur." Not true.

Measuring Talent

Measurement is critical so that you can distinguish among outperformers, performers, and nonperformers. Over the decades, this is how I measure talent when building high-performance organizations:

Talents can do the work of two to three regular employees.

How do you know before you hire someone if they are a talent or not? One of the most powerful methods I teach clients is behavioral-based interviewing. This approach works well because a candidate can't cut and paste answers. When hiring salespeople, it is legal (in most states) to ask to see a W-2. I have only had one sales candidate refuse to show me their W-2 out of several thousand interviews. Another technique is baking performance questions into the reference check process. Do your own reference checks. Do not rely on HR or others when filling critical positions.

Many entrepreneurs hit the wall, or their company becomes toxic, because they can't handle more layers of employee issues. Talent optimization is another power tool creating "more from less." More performance and production, with less headcount and headaches. When applied proficiently, this powerful framework prevents a large percentage of future people management nightmares.

When you attract and hire top performers, and provide them a well-designed system, they can usually do the work of two to three employees.

That is two more people you don't need to hire, compensate, and manage. Later in this chapter, I will share how to attract and hire proven talent.

Following the principles in this book, some clients in complex selling markets have sales talent who have produced up to 20 times the quota of a regular salesperson. That type of scaling is how your company will make huge profits and how you, your team, and your salespeople become embarrassingly rich.

Talent Myths

If you don't have talent in all positions in all roles, you're operating at a competitive disadvantage. I know that philosophy seems radical; however, I know entrepreneurs who've lost their fortunes because they've made mistakes filling critical positions. Here are some common myths you must reject.

Talent Costs Too Much Money

"Our salaries are more than competitive, and we don't want people coming here just for dollars."

Reality. High performers' base salaries will be at the upper end of pay scales. If not, is the applicant a *proven outperformer*? But talent isn't primarily looking for a job or money. They seek being "part of something special" and being rewarded in multiple ways. From a return on investment (ROI) standpoint, high performers are by far the best value.

We Don't Need Talent Everywhere

"We need some B players to balance the egos of too many A players," stated a potential prospect.

Reality. Yes, there are mission critical roles that are more important than others. Your reward programs must be designed and motivating for the value of that role. You may think you don't need a high performer at the receptionist desk. Yes, you do. Do you want a full-time person with a part-time attitude meeting, greeting, and fumbling prospect and client interactions? Don't assume that A players can't or don't want to work in a team construct. They do. The A players you should hire will thrive, working to make the team and company better and not putting themselves first.

Talents Are Hard to Manage

"We want people who get along and are manageable, not prima donnas."

Reality. An employee who behaves like a prima donna is a turkey, not a talent. Turkeys are toxic to business success. Many small companies are held hostage by that arrogant jerk in sales, marketing, operations, technology, or support. Hiring and tolerating employees who put themselves first is a leadership failure. I have many stories of entrepreneurs losing millions from allowing one individual to act as if he or she was more important than the company, which is another huge reason to transition quickly from being dependent on a people-based system, especially salespeople.

Talent Can Fix or Work in a Bad System

During a performance review, a top performer shared her frustration regarding many company challenges and problems. The VP leading the meeting responded by trying to be funny but came across as tone-deaf. "That's why we hired you," he joked. She turned to me with a look that said, "Save me!"

Reality. Many entrepreneurs try to hire people who will put up with a terrible system or will work to fix the issues. If plugging company holes isn't what the candidate will be paid to do, then two outcomes occur. First, you will never attract the highest performers, or second, you won't retain them.

Talent Will Be There "When You Need Them"

"Quick, get me two proven sales talents to fill this role," demanded the entrepreneur to the recruiter.

Reality. Acquiring outperformers is all about mutual timing. High performers always have a home and are rarely looking around because they are in demand. When top talents do become available, they're snatched quickly. You should always be recruiting.

Optimizing Your Talent

Now that you understand how to define and measure talent, are you ready to populate your whole company with outperformers?

I have bad news. No matter the economy—hot or cold—proven performers are always in tight supply. For most mission critical soft or hard skills, the talent pool is small. Plus, more companies are fighting to capture someone from the shrinking top performer list.

Business leaders have asked me, isn't more talent being developed than ever? Yes, in some areas of science and technology, but it's not keeping pace with demand. And there are some roles, like complex sales, where the candidate choices are in short supply. Incompetent salespeople are one of the biggest factors killing entrepreneurial ventures.

When I started keynote speaking 20 years ago, I shared with audiences this sad statistic from helping hire thousands of salespeople. Only 1 in 1,000 sales professionals can effectively manage all phases of a complex sale. Today, that number is only 1 in 2,500. This downward sales talent trend is one of the top reasons entrepreneurs never become rich with their business. Several times a year, prospects come to me close to tears from the costs, time, and damage of hiring salespeople who aren't producing.

Part I: Talent Acquisition

You can't hire talent if you don't attract them.

Pat, one of my favorite mentors, shared this story that locked in the importance of becoming a magnet for high performers. She told me about a dog show at which the audience and reporters were mesmerized by the stunts and superior skills the canines displayed. Jumping off pedestals, some animals caught plastic rings around their necks and balls in their mouths before landing. Others performed a somersault after leaping through a burning ring of fire. For the finale, a large dachshund ran around the ring with two small poodles riding sidesaddle on its back.

While the trainer was taking questions from the spectators, one of the reporters butted in and demanded to know the secret to the astonishing acrobatic performances. The trainer smiled without answering. The crowd joined in, "Is it the hours training? The rewards? The discipline when the animals don't perform properly?" The trainer kept smiling.

The reporter pushed, "What is your secret?"

The trainer moved closer to the crowd and said conspiratorially, "I start by finding *smart* dogs."

I love that story because it sets up the criticality of winning the war for talent. Later in the chapter, I will share ideas on how to attract and find the best performers.

Part II: Acclimation

After you find and convince talent to join your firm, don't make the mistake that many entrepreneurs make with new employees. The first few weeks should not be a time of simple transition or boring onboarding. Make sure those first days, weeks, or months have specific meaning. You must have clear deliverables, hard measurement, specific tasks, and sign-offs.

Unfortunately for new employees, especially the risky and high-cost salesperson, the first week or month typically ranges from waste to disaster. Here is a common sales question from entrepreneurs: "How soon should salespeople start producing?"

My answer: "All new hires should be productive the first day. For example, during sales acclimation, I require a new candidate to make a formal presentation at the end of each day, answering the questions, What did you learn? How will that insight make you more successful?

Effectively designed, tracked, and managed ramping programs create amazing short- and long-term performance. The normal times to production, like sales results, can be 50 percent faster. In addition, an intelligently designed acclimation program can dramatically lower turnover or failure rates over the life of employment.

Part III: Development

Have you heard this adage about employees? "It's important to develop your people." Does that mean to train, reskill, or something else? Many entrepreneurs and executives throw the words "training" and "development" around as if they're interchangeable. They're not. To become rich from your business, you must know the difference.

The meaning of training and development has morphed just as the US economy has moved from tangible to almost 90 percent intangible offerings. That shift from product focus to an emphasis on services means static training must transition to dynamic development. You train for skills, which made you competitive last century. To stay relevant today requires the ongoing development of competencies.

Skills Versus Competencies

A *skill* is knowing how to do something. A *competency* is the ability to apply a cluster of skills repeatedly and consistently to produce maximum results.

Entrepreneurial success requires hundreds of skills. You and your team's future wealth depends on mastering multiple skill sets, applied in the right order, and producing better results.

First, can you validate that your *people* have the right skill clusters? Second, can you prove your *company* has the right mix of competencies?

Every principle in this book is both a personal and company competency. Not a single concept in any chapter should be executed and completed by only one person. However, certain leaders are accountable for whether or not the department or company is competent.

For example, here is a core competency your firm and all entrepreneurs must have: *the ability to quickly convert products and services into contracts and cash.*

Training Versus Development

Training is short term, group wide, limited in scope, and can be auto tested. Development is longer term, specific to an individual, and broad in application, and it cannot be paper-based tested. You train for skills and develop competencies.

Skills are binary—a person can do something, or they can't. Testing employee skills is easy and becoming more automated. On the other hand, competencies are highly subjective. They should be tested by levels of ability. Those levels are usually ladder ranked as degrees of proficiency. It's impossible to automate or machine test proficiencies of competence, and that's what makes performance management so difficult today.

For example, a boardroom presentation requires many skill sets: organizing the meeting, crafting the presentation, facilitating the event, managing resistance issues, keeping control of the clock, and ending the presentation effectively. Winning a boardroom presentation is not based on how many skills someone has but how they *apply* the clusters of skills in the right order to produce results—a competency.

Effective hiring is a critical competency, and without achieving a high proficiency you will not build teams loaded with talent. As an entrepreneur dreaming of fast growth, you should not hire anyone if you don't thoroughly understand the critical competencies and levels of proficiencies required for each role. Every job description you create should list the required skill clusters for each position ranked in order of priority. During interviews, test and validate not only that candidates can apply those competencies but how proficient they are.

Part IV: Care and Compensation Systems

Most companies "pay for work" but don't "reward for performance." Many entrepreneurial leaders struggle with employee issues, and they try to fix or attack the person. Focusing on the individual rarely works and adds expensive management. If Mother Nature wants people to wear coats, does she send an email, reprimand them, or have HR call a meeting? No, she makes it cold outside. She changes the environment so that everyone exhibits the expected behavior. As an entrepreneurial leader, that is how you should think about leading and caring for your employees.

A well-designed, robust, holistic Care system, not just compensation, can enforce the right behavior and penalize the wrong behavior. Think of your reward system as the silent leader in your company. Yet, in 20 years, I have never walked into a company that didn't require anywhere from a modification to a total makeover of its reward systems. Most entrepreneurs and leaders don't have this expertise, which is why employees rate how they are compensated and recognized as either defective or demoralizing. A huge mistake is believing a reward system is all about money. It's not.

You must create and manage your Care system holistically, meaning you need three balanced parts: recognition, rewards, and reinforcement. Recognition can be formal or informal. It includes everything from shout-outs and emails to formal acknowledgments in front of teams or groups. Recognition is always positive. Rewards are tangible and include compensation and benefits, from fixed and variable pay to flexible time off or vacations. Reinforcement can be both "carrot and stick." The stick is highlighting the wrong behavior. This may include penalizing an individual or team. Reinforcement is usually quick or immediate, whereas rewards can be delivered at the end of a year or quarter. Formal recognition comes from superiors, while reinforcement may come from any employee.

Common Talent Mistakes

Talent blunders cost entrepreneurs fortunes and destroy companies. Here are the biggest talent gaffes to avoid.

No Strategic Talent Framework

It's no secret why leaders find the people areas of their business frustrating. Without the four parts working synergistically, maximizing performance is not possible. You must design, set up, manage, and adapt all four parts continuously to optimize your talent.

Missing Parts

Too many companies do not have robust Attraction or Acclimation parts of the framework. Even if Development and Care were perfect, they can't overcome the other missing components. Remember, your talent optimization is only as good as the weakest part.

Parts Go Stale

Rapidly changing market and cultural changes will render talent parts weak or ineffective. For example, employee compensation *wants and needs* are constantly changing. In the past, employees wanted cash, cash, and more cash. Today it's time off, work from home, career development, and even paying for personal hobby development.

Counterargument

Have you been taught or told a successful business starts with great people? How many sports franchises have the best and highest paid athletes and rarely win the championships? That's because even great people can't overcome bad systems.

Being terrific to work for, having low turnover, or being recognized as a "Best Place to Work" doesn't mean your business is close to tapping your talent potential. What is causing the gap? Entrepreneur leaders (the ones who make the final hire) are either delusional or deflective about talent.

Delusional

"We're already doing attraction and acclimation. Recruiters tell us our compensation is competitive."

Those are misguided comments I often hear. Please stop thinking you're proficient just because you're doing something. Entrepreneurs in our programs who made fortunes didn't argue or resist. Instead, ask questions like, "Which is our weakest talent area to improve first?" Another great strategy is to ask candidates what they are being offered by other companies, but don't ask for the name of the company.

Deflective

"It's HR's job to find good talent, screen them, and develop them. My role is to interview and select."

This flawed thinking might kill the talent part of your business more than being delusional. HR or recruiters can play critical roles in sourcing and screening once the talent optimization framework is in place.

I've reengineered hundreds of HR departments from small to large. Never has an HR person been able to give me a ranked list of complex competencies—for any job. Unless you do the job every day, you can't understand the nuances of skill clusters. But it's not HR's fault. You are accountable for talent, not them.

Why Acquire and Optimize Talent Now

Talent optimization adds another strategic piece to creating "more from less." Here are more reasons to implement this framework immediately.

More from Less

More production, more results, more performance using fewer direct and indirect employees, and much less management and costs. Fewer employees can mean less stress.

Quality Growth

Talent in the right framework creates a better, not bigger company. Proven talent will help provide the guardrails to becoming a big, bureaucratic, or procedural-driven business.

Profitability

Talent has the ability to get things done in the most efficient, effective, and lowest cost methods, further paying for themselves many times over while creating more profit.

Speed to Success

Next-level production and results will happen much faster and be more consistent.

Scalability

Talent can continue to produce more results using fewer company resources.

Competitive Advantage

If you have the best talent working for you using the principles in this book, you are positioned for dominance over your competitors.

Fun

Have you experienced being part of a dominant or championship team? How did it feel? Winning feeds winning. You win with winners, and winners in business are called "talents."

Sense of Urgency

This Talent Optimization framework is another manifestation of "more from less": more and faster growth, higher profitability, and setting your company up for dominating your space. However, too many entrepreneurs don't understand that real and proven talent doesn't come for the money or your wonderful personality. Talent is attracted and retained by a framework that allows them to grow, develop, and be rewarded for their performance. Many of our clients actually present their new talent optimization framework binder to candidates as a marketing tool. I have sat in many interviews in which a candidate has said that they have never seen anything so well laid out and how it has them even more excited about the opportunity.

Believing a high pay structure will entice and keep top talent is old and stale, as is believing you can go hire talent whenever you need them. In the best of times and the worst of times, talent always has a home. You will have to fight to find them and keep them.

To begin a conversation with proven talent, you need to know how to attract, compete for, and win those superior people to your business.

Throwing job offers out like seeds in a field, hoping to be lucky enough to hire a top performer, is not a superior practice. You must market and sell your company as a system for talent to come and be successful.

Remember you're not hiring superior talent;
they're buying into your system.

Talent Optimization Action Plan

Talent optimization starts with attracting top performers. Assess your website. Does it speak to or attract top talent? Where and how? Look through your job descriptions. Are they dull and boring like most, or are the descriptions power messaging tools (PMTs) creating demand for top performers?

Another place to find talent is your competitors. While running a fast-growth software organization, my salespeople were called almost daily by recruiters trying to steal them. That would upset most leaders. It proved to me that I had built a powerful team. In three years, no salesperson ever left to go to a competitor because they didn't want to leave our system.

Once those new hires start, how will you acclimate them for success? Is there a formal program with measurement and metrics? When I was hired as a sales executive by EDS back in the 1980s, my acclimation program was 13 months of grueling assignments, executive rotations, industry embedment, and stressful certifications. I had to complete over a year of duties before I was allowed to make my first sales call. The vaunted EDS acclimation program was the reason I left a high-paying sales management position. If you run a small company you don't need to spend months in acclimation, but you should invest weeks preparing your new hires for success.

Your acclimation should have three main parts. The first is competence: teaching the new recruit all that is necessary to be competent in your company. The second is proof of knowledge: testing, presenting, or role-playing. The third part is field application: the candidate must apply the principles in the field to prove results.

Create development paths for critical roles. What are the career paths in your company? If you want to attract and retain top talent, you must show them how and where they can go as they continue to develop and prove their skills. Every role should have a next-level position or opportunity for greater responsibilities and rewards.

Recently, I was asked to evaluate a client's Care system. I declined. I suggested that we allow the employees to evaluate it through an anonymous survey. The leaders thought their employees loved how they were rewarded and would give it a score of 8 or 9. The average score was 4.5. Included in the survey was a question asking for three ways to improve the current care system. I helped the leaders implement almost a dozen different ideas we received. The same survey less than a year later resulted in a huge increase to a 7.5 rating. You should do that in your company right now.

You have now read, completed, learned, and maybe even implemented over a dozen core revenue growth principles and hundreds of concepts and ideas. Great job! How do you feel? Are you more excited about business than ever? Are you like many clients who asked me, "Where were you 20 years ago when we started this business?" Or maybe like other clients who have seen immediate results just by thinking differently?

Some of you might be overwhelmed and not know where to start. Don't worry. Besides the Action Plans at the end of chapters, the next chapter offers additional steps in how to implement these ideas easier and "culturalize" my road map in your company faster.

The number one request I receive after speaking engagements is this: "Will you help us implement these principles?" Not only can we help you, but our model will "teach you how to fish," so that you and your team can do these things for yourselves—*forever*. In addition, we look forward to hearing about you starting, running, and leading many highly successful companies using this *Entrepreneur to Millionaire* road map.

CHAPTER 16

From Learning to Implementation

Moments after finishing a keynote speech at a resort in Cebu City, Philippines, for an Asia-Pacific CEO summit, a woman from the audience rushed up to the stage. I could tell she was excited by her gait. I couldn't wait to hear what part of the speech had resonated most.

She said, "I just called my executive team and told them to ditch the whole agenda for our business growth retreat starting tomorrow. I'm using this content as our agenda for the off-site and the next 12 months."

"Perfect," I responded. "What in particular has you so excited?"

"We've been following an extensive strategic plan, but that plan isn't going to make us wealthy from our hard work, it's only going to make our company incrementally bigger. You have given me a road map to deliver more value to our clients and make a lot of money with what we offer. That's a hundred times more valuable than a business growth plan," she beamed.

She continued, "I have many questions, but you're flying back to the States and won't be available for 48 hours. How do I present this to my team? How do I engage my employees as that's become a huge issue lately? Also, what do we do first? And is there a secret to making this all work?"

This is what I shared with her.

Presenting This Road map to Your Team

Tell your team you've learned about a proven road map to deliver more value to clients, generate a lot more sales and revenues, and create more rewards for team members. If you want to, add this part (many clients like it): and make our competitors go nuts.

Let them know, whether you follow a strategic plan or not, this new path is not focused on business growth but more profitable *revenue growth*. Let them know at every turn, the company will no longer be focused on "more from more," but on "more from less" in a way that benefits everyone.

Whether your organization is a small business, a medium-size company, or a large mature multinational, this new approach has this proven value proposition: dramatically increase sales, revenue, and profits without spending more money, hiring more people, or working more hours.

No Secret or Guarantees to Success— Only a Methodical and Sequential Approach to Making More Money

Another key point to make to your team is that our clients around the world have proven that every type and size of company has bundles of cash hidden in their walls. Yes, even companies with average products and so-so services. Those fortunes are just waiting to be discovered. However, the mistake businesspeople make is following false beliefs. They're told that there is some magic wand (more SEO), a secret to success (do more marketing or hire more salespeople), or some golden key (lower your prices) to open the padlock to riches. Others falsely believe that if you work smarter not just harder, you will achieve your financial dreams. Those solutions can *never* optimize revenue growth.

The lock keeping you, your team, and your company from realizing embarrassing wealth does not require a key. It's a combination lock, which requires knowing and following the perfect sequence. You must follow the right numbers, the right and left turns, and the full rotations. One mistake and the lock to riches won't open. This is the point of most entrepreneurial failures and frustration—trying to use a "key" to open a combination lock. Consistent, sustainable, highly profitable success comes from a methodical and proven approach that is the combination: the Entrepreneur to Millionaire road map.

Using Revenue Growth® Language in Your Company

Your leaders and employees will need to read this book for many reasons. First, to know and learn the phases, principles, and sequence. But maybe even more important is the language and lexicon. Imagine flying to a foreign country and not speaking the language. You might get around, but it can be frustrating and challenging, and waste a huge amount of time. Don't have meetings to explain the words and definitions before the teams have read this book. Make sure your people are prepared and ready for explosive revenue growth.

Many clients have told me that they needed to look through their notes or listen to my past speeches three to five times before the "aha" bells started ringing. That's normal. Most people hear a new or radical concept and believe they get it, but they don't. Rewiring how you think (which is required for everything in this book) will take time and commitment (the will). Absorb and apply the necessary deep learning to produce results. Remember, it's not just the power in the principles, but the power in the *sequence*, *integration*, and *synergy* of the phases and concepts that will unlock a massive fortune.

You and your team must know and understand the words and their exact definitions. For example, the definition of *business growth* versus *revenue growth*. You now know those terms have two completely different meanings. Not knowing the subtle difference and executing them congruently can cost small businesses millions.

It's critical that your team knows the lexicon (unique words to this methodology), the phrases, and the abbreviations—from FMP, PCP, PMT, and PPP to modeling, sweet spot, power messaging tools, blueprinting optimization, and talent optimization; from tiered pricing strategies and sales conversion system to multiple revenue streams. When your team knows and uses these terms properly, they will think faster and act smarter, being more efficient and effective. Plus, it's more fun and harmonious, like a great karaoke party where everyone knows the songs and the words.

It would also be helpful to have stakeholders, board members, investors, or vendor partners read this book, so that they, too, know and use the same language, terms, and definitions.

Multiple Applications for This Road map

Most clients use this road map for their whole enterprise, which is what I would recommend. However, there are three other ways to use it.

Divisions or Units

If your company is large, like a multibillion-dollar multinational or holding company, you can apply it in different divisions or business units. When we work with extremely large corporations, we start with divisions, product groups, or specific geographies. This divisional approach versus a "boil the ocean" plan of attack can create quick and proven wins. Other divisions will be faster to adopt the principles if they see results and they don't want to be left behind.

New Products and Services

This is a great road map for bringing new products and services to market. I know it's not possible to dominate the market with every product or service, but there is no reason that can't be the goal. These principles can dramatically improve the launch and sustainable traction of any new idea or venture.

Expansion

As companies expand into new regions or geographies, this road map provides a great checklist for success. I have helped start new organizations in many countries using these ideas. For example, one of the most important principles is power messaging tools (PMTs). Messages do not easily translate from one country to another, so it's important to create PMTs that are rooted in the local culture.

The Secret to Making Your Revenue Growth® Transformation Work

Be inclusive. Leverage insights and input from all areas and departments.

The biggest mistake in applying these principles is assigning them to a department that operates in a silo or a person that works solo. There is no principle in this book that a single person or department should own and implement by themselves. Use cross-functional teams for every step of this sequence, from FMP to talent optimization. However, although all the departments must be responsible, I do recommend that a single person—individual or leader—be accountable for results.

The Meaning Behind the Words in the Book Title

Most believe the word "entrepreneur" only refers to the person who starts or runs the business. That thinking is way too narrow. Then there's the term "intrapreneur," which was coined by Gifford Pinchot III. I don't think we need another word to define someone. I'm happy for employees to keep their titles, but to be more *entrepreneurial* in their thoughts, actions, and behavior.

Today, successful companies need *all* employees to be *entrepreneurial*. But to be entrepreneurial does not mean to run off and start new ventures. And it doesn't mean being a maverick, prima donna, or cultural misfit. It means being a problem solver, creative thinker, innovator, smart risk taker, and thoughtful investor of company resources. It means taking responsibility for your own personal development—and, above all, being a team player. Being entrepreneurial is about putting the client and the company first and making things better for everyone.

Some of the best, most rewarding, and least stressful periods in my corporate career happened when I was being entrepreneurial. At different career points, I was given jobs without titles, without structure, and without barriers to go do what I felt was best to help the company. I didn't worry about the pay or compensation; I focused on solving the problem. I was confident my great leaders and mentors would take care of me—and they did. Thank you, Mickey, Ed, Val, and Pat.

I am only able to write this book with decades of knowledge for this reason. Back in 1995, leaders of a multinational came to me and asked me to form a team of any experts I wanted with no limits on budget to solve a multibillion-dollar problem: why weren't our strategic business units growing faster, making more money, and growing more consistently?

I was asked to be entrepreneurial. The success of those projects fast-tracked my career to becoming a chief strategy officer (CSO) and a chief marketing officer (CMO) of an international billion dollar organization with overseas assignments in my mid-thirties. That's an embarrassingly rich reward. In this way, being "rich" isn't just about the money. (Although I have helped many direct W-2 employees become millionaires, some within 12 months, without all the headaches of running a business.) A rich career can mean more opportunities, development paths, promotions, special and prestigious projects, as well as more free time in the form of vacations and sabbaticals.

So whether you are an individual employee, supervisor, or leader of a division, this is what you must know: Your job is not only what you do, but the value you bring every day to your role, team, and company. Be entrepreneurial. Raise your hand, throw in your hat, and help implement the principles in this book, and accelerate your company to achieve optimized revenue growth. Being entrepreneurial in a team construct can help you become richly rewarded—maybe even embarrassingly so.

Sense of Urgency

Bust your collective butts to learn, apply, and master these phases and principles as quickly as your team can, not only because your competitors are doing it but because there is more to learn to make you even more money. Think of mastering this book as halfway to your black belt. You'll be ready for the more powerful and sophisticated concepts once you are proficient in these principles.

I want to hear about your successes and struggles. Every entrepreneur or leader gets stuck at some point. Reach out for help. Contact us at: info@revenuegrowthcompany.com.

To further accelerate your journey from *Entrepreneur to Millionaire* or transform your good business into a ridiculously profitable, fast-growth company, refer to the Appendix, "Additional Resources," for templates, tools, strategies, and methods, all packaged in modules and delivery methods to help you do all of this work 10 to 100 times faster and better.

My company's mission is to help a million entrepreneurs become millionaires. I hope you and your employees will be among them.

I hope this book helped you and your employees become smarter and more successful entrepreneurs. Maybe even embarrassingly rich.

Now I hope you will use your new riches to make the world a better place.

APPENDIX

Additional Resources

I f you want help accelerating your revenue growth and unlocking the fortune in your company, please visit revenuegrowthcompany.com or contact us at info@revenuegrowthcompany.com. We have invested more than $1 million creating, testing, validating, and continuously evolving our templates, tools, methods, and IP. Make sure to look for the Revenue Growth® registered trademark on all materials. Do not hire someone or believe a business is associated or affiliated with The Revenue Growth® Company (TRGC), LLC, just because they speak our language.

Resources and Programs

TRGC® offers support from free and no-obligation to enterprise transformation delivery options. We have more than 600 modules (prepackaged content of templates, tools, methods, and processes) ready and available to deliver in many public and private formats. Here is an overview of options to help you achieve explosive revenue growth.

Online

Visit revenuegrowthcompany.com, and sign up for a complimentary business transformation session. Schedule a no-obligation phone call to discuss your situation and strategize a plan. The website also includes dates for local and public events.

Assessments/Audits/Analysis

These are half-day to multiday sessions to help you and your team identify areas to leverage and areas to fix, build, or eliminate. They include: Enterprise, Function/Department, Leadership, Individual, and New Product Development/Launch.

Revenue Growth® Workshops and Executive Retreats

We offer public and private workshops and executive retreats. We can cover more than 170 disciplines and principles and leverage any of our 600 modules. Public workshops are free for individuals and fee-oriented for groups or multiple companies. Private workshops are for single firms. Executive retreats on Strategic Business Transformation, Leadership Transformation, and Strategic Sales Optimization for executives and teams are available in one- to four-day agendas.

Structured 90-Day and 12-Month Programs for Groups

We offer public and private group programs that are delivered in 90-day and 12-month periods. These are among the most affordable but highly accountable options for Revenue Growth® programs available. They include:

- ▸ P.E.R.F.E.C.T. Selling®: a highly sophisticated, complex seven-phase sales methodology—when you have to win million- or billion-dollar pursuits.
- ▸ Monetizing Value®: unlocking and leveraging the value of your offerings to maximize sales, revenue, and profit production—excellent for startups and small firms.
- ▸ Explosive Revenue Growth® 12-Month Program® and Entrepreneur to Millionaire™ (E2M™): This set of programs is designed to follow the road map in this book and is delivered to business leaders in groups of 8 to 12.
- ▸ RAMP®: Our highest intensity, on-site, exclusive, customized business and enterprise transformation program.

Keynote Speeches to Associations, Groups, or Individual Companies

Billingsley can deliver on any of the principles in this book, in addition to more than 170 business topics and functional disciplines. All of our content focuses on this value proposition: more sales, revenue, and profits using fewer resources.

Revenue Growth® Content License Rights

We offer a "Lead the Leader" program to certify your account people in our methods, templates, and tools. This can be a one-time event or ongoing certifications. Once certified, your people have the right to teach, train, develop, and implement these principles throughout your enterprise. Our extensive and robust library is filled with methods, formulas, processes, and tools to provide optimized performance and maximum scalability.

Combination Packages

A typical combination event includes a speech for insight, half- or all-day assessment for learning and planning, and then a one- or two-day private workshop to accelerate implementation. Contact us for budget and package customization for your group.

Certified Affiliations

We are looking for driven executive-level leaders who have an interest in being part of our efforts to help entrepreneurs and employees become millionaires. If you are interested in becoming certified and licensed to market, sell, and/or deliver our offerings, please contact us.

Partnerships

Please contact us regarding your specialty (marketing, SEO, recruiting, PR, advertising, etc.) services and how we might partner to bring more value to our mutual clients and the marketplace. See revenuegrowthcompany.com for details.

I hope this book helped you and your employees become smarter and more successful entrepreneurs. Maybe even embarrassingly rich.

Now I hope you will use your new riches to make the world a better place. And please help me turn a million entrepreneurs and entrepreneurial employees into millionaires.

INDEX

Above market pricing, 124
Abuse, in pipeline management, 184–187
Accenture, 174
Acclimation of talent, 225, 231, 237
Account coverage, 87
Accounting, 54
Action plan:
  for blueprinting optimization, 208
  for business modeling, 57
  for competitive dominance, 221–222
  for marketing demand creation, 146–147
  for packaging for value, 100–101
  for partnering for demand, 178
  for pipeline acceleration, 191
  for power messaging tools, 113–114
  for revenue streams, 72
  for sales conversion system, 165
  for solving FMPs, 41
  for talent optimization, 237–238
  for targeting, 88
  for tiered pricing strategies, 127–128
Adaptability, continuous, 198–204 (See also Blueprinting optimization)
Adaptive systems revenue growth model, 204–205
Adding, 3–5, 10
Addresses, 105
Addressing your audience, 105–106 (See also Power messaging tools (PMTs))

Aerosmith, 187
Affiliations (see Partnering for demand)
Amazon, 38, 52, 62
American Marketing Association, 136
Apple, 37–39
Approved Vendor List (AVL), 52
Arrogance, in modeling, 55
At-cost offerings, 124
Attraction:
  rethinking business model for, 56
  of talent, 225, 230, 237
  with targeting, 83, 87
  tiered pricing for, 126
Audience, addressing, 105–106
Audio.net, 36
AVL (Approved Vendor List), 52

Barriers to successful entrepreneurship, 11–13
Behaviors, of perfect clients, 86, 88
Below-cost offerings, 123–124
Bezos, Jeff, 38
Block growth model, 3–5, 53–54, 201–203
Blueprinting optimization, 195–208
  action plan for, 208
  as adaptive system, 204–205
  continuous improvement versus, 199–200
  for continuous transformation, 199–200

Blueprinting optimization (*continued*)
  counterargument to, 205–207
  for dynamic transformation, 203–204
  and flaws in basic block growth model,
    201–203
  reasons for, 207
  root problem for, 200–201
  sense of urgency for, 207–208
BMW, 159
Bookkeeping, 54
Brand, 141–142, 190
Breakeven point pricing, 124
Broadcast.com, 36, 37
BSA (Scouts of America), 59
B2B model, 52, 85
B2C model, 51–52, 61–63, 85
B2G model, 52, 85
Bundling, 91, 93 (*See also* Packaging for
  value)
Business growth:
  classic model for, 3–5
  ineffective strategies for, 1–2
  partnering for, 168–170
  revenue growth versus, 7, 9–11
  with talent optimization, 235
Business modeling, 43–57
  action plan for, 57
  criteria for, 48
  effective modeling design, 45–46
  evolution of, 46–47
  examples of, 49–51
  external market models, 51–52
  internal enterprise model, 53–54
  mistakes in, 54–55
  product or service or both models, 52–53
  reasons to rethink, 55–56
  sense of urgency with, 56–57
  visualizing, 49
Business to business (B2B) model, 52, 85
Business to consumer (B2C) model,
  51–52, 61–63, 85
Business to government (B2G) model,
  52, 85
Buyer acceleration path, 109–110
Buying process, 188, 189

Cadabra, 38
Callaway, Ely, 30, 81

Callaway Golf, 30
Care, of talent, 225, 233, 238
Carney brothers, 49–50
Casualties in business, 74
Cause of problems, 32–33
Change:
  designing companies for, 198–199 (*See
    also* Blueprinting optimization)
  in external market, 47, 197–198
  unwillingness to, 196
  in the world, 200–201
Characteristics:
  of perfect clients, 86, 88
  of RAMP participants, 15–17
  for revenue growth, 203
Cheapness, 55
Cisco, 174
Clients:
  identifying, 76–77
  in partnering, 176–177
  quality of, 145–146
  use of term, 76
Closing dates, 191
Commoditization, 98
Communication strategies (*see* Power
  messaging tools (PMTs))
Compensation, 225–226
  costs of, 157–158
  in partnerships, 172
  of talent, 233, 236
Competencies, skills versus, 231–232
Competency, delusions of, 55
Competitive data/playbook, 215–220
Competitive dominance, 209–222
  action plan for, 221–222
  competitive data for, 215–220
  from opponent's perspective, 214
  reasons for mastering, 220–221
  sense of urgency for, 221
  for winning all the time, 211–213
Competitors:
  assessing, 177
  in crafting business model, 48
  dominating, 194 (*See also* Own the
    Market [dominating] phase)
  finding talent from, 237
  intensity of, 206
  partnering with, 169–170

seeing from perspective of, 214
and talent optimization, 236
Complex sales, 156, 191
Content, in messaging, 105
Continuous adaptability, 198–204 (*See also* Blueprinting optimization)
Continuous improvement, 199–200
Continuous transformation, 199–200
Contract size, 190, 199
Coopetition, 170
Corporate sales, 156
Cost plus pricing, 116–117, 124
Costco, 120, 123
Costs:
  of each salesperson, 156–158
  as FMP, 40
  and revenue growth scaling, 10
  of sales pursuit, 8–9
  of talent, 228
COVID-19 pandemic, 64
CRM (*see* Customer relationship management)
Cross flow, 205
Cuban, Mark, 35–37
Customer relationship management (CRM), 162, 181–183, 190
Customers:
  identifying, 76–77
  in partnering, 176–177
  use of term, 76

Data:
  for competitive dominance, 215–220
  in sales pipeline, 180–182, 186–188
Degree of pain, 34
Delivery:
  adaptation by, 208
  in internal enterprise model, 53, 202
Demand:
  filtering, 113
  partnering to create (*see* Partnering for demand)
  speed in creating, 112–113
Demographics, 86, 88
Development:
  of talent, 225, 231–233, 237–238
  training versus, 232–233
Digital marketing, 140

Disruptive market changes, 47
Dominating, 214 (*See also* Own the Market [dominating] phase)
Domino's Pizza, 50
Durango & Silverton Narrow Gauge Train, 65
Dynamic transformation, 203–204

Earnings, marketing demand and, 145
EDS, 29
Einstein, Albert, 20
Electronic stores, 68–69
Elevator pitches, 108–109
Elimination, avoiding, 215, 218–219
Emotions, 82–84, 93
Engagement, tiered pricing for, 126
Enterprise modeling, 53–55 (*See also* Business modeling)
Enterprise selling, 156
Entrepreneurs, 16–17, 21, 243–244 (*See also* Successful entrepreneurship)
Expansion, 242
Expectations, 17
External market models, 51–52
External resistance, 11

Filtering demand, 113
Finance function, 54
FMPs (*see* Fundamental Marketplace Problems)
Forecasting, 182, 188, 189
Formal partnerships, 172, 178
Four Ps of marketing, 138–139
Framing FMPs, 34, 39–41
Fraud, in pipeline management, 184–186
Free offerings, 123, 128
Frito-Lay, 215
Fundamental Marketplace Problems (FMPs), 29–41
  action plan for solving, 41
  for Amazon, 38
  for Apple, 37–38
  in crafting business model, 48
  Cuban's solving of, 35–37
  degree of pain for, 34
  evolution of, 34–35
  for family tent camping, 60–62

Fundamental Marketplace Problems
(FMPs) (*continued*)
foundational cause of, 32–33
as foundational to success, 32–34
framing, 40–41
Google's solving of, 38
marketplace scope and scale of, 33–34
mistakes made with, 39
reasons to focus on, 39–40
sense of urgency with, 40–41

Glamping, LLC, 62–63
Go to Market (winning) phase, 23,
129–130
marketing demand creation, 131–147
partnering for demand, 167–178
pipeline acceleration, 179–191
sales conversion system, 149–165
Goals:
for marketing, 147
for sales pipeline production, 191
in targeting, 78–79
for winning, 210
Google, 38

Halo products, 120
Helen's fine dining, 50
High spectrum entrepreneurial traits,
15–16
Hiring, 224–228 (*See also* talent
optimization)
HP, 174
Human resources (HR), 54

IBM, 37, 174
Income streams, 63 (*See also* Revenue
streams)
Incremental growth, 4–5
Indiana University, 36
Informal partnerships, 172–173, 178
Infrastructure costs, 158
Insurance companies, 68
Intent, in messaging, 105
InTents Glamping, 62–63
Internal enterprise model, 53–54
Internal resistance, 11–12
Internet sites, 110–112
Intrapreneur, 243

Jobs, Steve, 39

Kaizen, 199–200

Language of revenue growth, 241
Lead generation (*see* Marketing demand
creation)
Legal counsel, 54
Long-term production, 141–142
Losing, impact of, 213

Management costs, 158
Market growth, 206
Market Ready (preparation) phase,
22–23, 73–74
packaging for value, 89–101
power messaging tools, 103–114
targeting, 74–88
tiered pricing strategies, 115–128
Market segments, 80, 81, 84–85, 193
Marketable database, 141
Marketing:
competitive insights in, 215–217
internal attitudes toward, 132–133
in internal enterprise model, 53, 202
lack of strategic leadership in, 133–135
as noun or as verb, 136
sales versus, 132
typical fix for, 135
weak, persistence of, 135–137
word-of-mouth, 143–145
(*See also* Go to Market [winning] phase)
Marketing Activities, 140–141
Marketing demand creation, 131–147
action plan for, 146–147
biggest mistake in, 143–145
changing thinking about, 145–146
and persistence of weak marketing,
135–137
responsibility for, 143
sense of urgency for, 146
and strategic leadership, 133–135
transforming marketing for, 137–143
and typical marketing fix, 135
Marketing Function Roles, 138–140
Marketing Performance Management,
142–143
Marketing Production, 141–142

Marketing sales support role, 139–140
Marketplace, scope/scale of FMP and, 33–34
Marketplace problems (*see* Fundamental Marketplace Problems (FMPs))
McDonald's, 68, 96, 98, 175–176
Measurement:
　in marketing management, 142
　of revenue growth, 8
　in sales conversion system, 162
　of sales pipelines, 187, 189
　of talent, 227–228
Messaging:
　for fast growth, 103
　power of, 106 (*See also* Power messaging tools [PMTs])
　weak tools for, 111–112
Metrics:
　in marketing management, 142
　in sales conversion system, 162
Micromuse, 14
Mid-term production, 141
Modeling (*see* Business modeling)
Money:
　as a goal, 19
　road map for making more, 249
　spending money to make money, 5
　worry about, 18
More from less:
　as counterintuitive, 9
　downsizing as, 200
　misapplication of, 5–6
　with partnering, 176
　in pipeline acceleration, 185, 189
　in pricing, 118
　in sales, 163, 212
　by scaling revenue growth, 6–9
　with talent optimization, 235, 236
More from more:
　and blueprinting optimization, 200
　in hiring, 224
　in marketing, 134, 135
　as model, 4–5
　in sales, 151, 212
　in targeting, 79–80

Naked and Afraid (television show), 71
New will, 16, 19–21

Offerings, 48
　grouping (*see* Packaging for value)
　in pricing, 120 (*See also* Tiered pricing strategies)
Onboarding costs, 157
Operations:
　adaptation by, 208
　competitive insights in, 215–216, 219–220
　in internal enterprise model, 53, 202
Outsourcing, 135
Own the Market (dominating) phase, 23, 193–194
　blueprinting optimization, 195–208
　competitive dominance, 209–222
　from learning to implementation, 239–244
　talent optimization, 223–238

Packaging, 93, 95
Packaging for value, 89–101
　acting like a buyer in, 91–93
　action plan for, 100–101
　client case study of, 96–97
　counterargument to, 98–99
　effectiveness in, 97–98
　intent of, 93–94
　mistakes in, 95–96
　reasons for, 99–200
　sense of urgency with, 100
　when to offer, 94–95
Pain, degree of, 34
Papa John's, 50
Papa Murphy's, 50–51
Partnering for demand, 167–178
　action plan for, 178
　for explosive profits and growth, 168–170
　mastery examples of, 175–176
　mistakes in, 174–175
　and Perfect Partner Profile, 170–171
　power of, 173–174
　reasons for, 176–177
　sense of urgency for, 177–178
　types of partnerships, 172–173
Partnerships:
　in crafting business model, 48
　Perfect Partner Profile, 170–171
　types of, 172–173

Patterns to success, 71
PCP (*see* Perfect Client Profile)
Penetration, with targeting, 87
PepsiCo, 215
Perfect Client Profile (PCP), 77–80
  aligning buyers' perception of value
    and, 96
  changing, 88
  elements of, 85–86
  excuses for not effectively identifying,
    84–85
  in looking for partners, 177
  reasons for using, 87
  targeting your, 77–80 (*See also*
    Targeting)
Perfect Partner Profile (PPP), 170–171
Performance adaptability, 205
Perot, Ross, 29
Physical address, 105
Physical marketing, 140–141
Pipeline acceleration, 179–191
  action plan for, 191
  and customer relationship
    management, 181–183
  effectiveness in, 187–189
  mistakes in pipeline management, 189
  reasons for mastering, 189–190
  and sales pipeline, 181–183
  sense of urgency for, 190–191
  thinking for, 184
  and waste/fraud/abuse in pipeline
    management, 184–187
Pipeline management, 184–189
Pitches, 108–109
Pizza Hut, 49–50
Pleasure, level of, 34
Positioning, 215, 217
Power messaging tools (PMTs), 103–114
  action plan for, 113–114
  and bad elevator pitches, 108–109
  in creating buyer acceleration path,
    109–110
  and excuses for weak messaging tools,
    111–112
  getting started with, 110–111
  how to address audience, 105–106
  reasons for creating, 112–113
  sense of urgency with, 113

PPP (Perfect Partner Profile), 170–171
Premium pricing, 124–125, 128
Preparation (*see* Market Ready
  [preparation] phase)
Pricing:
  basic strategy for, 119
  mistakes in, 125–126
  most common approach to, 116–117
  tiered (*see* Tiered pricing strategies)
  unlocking power of, 117–118
Problems, 30 (*See also* Fundamental
  Marketplace Problems (FMPs))
Product models, 52–53
Product sales, 155
Products:
  in crafting business model, 48
  new, road map for, 242
  range of, in pricing, 120 (*See also*
    Tiered pricing strategies)
Proficiency, 23–25
Profit(s):
  and business growth, 3
  and incremental growth, 4–5
  packaging to protect, 99–100
  with partnering, 168–170, 176
  in pricing strategy, 120
  and sales conversion system, 164
  from scaling revenue growth, 6–9
  and talent optimization, 235
  with targeting, 87
  tiered pricing for, 126–127
  when dominating competitors, 220
Profit margin, 120 (*See also* Tiered
  pricing strategies)
Project revenue, 66–67
Prospect management, 180 (*See also*
  Pipeline acceleration)
Protection of client relationships, 215,
  219–220
Psychographics, 86, 88
Pursuit status, 188

Quality of clients, 145–146

RAMP (*see* Revenue Growth program)
Recruiting costs, 157
Recurring revenue, 67
Referrals, 171

Resistance to successful
    entrepreneurship, 11–13
Resources, 245–247
    from author, 128
    fewer, tiered pricing for, 126–127
    more income using fewer resources,
        70
    for sales support, abuse of, 186–187
Retail electronic stores, 68–69
Retention of clients, 87
Revenue, 63, 87
Revenue growth:
    adaptive systems model for,
        204–205 (*See also* Blueprinting
        optimization)
    business growth versus, 7, 9–11
    business modeling for, 47–48
    characteristics for, 203
    as focus of road map, 240
    leveling/shrinking of, 199
    optimizing, 12
    scaling, 6 9
    successful transformation for, 242
    using language of, 241
Revenue Growth program (RAMP),
    15–25
    characteristics of participants in,
        15–17
    different Way presented in, 21–25
    new will presented in, 19–21
    reasons for participating in, 17–19
Revenue Ready (validation) phase, 22,
    27–28
    business modeling, 43–57
    Fundamental Marketplace Problems,
        29–41
    multiple revenue streams, 59–72
Revenue streams, 59–72
    action plan for, 72
    forms of, 66–67
    meaning and importance of, 63–64
    mistakes when creating, 69
    multiple, 63–66
    reasons for creating, 69–70
    river metaphor for, 64–66
    and traditional B2C model, 61–63
    unconventional, 67–69
Reverse flow, 205

Risks:
    as FMP, 40
    with multiple revenue streams, 70
    value greater than, 123
Road map, 239–244
    achieving proficiency of, 23–25
    applications for, 242
    as different way, 21–25
    Go to Market (winning) phase in, 23
    Market Ready (preparation) phase in,
        22–23
    Own the Market (dominating) phase
        in, 23
    presenting team with, 240–242
    and proficiency levels, 24–25
    Revenue Ready (validation) phase in,
        22
    value of, 239
Rogers, Will, 195

Sales:
    adaptation by, 208
    competitive insights in, 215–216,
        218–219
    costs of, 158
    environments for, 154–156
    in internal enterprise model, 53, 202
    marketing versus, 132
    new, 141
    optimizing and scaling, 211 213
    partnering versus, 173–174
    and relationship management, 183
    selling environments, 154–156
    with targeting, 87
    as weakest link, 151–154
    when dominating competitors, 220
    win rate in, 8, 153
Sales conversion system, 149–165
    action plan for, 165
    and costs of each salesperson, 156–158
    counterargument to, 163
    hard areas in, 161
    price as strategy in, 119
    reasons to focus on, 163–164
    and sales as weakest link, 151–154
    sales transactions versus sales
        conversions, 158–159
    and selling environments, 154–156

Sales conversion system (*continued*)
  sense of urgency for, 164–165
  soft areas in, 160–161
  support tools areas in, 162
  talent areas in, 161–162
Sales funnel, 179–181 (*See also* Pipeline
  acceleration)
Sales leads, 141
Sales management, 154
Sales pipeline, 181–183 (*See also* Pipeline
  acceleration)
Sales transactions, 158–159
Salespeople:
  costs of, 156–158
  hiring, 152–154
  old sales model based on, 150–151
  training for, 151, 154
Sam's Club, 123
Scale of FMPs, 33–34
Scaling:
  common misunderstanding of, 10
  for growth and profit, 21
  rethinking business model for, 55–56
  of revenue growth, 6–9
  with talent optimization, 236
Schnatter, John, 50
Scope of FMPs, 33–34
Scouts of America (BSA), 59
Selling:
  costs of, 158
  environments of, 154–156
  as mistake in sales role, 89–90
Service models, 52–53
Services:
  in crafting business model, 48
  new, road map for, 242
  packaging, 93
  range of, in pricing, 120 (*See also*
    Tiered pricing strategies)
Services revenue, 67
Short-term production, 141
Simple sales, 155–156
Skills, competencies versus, 231–232
Small business owners, entrepreneurs
  versus, 16–17, 21
Speed:
  to buying decisions, packaging for, 99
  in creating demand, 112–113

  as FMP, 40
  marketing demand creation for, 145
  to new sales and revenue, 163–164
  with partnering, 176
  to profitable growth, revenue streams
    for, 70
  rethinking business model for, 55
  to sales and revenue, 87
  with talent optimization, 236
  tiered pricing for, 126
  when dominating competitors, 221
Spending money to make money, 5
Strategic leadership, 133–135
Strategic marketing role, 138–139
Strategic talent framework, 225–226,
  234
Subscription services, 67
Substitutions, in crafting business
  model, 48
Subway, 50
Successful entrepreneurship, 1–14
  barriers and resistance to, 11–13
  and business growth versus revenue
    growth, 9–11
  classic business growth model for,
    3–5
  and misapplication of more from less
    concept, 5–6
  patterns for, 71
  revenue growth model for, 6–9
Suppliers, 48
Support:
  adaptation by, 208
  in internal enterprise model, 54, 202
Sweet spot, 80–81 (*See also* Targeting)
Systems thinking, 205

Tactical marketing role, 139
Talent, 226–227
  measuring, 227–228
  myths about, 228–229
  in sales system, 161–162, 164
Talent mapping exercise, 223–224
Talent optimization, 223–238
  action plan for, 237–238
  common mistakes in, 233–234
  counterargument to, 234–235
  and meaning of talent, 226–227

measuring talent, 227–228
myths about talent, 228–229
populating company with
outperformers, 229–233
reasons for, 235–236
sense of urgency for, 236–237
strategic talent framework for,
225–226
Targeting, 74–88
and accepting new business, 85
action plan for, 88
effective and accurate, 76, 77
identifying customers and clients,
76–77
identifying sweet spot in, 80–81
mistakes in, 75, 82–85
and Perfect Client Profile, 77–80,
85–86
reasons for using, 87
sense of urgency for, 87–88
Teaming (*see* Partnering for demand)
Technology, sales and, 152
Technology function, 54
Thought leadership, 12
Thresholds, 142–143
Tiered pricing strategies, 115–128
action plan for, 127–128
and basic pricing strategy, 119
and mistakes in pricing, 125–126
reasons for implementing, 126–127
sense of urgency with, 127
to unlock power of pricing, 117–118
variables in, 119–125
Tiered pricing wheel, 120–122
Toys 'R' Us, 123–124
Traditional B2C model, 61–63
Traditional marketing, 140
Training, development versus,
232–233
Trampoline effect, 81
Transaction revenue, 66
Transaction selling, 155
Transaction size, 99
Transformation:
continuous, 199–200
dynamic, 203–204
for revenue growth, 242

Unconventional revenue streams, 67–69
Underperformance, 196–198, 224
URLs, 106

Validation (*see* Revenue Ready
[validation] phase)
Valuation:
revenue streams to increase, 70
and sales conversion system, 164
Value, 1
buyer's perception of, 96
packaging for, 93 (*See also* Packaging
for value)
of road map, 239
in tiered pricing, 122–123, 128
Value proposition, 81–84
Vendors, 48
Visualizing, in business modeling, 49

Wagner, Todd, 36
Walmart, 119, 123–124
Waste, in pipeline management,
184–185
The Way, 21–25 (*See also* Road map)
Weak messaging tools, 111–112
Wealth creation:
myth about, 3–5
personal characteristics for, 15–16
and sales pipeline competency, 182
Web address, 105
Websites, 110–112
Wendy's, 96, 98
Will, 11, 16, 19–21
Winning (*see* Go to Market [winning]
phase)
Winning all the time, 211–213 (*See also*
Competitive dominance)
Word-of-mouth marketing, 143–145
Work:
harder versus smarter, 19–20
leveraging parts of company for,
20–21, 25
Working capital, 206–207
Wozniak, Steve, 39

Yahoo, 37
YouTube, 62

ABOUT THE AUTHOR

Kent Billingsley is the founder and president of the The Revenue Growth® Company, LLC (TRGC). He has become America's Revenue Growth® Architect by helping thousands of entrepreneurs and small businesses (representing hundreds of thousands of employees) generate several billion dollars in new sales, as well as tens of billions in new revenue and profit for large corporations. He has personally designed, built, transformed, and turbocharged more than 1,000 organizations in 36 countries. His corporate experience includes roles such as founder, president, senior executive officer, chief strategy officer, chief marketing officer, and chief sales officer in start-ups and billion-dollar firms alike. Over the past 20 years, his original content and trademarked programs have turned thousands of entrepreneurs and employees into millionaires and multimillionaires by helping them achieve explosive profitable growth using the resources they already have.

For more information on creating wealth in your company and for you and your employees, visit revenuegrowthcompany.com.